Animals in the Wild

Bear

by Mary Hoffman

RAINTREE
STECK-VAUGHN
L I B R A R Y
A Division of Steck-Vaughn Company

Bear cubs are very tiny when they are first born. They weigh less than a pound. Their eyes are closed and they have no fur. But they grow quickly. These two American black bear cubs are about two months old.

Bears spend most of the winter sleeping in dens like this one. They eat a lot in autumn so they can live through the winter on food stored in their bodies. During this resting time, cubs are born.

Once the cubs have been brought outside
the den by their mother, they start to
explore. Black bears are very good climbers.
This young cub can already get up a tree—
even if it is not sure how to get down!

But little cubs stay close to their mother
most of the time. They will live with her
until they are about two years old and able
to find their own food. This family of brown
bears lives in North America. Brown bears
are bigger and shaggier than black bears. 5

This mother brown bear shows her cubs
how to catch fish. They learn by watching
her. Bears stand in the shallow part of a
river, then quickly pounce on a fish.

This big brown bear has just caught a salmon. Most bears are omnivorous, which means they eat both plants and animals.

Both black and brown bears live in North America. In the last picture, a black bear was standing on a beaver dam. This big brown bear is called a grizzly. Grizzly bears are very big and dangerous.

There are brown bears in Europe too,
especially in Russia. There used to be
many more European brown bears, like
this one, even in the British Isles. But now
bears live only in the wildest places.

11

Polar bears live in the Arctic. They spend a lot of time in the water and are the best swimmers of all bears. Polar bears are very good hunters. They eat fish, seals, and other sea animals.

Polar bears have very thick fur because they live in such a cold climate. Their fur is coated with oil so they can shake water off easily. They have pads of fur on the soles of their feet to help them walk on the ice.

15

These cubs are only four months old, but their fur is already quite thick. It blends with the snow, keeping them hidden from enemies.

Polar bear cubs are born in a den under
the snow. When they grow old enough to
come out and explore the world, the
mother keeps a close watch out for danger.

17

Like all bears, young male polars spend a
lot of time play-fighting. They don't hurt
each other, although they could. It is a way
of keeping fit.

The polar bear on the right is almost fully grown. It is nearly ready to leave its mother. It will live alone, as other adult bears do.

Bears live in other parts of the world, too.
In South America, there are bears with
large white circles of fur around their eyes,
called spectacled bears. The bears in this
picture are sloth bears from India.

This Asiatic black bear is often called a moon bear because of the white crescent on its chest. It is much smaller than the American black bears. Sun bears, the smallest of all bears, live in southeast Asia.

Bears do not have many animal enemies.
They are too big and fierce. But this
American black bear is no match for the
puma that is attacking it. Bears' worst
enemies are people who hunt them for
sport and for their fur.

In Canada, polar bears can be a problem
for people. They sniff through the garbage
for food and come quite close to houses.
At one time, many people hunted polar
bears for their beautiful fur. But now these
bears are protected in some countries.

First Steck-Vaughn Edition 1992

First published in the United States 1986
by Raintree Publishers, A Division of Steck-Vaughn Company.

Reprinted in 1989

First published in the United Kingdom under the title
Animals in the Wild—Bear
by Belitha Press Ltd.
31 Newington Green, London N16 9PU
in association with Methuen Children's Books Ltd.

Text and illustrations in this form © Belitha Press 1986
Text © Mary Hoffman 1986

Dedicated to Shilpa and Kamini

Scientific Adviser: Dr. Gwynne Vevers. Picture Research: Stella Martin.
Designer: Ken Hatherley.

Acknowledgments are due to the following for the photographs used in
this book: Bruce Coleman Ltd pp. 2, 3, 4, 6, 8/9, 11, 14, 15, 16, 18, 19, 22,
and 23; Eric and David Hosking pp. 12/13; Frank Lane Picture Agency Ltd.
pp. 5, 7, and 21; NHPA pp. 10 and 20; Survival Anglia Ltd pp. 1 and 17.
Front cover: NHPA. Back cover: Bruce Coleman Ltd.

Library of Congress number: 86-6775

Library of Congress Cataloging in Publication Data

Hoffman, Mary, 1945–
  Bear.

  (Animals in the wild)
  Summary: Describes the physical characteristics, behavior, and natural
environment of different kinds of bears throughout the world.
  1. Bears—Juvenile literature [1. Bears]
I. Title. II. Series.
  QL737.C27H64   1986   599.74′446   86-6775

ISBN 0-8172-2396-7   hardcover library binding

ISBN 0-8114-6871-2   softcover binding

4 5 6 7 8 9   99 98 97 96 95 94 93 92

TRUE CRIME

Crimes of
Passion

BY
THE EDITORS OF
TIME-LIFE BOOKS
Alexandria, Virginia

Crimes of Passion

COVER: JEAN HARRIS

1

Appearances

They were a sophisticated-looking couple—he tall, trim, and well-tailored; she petite and coolly blond, her clothes and jewelry a study in understated good taste. They seemed well suited to their setting that October in 1976: the luxurious Ritz Hotel in Paris, where they followed a porter down the hallway toward their elegant suite. Accustomed to worldly and well-heeled guests, the porter nevertheless might still have been impressed by this pair. The man seemed so obviously well-to-do—born to money, most likely—and the pretty woman looked so confident and self-possessed, a lady who clearly knew who she was and where she belonged in the world. That was how things appeared, anyway. The problem was that with Herman Tarnower and Jean Harris appearances were often deceiving; things were so seldom what they seemed.

Harris stepped inside the door of the suite, studiously ignoring the fat manila envelope on the rug. Mail tended to follow them on the round-the-world travels that they both enjoyed. And Harris, who had been this man's lover for 10 years, knew that the mail was often from other women, although the one time Tarnower offered an explanation he said it was from the medical group that he, a highly successful cardiologist and internist, had founded in the tony New York suburb of Scarsdale. Harris had pretended to accept the lie. It wasn't her habit to make a fuss.

On this particular occasion, Tarnower scooped up the envelope without comment. Then he took off his cuff links, a handsome gold and malachite pair that he wore often. Harris had seen them many times; he'd told her they were a gift from a grateful patient. He dropped them on the mantelpiece and went to his room to change for dinner. Alone, Harris took off her earrings and pearls, laid them by the cuff links, and noticed for the first time that the cuff links were engraved. "All my love, Lynne. February 23, 1974," the inscription read. Lynne was Lynne Tryforos, and she was no grateful patient, as

Harris well knew. Tryforos, like Harris, was Tarnower's lover, and she was an increasingly formidable rival for the doctor's attention and affection. Unlike Harris, who was soon to be headmistress of a posh girls' school, Tryforos had no particular social credentials. But like Harris, she was blond and pretty—Tarnower's preferred physical type. She was also considerably younger than Harris and, as the doctor's assistant at the medical group, considerably closer to the work that was the real center of his life.

Harris suddenly lost the tight grip she normally held on her emotions and began shouting at Tarnower. Then, astonishingly, she slammed a closet door with such vicious force that its full-length mirror shattered. Tarnower came in and quickly assessed the damage—both to the mirror and to his prospects for an unruffled evening. Then he, an absolute autocrat with the women in his life, also did an uncharacteristic thing. He apologized; he was sorry for bringing the cuff links.

No more was said. The doctor and his lady dressed and set out for their evening in Paris. By the time they returned to the hotel, the Ritz had already replaced the mirror, so there was no unseemly shattered glass to remind them of shattered calm. And they went serenely on, this handsome, well-matched pair, enjoying each other as they'd always done, savoring the best that life had to offer. To all appearances.

Jean Harris had understood about appearances all her life. She'd learned about them from both her parents, although in different ways. Born Jean Struven in Chicago on April 27, 1923, she was the second of four children of a solidly middle-class Episcopalian family. Albert Struven, her father, was a successful engineer and, at six-feet-two-inches, an imposing physical presence. He was also a mean-spirited, hot-tempered bigot, quick to criticize, slow to praise, opinionated with his friends, and often tyrannical to his family. Frequent tar-

---

At the West Palm Beach, Florida, home of friends in December 1978, cardiologist and diet doctor Herman Tarnower and school headmistress Jean Harris strike a companionable pose that belies the mounting tensions in their 12-year affair.

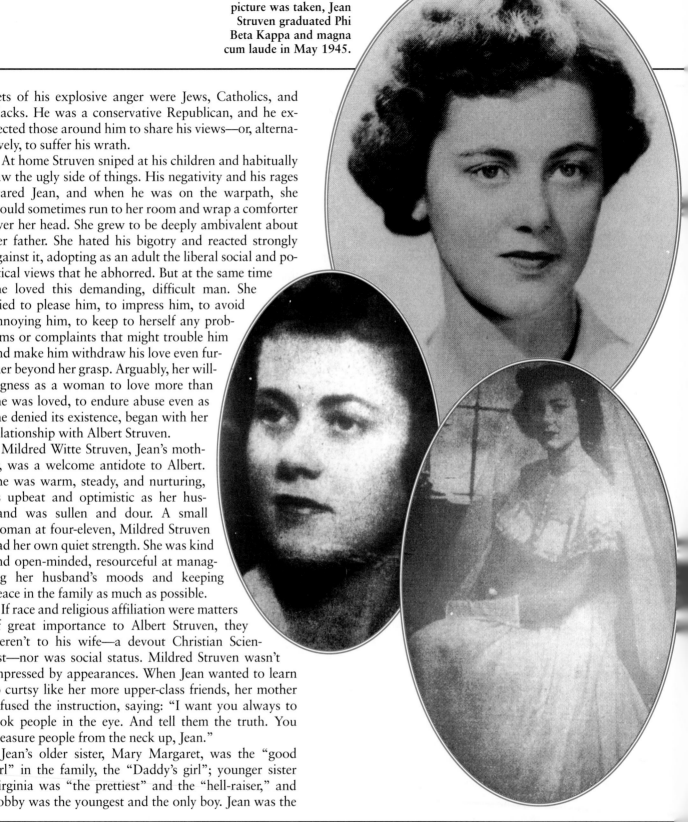

A steady-eyed economics major at Smith College when this senior picture was taken, Jean Struven graduated Phi Beta Kappa and magna cum laude in May 1945.

gets of his explosive anger were Jews, Catholics, and blacks. He was a conservative Republican, and he expected those around him to share his views—or, alternatively, to suffer his wrath.

At home Struven sniped at his children and habitually saw the ugly side of things. His negativity and his rages scared Jean, and when he was on the warpath, she would sometimes run to her room and wrap a comforter over her head. She grew to be deeply ambivalent about her father. She hated his bigotry and reacted strongly against it, adopting as an adult the liberal social and political views that he abhorred. But at the same time she loved this demanding, difficult man. She tried to please him, to impress him, to avoid annoying him, to keep to herself any problems or complaints that might trouble him and make him withdraw his love even further beyond her grasp. Arguably, her willingness as a woman to love more than she was loved, to endure abuse even as she denied its existence, began with her relationship with Albert Struven.

Mildred Witte Struven, Jean's mother, was a welcome antidote to Albert. She was warm, steady, and nurturing, as upbeat and optimistic as her husband was sullen and dour. A small woman at four-eleven, Mildred Struven had her own quiet strength. She was kind and open-minded, resourceful at managing her husband's moods and keeping peace in the family as much as possible.

If race and religious affiliation were matters of great importance to Albert Struven, they weren't to his wife—a devout Christian Scientist—nor was social status. Mildred Struven wasn't impressed by appearances. When Jean wanted to learn to curtsy like her more upper-class friends, her mother refused the instruction, saying: "I want you always to look people in the eye. And tell them the truth. You measure people from the neck up, Jean."

Jean's older sister, Mary Margaret, was the "good girl" in the family, the "Daddy's girl"; younger sister Virginia was "the prettiest" and the "hell-raiser," and Bobby was the youngest and the only boy. Jean was the

One week after graduation, Struven's photo (*center*) and news of her engagement to James Harris appeared in her hometown paper. A year later, on May 25, 1946, she wed (*above*).

"smart one." However peculiar their father or conflicted their family life, the Struven children were in most ways privileged beneficiaries of the American Dream. They lived in the better suburbs of Cleveland—Cleveland Heights and, later, Shaker Heights—and they went to fine schools. After eight years of public schools, Jean put on the green skirt and middy blouse of the Laurel School in Cleveland, as did her two sisters. She did well in her studies and was popular with her classmates. Good-natured and trusted, she was elected secretary of her freshman class and class president in her senior year. Three years in a row she was Laurel's winner of *Time* magazine's challenging Current Events Contest. She liked school—but not as well as she liked the family's yearly summer vacations.

Around Memorial Day the Struvens, with maid and cook in tow, drove both their Packards into Canada to a posh cottage in Rondeau Shores Estates, the stretch of shoreline by Lake Erie that the media dubbed Millionaires' Row. The Struven children would long remember these summers as innocent idylls full of ghost stories, canoeing, home theatrics, taffy pulls, and their mother's cinnamon toast with milk. An older girl, Marge Richey, was the leader of the children whose families summered there, and Jean tagged around after her. Even more than hobnobbing with Marge, however, Jean liked to visit with the Harris family, who had a cottage nearby. Patriarch Albert "Butts" Harris consistently voted Democratic, thus earning the ridicule of Albert Struven. But Jean adored Butts. He was short and funny, so much more relaxed than her father and such a reader. His home exuded warmth and a kind of informal intellectuality. Butts enjoyed sharing such writers as the irreverent H. L. Mencken and philosopher and psychologist William James with the keen and curious Jean.

Jean also liked Butts Harris's son Jim, a tall, handsome boy who possessed his father's goodness, if not his brilliance. When Jim was off at the University of Michigan, Jean remarked to friends at Laurel that she guessed she'd marry him, even though he was so predictable that her life would probably be boring.

World War II was raging in Europe when Jean traveled east in 1941 to prestigious Smith College. Jim Harris was navigating Pacific rescue missions for the Naval Air Corps at the time, and he and Jean were writing each other steadily. At Smith she majored in economics and minored in Spanish. In her junior year Jim presented her with a diamond ring.

In the spring of 1945, Jean Struven was graduated magna cum laude from Smith with a Phi Beta Kappa key in hand. Had she been born 30 years or so later, she might have looked forward to a future of nearly limitless options. But, however gifted, she wasn't thinking uppermost of a career. She was very much a product of her times and her circumstances—a traditional girl with traditional expectations. And that meant that she expected to get married—soon. In those days anyone left single at 25 was an old maid, viewed by most of society as being eccentric or impaired or both.

Jean Struven wasn't worried. She had her engagement ring, and she spent the better part of the next year making plans for her wedding and looking for a teaching job. Albert Struven considered schoolteaching the lowliest job on earth.

As the date for the May 1946 nuptials rolled around, Mildred Struven assembled a trousseau of dresses with matching hats for her daughter, while Albert Struven railed that the groom wasn't bright enough or ambitious enough for his daughter. Struven escorted 23-year-old Jean downstairs to the backyard ceremony, but he cried during much of it, perhaps because his will was being thwarted. The bride would say long afterward that she married the groom to defy and escape her father and because, unlike her father, Jim Harris was quiet. If he didn't sparkle, neither did he rage. He seemed to offer her a safe haven.

Jim and Jean Harris began their married life in Grosse Pointe, Michigan, a wealthy WASP town where the privileged churlishly guarded their prerogatives: It would be one of the last American municipalities to strike down restrictions against Jews at its golf and yacht clubs. The young Harrises, although they were adequately pedigreed, were not part of Grosse Pointe's elite; they lacked the wealth of the favored class, and even, for that matter, of their own parents. They lived first in a garage apartment, then moved into an unpretentious colonial-style house on a street not far from a Sears shopping center.

Making automobiles was the economic lifeblood of

Detroit and its suburbs, and many of the industry's aristocrats lived in Grosse Pointe. Jim Harris wasn't among them. He found a modest job at Holley Carburetor and never excelled. He was considered easy and relaxed, a man of sunny disposition and simple pleasures. He liked to mow his lawn, wash his car, and, later, play ball with his sons. Jean Harris found a job teaching history and social studies to secondary students at the Grosse Pointe Country Day School, now called University-Liggett School. She worked long hours preparing classes and correcting papers, then turned her energy to her home, where she scrubbed her own floors, housed her widowed mother-in-law, and entertained other young couples in Grosse Pointe's lower strata of professionals and working people.

Harris was 27 in 1950 when her first child, David, was born. The new mother fell into a two-day postpartum depression that she handled by driving around in a car, crying quietly. Two years later, her son Jimmy was born. By this time Jean was beginning to realize that some of the hollowness she felt was actually discontent with her marriage, but she soldiered on with it for 12 more years. In the process, she came to certain stiff-upper-lip conclusions: If things go wrong in life, you must examine yourself first and not blame others. If she'd made a mistake in marrying Jim, she'd not complain. She'd play her part. She'd be jolly, a good companion, the committed wife. She was genuinely happy with her children, at least, and with her teaching. She was a splendid teacher.

Harris had started off teaching middle school and high school, then switched to a lighter schedule as a kindergarten teacher until her first child was born. After the birth of her second son she'd resumed full-time work, teaching first grade for 11 years. Her own boys attended the private school free. Of all her teaching experiences, she best loved watching six-year-olds begin to read, write, and reason. Small as they were, Harris encouraged her pupils to explore their world boldly; she delighted in those who plunged with gusto into the finger paints and responded with wonder when she played records of whales singing.

When her boys were 11 and 9 and off to a summer camp paid for by a fellowship she'd won, Harris took a break herself. She chaperoned a group of boys from the exclusive Choate School on a trip to Russia. Passing through New York en route, she visited her old friend Marge Richey, who was now married to a Jewish lawyer. Marge and Leslie Jacobson were living on Park Avenue, and Harris was impressed not only with Marge's husband and her elegant home but also with the fact that Marge had forged a career as an interior decorator. Women working if they didn't have to weren't all that numerous in 1961.

The visit with the Jacobsons and the trip abroad offered tantalizing glimpses of wider vistas—glimpses that may have helped crystallize the discontent that was growing inside Jean Harris. She returned to her life as a wife, mother, and provincial schoolteacher, but the confines of her world seemed even narrower than before. She presented her usual cheerful face to the world; she kept up appearances. But there were nights when she lay on the summer grass and looked at stars and asked herself if this were all.

One night in 1964 Jim Harris discovered that his two sons had gone to bed without brushing their teeth. He came downstairs to lecture his wife on this obvious neglect of her maternal duties. And in that one inane confrontation, the aridity of her life was, to Jean Harris, suddenly clear and inescapable: The sum of her whole existence was a pair of dry toothbrushes, pointing blame from their tidy holders. Calmly, she told her husband their marriage was over.

Harris saw a lawyer and filed for divorce. She wouldn't say anything bad about Jim Harris; he was a fine man, a wonderful father. She didn't want alimony, and she said that child support of $200 a month would be fine. The divorce became final on June 11, 1965.

Harris was 42 when the divorce came through, a softly pretty woman with a luminous complexion, shiny blond hair, and a trim figure. Social mores were changing as the 1960s moved toward the turbulence that would be their hallmark. But even so, divorce was not common among the people Jean Harris knew. It was still regarded as vaguely improper, and divorced women were faintly déclassé, creatures who often foundered alone in a world that was made up of couples. Still, Jean Harris wanted her independence and a chance for a more meaningful life, and she went after them with her customary grit.

After her 1965 divorce, Harris, shown in her office at Philadelphia's Springside School, took an administrative post.

She and the boys could live on her $8,500 annual salary, Harris figured, but she needed to save for her sons' education. At 15 and 13, brawny, football-playing David and Jimmy looked to their diminutive mother to handle things, affectionately calling her Big Woman, or Big for short. In an effort to bolster their future as well as her own, she looked for a better-paying job. As much as she loved teaching, she knew that she'd have to abandon it in favor of administration, which offered slightly more money.

Harris consulted the Smith College Vocational Office and found a job paying $10,000 as director of the Middle School—grades five through eight—of the Springside School, a private girls' school in Chestnut Hill, the Philadelphia suburb where ran some of the bluest blood in America. Jean and the two boys moved into an old house she'd rented. It had squirrels in the attic, but its seven fireplaces were atmospheric. David and Jimmy were able to get scholarships at nearby Chestnut Hill Academy. Their diminished family might be financially strapped, but the boys' education continued to be first rate.

In the fall of 1966 Harris began learning the difference between teaching and running a school. Gone was the joy of watching understanding spread across a small face. Rather, her time was spent holding the line against beer and marijuana, counseling parents who'd lost control of their children, and recruiting new students to keep the coffers filled. A school director, Harris later quipped, needed the hide of an iguana, the ability to get along on four hours' sleep, a law degree, and a wife.

So relentless was the work that Harris began to feel like a nonperson; she was known to others only by what she did, not who she was. She had no social life, and she needed one. She'd always enjoyed the company of men, and she had never meant to give them up. After her divorce, Jean had even fantasized to a friend about the perfect second husband. He'd be a Jewish doctor, she said: Such a man would be ideal because as a Jew he'd be intellectual and warm-hearted, while as a doctor he'd be protective and caring. If she realized that she was dealing in stereotypes no less than her father had done, the irony of it apparently escaped her.

Early in December 1966 Harris spoke on the tele-

SYRACUSE UNIVERSITY
MEDICAL COLLEGE
JUNE 1933

Photos By Doust

phone with her old friend Marge Jacobson. Marge invited her to that weekend's dinner party, adding, "I've got a guy for you!" It was then that Jean Harris met her Jewish doctor. And he was everything she could have wished for—to all appearances.

Working as a camp counselor to help earn his tuition, Herman Tarnower (inset) graduated from medical school in 1933.

Whatever impression he managed to give later in life, Herman Tarnower was not a child of wealth and privilege. On the contrary, he was the son of Eastern European immigrants who were among the approximately 90,000 Jews who fled to the United States each year during the early part of the 20th century to escape poverty, grinding labor, and bloody massacres in their anti-Semitic homelands. This influx greatly boosted New York City's Jewish population and caused considerable social upheaval: Rather than welcoming their coreligionists with open arms, the long-assimilated German Jews who'd prospered in America were appalled by

them. For the most part, members of the Jewish gentry did all they could to dissociate themselves from the unwashed, unlettered tide of new Jews, whom they referred to as "Orientals." There was fear among the old-line Jews that these hordes of unsightly newcomers might threaten the hard-won position that they, the Jews long established in American culture and commerce, had carved for themselves among the nation's WASP aristocracy.

Herman Tarnower was born in Brooklyn on March 18, 1910, the only son among four children and therefore, in his patriarchal environment, automatically the pampered darling of the family. His mother and three sisters doted on him, instilling in him early, perhaps, the notion that the affection of women was his by right. Harry Tarnower, Herman's quiet, gentle father, made a decent living as a manufacturer of hats. His mother, Dora, was a homemaker, a woman as talkative as her husband was silent. Like Jean Harris among her siblings, Herman Tarnower was apparently the smart one. He did well in public school and finished up with excellent grades at James Madison High School.

Not only was he smart, but Herman Tarnower—Hi, as he was nicknamed—was in some respects acutely sensitive. He was, for instance, painfully aware of the limitations inherent in his birth. And he was equally mindful that somewhere beyond Brooklyn another world existed—a world of money and perquisites, of sleek, scented, soft-voiced women and polished, powerful men. This world was a fortress whose every gateway was barred to the likes of Herman Tarnower, but he was young and bright and, above all, determined. He would somehow scale the walls. He would belong.

After high school Tarnower threw a few things into a bag—including some rather handsome winnings from cards and pool—and hitchhiked upstate to Syracuse University. His father paid as much of the tuition as he could, and Hi made up the rest with his gambling earnings. One of the courses he chose at Syracuse was speech. He bought a mirror and practiced in front of it, gradually losing the Brooklyn accent that advertised his origins. He also worked to expand his cultural horizons; he read widely and voraciously.

Tarnower was still at Syracuse in 1929 when the stock market plummeted and took America into the Great Depression. His father's business failed, but Hi somehow managed to launch himself into medical school at Syracuse. His keen mind and relentless drive allowed him to finish his studies on an accelerated schedule, and he graduated in 1933. With the help of a fellowship, he studied the new discipline of cardiology in London and internal medicine in Amsterdam. He was in Europe when Harry Tarnower died at the age of 54 of a heart attack. Dora Tarnower withheld the news from her son for weeks, waiting until he finished his studies and returned to the United States.

Dora managed to keep intact a $5,000 life insurance benefit for Hi to use to set up a practice, but if her son was grateful, his appreciation seemed tempered with distaste. Now the man of the family in his mid-20s, Hi reportedly made a deal with his sister Billie regarding their mother. "You listen to her," he said, "and I'll pay the bills." Thereafter, he supported Dora and visited her fairly frequently, but the visits were always brief. According to some people who knew him, he regarded his mother as a burden.

After completing his internship and residency at Bellevue Hospital in 1936, Tarnower set up an internal medicine and cardiology practice in the stylish, predominantly WASP suburb of Scarsdale, located in Westchester County north of New York City. The town's first Jewish doctor—according to Tarnower—he rented an office with a tiny living space behind it and bought equipment on the installment plan. He stayed by the phone, waiting for patients.

Gradually they appeared. They weren't always wealthy, but if his patients couldn't pay in cash, Tarnower was willing to accept fresh flowers or vegetables instead. People liked him—women especially. He wasn't handsome in a conventional way, but he kept himself fit and he had warm, deep-set brown eyes. He was witty and a wonderful dancer, and when he cared to be, he was marvelously attentive: He could make a woman feel important and admired. He was good company and a more-than-presentable escort or dinner partner; he'd acquired a lot of polish in school and in Europe, and Brooklyn was far behind him.

But if Hi Tarnower enjoyed women, he didn't seem to value them very highly. Cold and warm, pragmatic and romantic, he was full of contradictions—a pull-push man who'd charm a woman only to drop her instantly if she failed in any way to meet his needs or expectations. He had no patience with women who made demands on his time or attention, and he was acutely marriage shy. Professional success was at the top of his agenda.

When the United States entered World War II, Tarnower joined the army. By mid-1942, the self-assured young captain was stationed in Kentucky, where he learned to hunt birds. Game shooting had a genteel air that appealed to him; it was the sort of sportsman's pursuit that might one day help endear him to wealthy patients. But if Tarnower began his military service with one of the cushiest assignments, he ended with one of the worst. Promoted to the rank of major, he was one of a contingent of doctors sent on the first air mission to assess the damage at Nagasaki after that Japanese city had been leveled by an American atomic bomb. The devastation shook him; he had difficulty talking about it.

After the war—he left the military as a lieutenant colonel—Tarnower returned to Scarsdale and started a small group medical practice. He moved into a new apartment, where he ordered the gas stove disconnected: He didn't cook and he didn't want to encourage any woman to cook for him. He worked six long days a week, making himself available to patients before their workdays started if necessary. He made house calls in his Chevrolet and bought a Cadillac for his social life. The ambitious young doctor was prospering, but he hadn't yet located the toehold that would boost him toward the rarified social stratosphere to which he aspired. He was in his late thirties when he finally found it.

Frieda Schiff Warburg of New York City and the Westchester country estate of Meadow Farm had long been a mainstay of New York's German Jewish aristocracy. The daughter of one influential banker and wife of another, she was a woman whose patronage was potentially a key to the fortress's highest towers. One day Warburg came into White Plains Hospital, with which Tarnower was affiliated, for some electrocardiograms, and Tarnower read them. He suggested—though fellow doctors scoffed at the idea—that the great lady would profit from taking her digitalis by injection rather than by mouth. He himself would be most happy to come by Meadow Farm every day to inject her.

Not surprisingly, they became friends. Tarnower paid court daily, usually around noon. Warburg affectionately dubbed him Dr. Lunch Hour. Ever attentive, Tarnower was a superb listener, helpful, full of amusing stories interspersed with erudite conversation. Soon he was tending the ills of the entire Warburg family, its servants, and its friends—including the profoundly wealthy bankers, industrialists, and publishers, and the gifted artists who dwelled at the glittering pinnacle of Jewish society.

Over the years, members of the German Jewish aristocracy had taken to spending their weekends in Westchester County, golfing at their own Century Country Club, which in the not-too-distant past had excluded "Oriental" Jews as thoroughly as WASP country clubs of the day excluded Jews of any kind. Hi Tarnower was one of the first Jews of Eastern European descent to be invited to join Century, just before he turned 40.

Dr. Herman Tarnower had arrived; he'd joined the club both literally and figuratively. It was belonging that mattered most, but the money that came with his new-found social acceptance was also welcome. He would never be wealthy in comparison with many of the super-rich with whom he now hobnobbed, but he would live very comfortably.

By his late forties, Tarnower had enough money to attract a group of doctors and build the Scarsdale Medical Center. The group practice did well. Tarnower himself was usually beloved by patients, but he was not always admired by fellow physicians. Some of his colleagues found him autocratic, testy, and controlling.

Hi Tarnower fished for marlin in the Bahamas and for bonefish off Mexico. He golfed with his country club friends. But if he was good at sports, it sometimes seemed that he never truly understood sportsmanship. A Century Club member remarked that in 20 years of playing golf with him, Tarnower never once called out "good shot." He played with the same single-minded intensity that he applied to his work or to social climbing. He played to win.

Nevertheless, Tarnower's wit and charm brought him many invitations from wealthy friends and patients. Some invited him on exotic trips, and occasionally a woman went with him. There were plenty of women, although Tarnower's ex-lovers seldom remembered him with much fondness.  "In bed, he was completely unemotional, uninvolved," one former mistress told author Shana Alexander, who wrote a 1983 book about Harris and Tarnower. "It ended because I got too possessive and Hi dropped me flat. He's the kind of guy that starts fast and finishes fast. Then he gets into the other bed and goes to sleep while you just lie there and feel bad."

Still, an affair with Hi—while it lasted—could be enormously exciting. He took his lady friends on expensive trips, gave them lit-

SCARSDALE
MEDICAL CENTER

Hi Tarnower set up
practice in Scarsdale,
New York, and by
1959 he had built the
Scarsdale Medical Cen-
ter *(above)*. In 1963,
Tarnower *(left, circled)*
joined former medical
school classmates for
their 30th reunion.

At Tarnower's Purchase, New York, home the central kitchen and dining room were flanked by servants' quarters—at left, in this aerial view—and, at right, by the main-level living room and, above that, his bedroom.

tle gifts, and accepted in return their devotion and their considerable output of monogrammed mementos. But he remained a bachelor. His treatment of women patients and the women he cultivated socially may have been infinitely gentle and caring. But his actions toward those he dated suggested that he didn't much respect women, or trust them, or even like them. He didn't take them seriously; he didn't feel they were equal to men. Female feelings, if he noticed them at all, were of little concern to him—or, worse, they were a troublesome trespass into his self-absorption. In love affairs he was, if charming and presentable, also selfish.

Approaching 50, Tarnower bought a home near Scarsdale that suited the status he'd attained. It was a portion of an estate, set on six acres in Purchase, the northeastern section of a small town called Harrison. It included a tennis court and pool, and a pool house that Tarnower converted into living quarters. He admired the formality and simplicity of Japanese art and architecture, and he remodeled the pool house to resemble, roughly, a Japanese-style dwelling. The house had a sort of dumbbell configuration. On the main level was a central entry hall, which included a small kitchen and was flanked on one side by a big dining room and on the other by a living room. Two rooms off the dining room, added later, were servants' quarters. There was a garage beneath the living room, and from it issued a spiral staircase that ran up through the living room and into Tarnower's bedroom on the second floor. The bedroom was the only room on that level.

The bedroom was a long, plain room divided into two even narrower areas by a massive carved room divider. The stairs emerged near the first of two single beds whose headboards were formed by the divider. Both headboards had padded armrests that could be lowered so that Tarnower and his guest could comfortably sit up to read or watch television. A sliding glass door on the front wall by the TV led out onto a balcony that overlooked a circular drive and beyond it a small pond. Tarnower had placed at the center of the pond a gold-painted Buddha. In an area behind the room divider were two bathrooms, his and hers, with a dressing room between them. In the dressing room a large window looked from the back of the house over the swimming pool and the tennis court.

By spring 1967 the romance between Harris and Tarnower
was in full flower, and he sent love letters to her in
Philadelphia like the one below—written following a conversation in which they "had settled the world's problems."

The doctor enjoyed entertaining in his new home. He played host from the head of the dining room table, his chair facing a cabinet that displayed his collection of guns. The dining room walls were hung with the mounted heads of Tarnower's kills: gazelle, wilde-beest, antelope, and a Cape buffalo, plus a pair of elephant tusks. His dinner parties usu-ally consisted of six to eight people and fea-tured his women friends —trophies in their own right, some might say.

The wines at these din-ners were good; the doctor had been coached in wines by his friend and patient, publisher Alfred Knopf. The credit for the cuisine belonged to his cook and housekeeper, Suzanne van der Vreken, the more companionable half of a Belgian couple Tarnower hired in 1964 to manage his domes-tic arrangements. Her husband, Henri van der Vreken, was pri-marily the chauffeur and gardener, although he sullenly chose to refer to himself as the estate manager.

Tarnower's lover at the time was Gerda Stedman, Ger-man born and half Jewish, half Catholic. She was slen-der, blond, and blue-eyed, and she knew how to live well. In 1961 her banker husband had died young, leav-ing her with two small girls and a great deal of money. She added greatly to Tarnower's sophistication, taking him to her husband's tailor and trying to interest him in museums and concerts. But while she guided him gently

in certain matters of taste, she un-derstood that Tarnower must not be criticized or controlled in any way, not even urged to leave a table before he was ready: "If you don't like it," he said once when she tried to hurry him, "let's call it quits." Toward the end of 1965, after three years with the doctor, she left him to marry somebody else. He turned 56 without a woman by his side. But he wasn't alone for long.

On December 9, 1966, Henri van der Vreken drove a blue Cadillac into Manhat-tan and stopped at a posh address on Park Avenue. The doors of the Jacobsons' ele-gant home were opened to their din-ner guests, and Jean Harris and Hi Tarnower came into each other's presence for the first time.

Harris felt the doctor's anima-tion and authority instant-ly—he reminded her of an Egyptian pharaoh, she said later—and Tarnower felt the small blond woman's energy and charm. They sat on a sofa and laughed and showed off for each other, trading sto-ries of their separate trips to Russia. But at 11 p.m. sharp, Henri van der Vreken arrived to whisk Tarnower off in a departure so abrupt that Harris dubbed it Cinderella-like and thought she'd never see him again.

Returning to life at Chestnut Hill, Harris soon found herself in bed with back trouble. A present arrived, a picture book about the ancient Judean fortress of Masada. The accompanying note said, "It's time you learned more about the Jews, Hi Tarnower." Next came a Christmas note: "You were a delight to be with. I kept wondering if you could keep up the pace." Then a dozen red roses, then silence.

In January, Harris got a letter from Tarnower, written just before he left for a safari in Nairobi, Kenya: "Is there any day you might be in New York in March?" he wanted to know. Indeed, Harris would be attending a meeting in New York in March, and the two arranged a date; she left her meeting early to splurge on a pair of shoes. That evening, Tarnower's Cadillac pulled up in front of the Barbizon Plaza Hotel to collect her. He took her to dinner at a small, expensive restaurant, where he'd carefully ordered the meal ahead. Harris loved having him make such decisions. For years her husband had turned to her to ask where they should go when they ate out. This man took charge.

The doctor found that Harris had no problem keeping up the pace. She made jokes, caught innuendos, and knew current events. Also attractive to Tarnower was the fact that she'd spent most of her adult life in that exclusive WASP enclave, Grosse Pointe—so impressive for keeping up appearances. After dinner the couple moved on to the Pierre Hotel for dancing. He found her a stiff partner, but it was a minor flaw. For the most part, he decided, she suited him very well. They both drank more than usual—two manhattans for him, two whiskey sours for her. But then, at 11 p.m., the chauffer arrived, and Tarnower made one of his deadline departures. The doctor did, however, escort his date back to her hotel, where, looking for the elevators after entering through a back door, the couple got caught momentarily in a hallway dead end.

"I guess we've gone about as far as we can go," she quipped.

"Oh, no," he said, "we haven't."

Harris enjoyed two weeks of intense long-distance courtship, complete with roses and telephone calls. At spring break she headed back to Manhattan with David and Jimmy. They stayed with the Jacobsons and joined Tarnower on Friday evening to see Angela Lansbury onstage in *Mame*. On Sunday, Harris and the boys drove out to Tarnower's home to enjoy Suzanne van der Vreken's curried shrimp. But the big event of the week-

end was on Saturday, when Harris joined the doctor and his friends to observe his 57th birthday. Jean Harris would celebrate 13 birthdays with Hi Tarnower. He never asked when hers was.

From March into May, Tarnower telephoned Harris every day at 6:30 p.m. She visited him in Purchase three or four times, staying in the town of Armonk with some friends of his, retired investment banker Arthur Schulte and his wife, Vivian. Tarnower rarely visited Harris in Philadelphia.

The pair continued to amuse and impress each other, presenting at all times their most urbane faces. But even in the heady early days of the affair, there were some problems. Many of Tarnower's Jewish friends didn't approve of Jean Harris, and her WASP world wasn't universally enthusiastic about him. Her mother gently cautioned Jean to stop mentioning Tarnower in letters; every time she did it her father got furious and called her a whore. But whatever the external difficulties, Tarnower was clearly in hot pursuit at that point. "I love you very, very much," he wrote to Harris. "How can I tell?—I miss you and want to share so many things with you—sharing that must be love!! Are most people who marry in love? What happens? So few are really happy. You will give me all the answers this weekend—drive carefully, you will be transporting valuable cargo."

Harris charitably declined, evidently, to correct her suitor's peculiar punctuation, nor did she quibble with a far less attractive trait that must have been an affront to her own good breeding: his name dropping. "The highlight of this week will be Sunday—cocktails with the Smiths and then dinner at the Seymour Toppings (foreign editor of the N.Y. times), with Knopf, Harrison Salisbury and Mr. Ronning (Canadian Ambassador-at-Large...)." Only after detailing his impressive acquaintances—complete with descriptions in parentheses, lest she not grasp their full importance—did Tarnower again wax romantic: "Darling my love for you grows deeper all the time—that's good?? I feel we could be very, very happy together."

Perhaps the affair reached its apex on Memorial Day weekend of 1967, when Tarnower gave Harris a $10,000, four-carat, emerald-cut diamond engagement ring. She had a few reservations: Would such a confirmed bachelor make a good husband and father?

Jean, I can't go through with it.

HERMAN TARNOWER

Should her sons be moved to another school so fast? But she was in love for the first time in her life, and besides, her doctor could take care of her, could enfold her in a world free of money worries and work problems, a world full of parties and dinners and exciting trips and interesting friends. All doubts faded at the prospect of spending the rest of her life with this fascinating man.

She gave notice at Springside and on the Fourth of July was dancing with her fiancé at the Century Country Club, the diamond sparkling on her hand. Several of the doctor's close friends doubted that he'd ever make it down the aisle. But Tarnower himself seemed to consider his blond WASP a plum social trophy. He often introduced her as "Jean Harris of Grosse Pointe," as though she were a doyenne of that town's charmed circle.

As the summer went on, however, Harris began to wonder herself whether Tarnower would ever set a date. By late August she had to know. And during a phone call, he told her: "Jean, I can't go through with it." He said he was sorry, but he just couldn't overcome his fear of marriage. She deserved to be married, but he couldn't do it. She hung up, devastated.

Everything was falling apart. Harris's back was giving her trouble again, and funny noises she heard in the walls at the Chestnut Hill house turned out to be masses of ticks. After she and the boys packed up to stay with a friend while the exterminator worked, she mailed the diamond ring to Purchase with this note: "You really ought to give this to Suzanne. She's the only woman you'll ever need in your life." Then, wearily, she called Springside and got her job back.

When Tarnower received the ring, he telephoned. She must keep it, he said. If not, he'd give it to her son David. She declined. He went to Philadelphia to see her. Her boys tried to figure out what was happening when their mother and the doctor locked themselves in her bedroom, from whence issued, hour after hour, the sounds of arguing. At the end of it, he left; she kept the ring.

Jean Harris started trying to put her life back together. In September she took Jimmy to Rhode Island for some sailing. But driving back on the Merritt Parkway, she saw the turnoff to Tarnower's house and impulsively took it. From a pay phone she called him. He invited them to have dinner with him and his sister Billie and

her family. The evening only made it clear that the old attraction held.

Late in November Harris wrote a letter to Tarnower on three-holed, lined, school paper; it essentially declared that she was a 1967 modern woman and free to enter a sexual liaison without marriage: "Everything about us is important to me Hi, because I've never experienced love before until you," she wrote. "Maybe I can never really know that you loved me, Hi, but I do know that for a little while you were a wonderfully strong, loving, desiring and desirable male animal, and as a rather odd but honest loving female I found every moment with you warm and satisfying and good.

"Maybe having too much money was the trouble," the letter went on. "If the bottom ever falls out of the market, darling, I'm really a very capable housekeeper." Tarnower's reponse was to call and invite her to Jamaica for Christmas.

The lovers returned to separate lives. Harris knew that the doctor saw other women. In response, she adopted her mother's approach with a difficult man: Accentuate the positive, don't whine, be jolly. After all, it was hardly unusual among the couples she knew, including the married couples, for the women to endure the men's infidelities. That's the way things were. The important thing was that the other women would come and go, while she, Jean, would remain. She'd be, if not the only one, at least Number One. She'd hang on; she'd learn to live with it and even to laugh about it—at least in public. And, though she wouldn't admit it to herself, there was some part of her that still hoped that someday he'd change, that he'd realize her devotion, tire of bachelorhood, and marry her.

And so the affair lurched on. They met as lovers, they traveled. In 1970, when Tarnower told Harris that he'd found a woman with four children and wanted to marry her, Harris laughed. She told him he ought to know by now that he wasn't going to do that: "So why don't you stop hurting so many women, and just concentrate on hurting me?" He laughed, too.

But beneath the laughter, Jean Harris was suffering a spiritual erosion from trying to keep up the appearance of affability and acceptance, from struggling to live a life that nothing in her background had equipped her to lead. She was trying her best to be a mistress, but she

18

couldn't help thinking like a wife. Sharing her man didn't come easily to her.

Harris was in her late forties when she began to lose her famous energy. Much later a psychiatrist would explain that this fatigue probably resulted from depression, but all she knew was that she was tired all the time. In early 1971, Tarnower prescribed Desoxyn, a powerful methamphetamine, in a moderate dose—5 milligrams a day. Since the drug was a controlled substance, he sent her the pills in bottles, or gave them to her, or sometimes mailed her prescriptions with false names on them. When the Madeira School doctor later refused to prescribe what he termed a "mind-altering drug," she confronted Tarnower, who told her not to worry, it wouldn't hurt her. Her energy returned. In fact, Harris was so wide awake that she occasionally depended on Tarnower's prescriptions for Valium so she could sleep.

In March of 1971, Harris and Tarnower left for the first of several world tours, seeing this time Kenya, Khartoum, Ceylon, Saudi Arabia, Vietnam, and Hawaii. Jean may have felt this was her due, the special treatment she deserved for tolerating Hi's philandering, but she wasn't the doctor's first choice for a traveling companion. He'd initially invited his former lover, newly divorced Gerda Stedman, whom he pursued for some six months in the middle of his relationship with Harris.

Back home in Chestnut Hill, Harris learned that the Thomas School in Rowayton, Connecticut, needed a headmistress. The job was a challenge, to put it mildly. Thomas, a school of some 115 teenage girls, had no accreditation and was more than $70,000 in debt. But for Harris it was superbly located—on Long Island Sound, only 20 minutes from Purchase. Her sons' lives would not be disrupted by the move: David was in college and Jimmy was in boarding school. So, in the fall of 1971, she settled in Rowayton, where she would live for four years, visiting Tarnower almost every weekend. On Fridays, the doctor's housekeeper would clear away any traces of other women from the master bedroom, and on Sundays she would perform the same rites to erase signs of Jean Harris.

Glad as she was to be close to Tarnower, Harris was increasingly put off by some aspects of her weekends at Purchase—the overly fancy dinner parties, in particular.

She cherished the moments when she was alone with him, walking arm in arm around his estate, admiring the trees and flowers. The pond was his favorite spot; it became hers. They both loved it most in the spring when the daffodils bloomed.

Such peace as she found on weekends was relief from hectic workweeks wherein Harris tried to raise standards at the Thomas School, set up retirement funds, and hold a firm line against the girls' agitation for a smoking room. More and more, it was as though she were two people: for five days a week the harried headmistress, transforming herself on Friday afternoon into the stylish, freshly coifed woman who stepped into a blue chauffeur-driven Cadillac that would take her to a different universe.

In 1972 there was another round-the-world trip for Harris and Tarnower, who flew this time to Iran, Nepal, Burma, Thailand, Hong Kong, and Hawaii. But even such lavish distractions could not obscure the fact that time was passing for Jean Harris, and with it her prime. In the spring of 1973 she turned 50. Her sons were by her side for that birthday. Her lover was not.

Tarnower had begun seeing another blue-eyed blonde with two children—his office assistant, Lynne Tryforos—and that romance waxed as his affair with Harris waned. Sometime in 1974, he stopped saying he loved Harris. He didn't love anyone, he told her; he didn't need anyone. Harris countered with her old who-cares-I'll-be-jolly act, but there was mounting evidence that all her forbearance and good nature were failing to hold on to the doctor's affections.

Marjorie Lynne Brundage was born in Ossining, New York, in 1943. After finishing high school in Scarsdale, she went on to Endicott Junior College but soon dropped out. She married a young florist, Nicholas Tryforos, and at 21 she gave birth to Laura; at 25 Electra was born. Lynne worked part-time in the florist shop and part-time as a secretary-receptionist at the Scarsdale Medical Center. When her marriage fell apart—her husband moved in with another woman—she apparently transferred her affection to Tarnower. She adored her boss. She and her daughters made buttons that

So why don't you stop hurting so many women, and just concentrate on hurting me?

read "Superdoc." Eventually, she began working for the Medical Center full-time.

Lynne Tryforos would become, in time, the bane of Jean Harris's existence. Harris would try in the early days to airily dismiss her as someone tacky and trivial, a woman not up to the doctor's usual standards. Later, she would accuse her rival of everything from sluttishness to psychosis. Tryforos herself has never spoken publicly about Harris, Tarnower, or the role she played in their lives. But if she declined personally to take issue with the lurid portrait that Harris painted of her, Tryforos was defended by others. Some close friends of Tarnower would speak glowingly of her to the press. For example, Iphigene Sulzberger, matriarch of the family that owns the *New York Times,* said Tryforos was "a very nice young woman" and "a perfectly wonderful person." And Tarnower's sister, Billie Schwartz, would call her "giving, good, and loving."

Of course, when Harris first heard about Tryforos, she didn't worry: She'd seen a lot of women come and go in her doctor's life, and she, Jean, was still Number One; she got the weekends and the trips. Besides, Tarnower was, increasingly, the brightest part of her life.

Since Harris had quit teaching and taken up administration, her career was more a burden than a pleasure. Unable to patch up the Thomas School, she worked out a plan during the 1974-1975 school year for having it merge with another academy. But the end of the process left her drained of energy. She'd had it with headmistressing. From guests at the Purchase dining table, she got a line on a new kind of job. For a salary said to be $32,500 a year, she went to work writing up bids on contracts for the Allied Maintenance Corporation in New York City, a large cleaning service for office buildings, industrial sites, and airports. When the Thomas School closed in the spring of 1975, she refused Tarnower's offer to buy her an apartment in New York, stored her extra furniture in his basement, and rented a small place in Manhattan's East Sixties. She continued to spend most weekends with him.

The next February, Tryforos, then 33, came to a final parting of the ways with her husband, and they were divorced in the summer of 1976—the summer that she and Jean Harris started running into each other. According to Harris, the younger woman came by Tarnower's

pool with her daughters one July day while Harris was sunning. The girls jumped into the pool, and Tryforos opened a can of paint and began to freshen up the garden furniture. Harris told her rival that it was bizarre for the two of them to be at the doctor's at the same time. As Harris told it, Tryforos didn't know what the word bizarre meant. Harris told her to leave, and she did.

The two women already had a strange history and one that would remain something of a mystery. A year or so earlier, Harris had begun getting anonymous phone calls; they usually came when she was asleep. The phone would wake her, and when she answered, a man's voice might describe Tarnower making love with another woman, or it might advise Harris to take sex lessons, or tell her that she was old and pathetic. Often the calls came to Harris's office when she was traveling with Tarnower, and when Harris returned to work, there'd be a message for her to call a certain number. When she dialed it, Lynne Tryforos would answer. Stop harassing me, Tryforos would tell Harris.

Both women would complain to Tarnower, who, according to Harris, would then tell his older mistress to leave his younger mistress alone. If she didn't, he threatened Harris, he'd banish her from Purchase. So emotionally dependent on Tarnower had the once-proud Harris become by then that she endured even this indignity. As for the doctor, he seemed to enjoy having his women fight over him.

On the night of September 15, 1976, Tarnower invited Tryforos to stay over. On the 16th he rose, dressed, and met Harris for their flight to Eastern Europe, where Tarnower wanted to search for his father's birthplace. They visited Poland, Romania, Hungary, and Bulgaria, and then they went to Paris and the Ritz, the scene of Harris's small gust of protest—her shattering of the mirror after she read Tryforos's adoring inscription on Tarnower's cuff links.

Back at home, her love life still unsettled and unsettling, Harris did, at least, encounter a new job opportunity, one that seemed to suit her intellect far better than writing cleaning contracts. On December 15, 1976, the search committee of the elite Madeira School outside Washington, D.C., offered Harris its headship over some 325 girls. The position carried a salary of $25,000, with $5,000 raises each year that her annual contract

In 1976, Jean Harris *(above)*, was selected from among 100 candidates to become the new headmistress of the prestigious Madeira School for girls in McLean, Virginia *(top)*.

was renewed, plus a house and a car. The job offer was quite an honor; Madeira had chosen her from among 100 applicants. However, accepting meant putting more geographical distance between her and her lover at a time when her hold on him was very shaky. Moreover, she wasn't sure she was up to the challenge of running a school as big and as prominent as Madeira. But she felt a need to try to regain some control over her circumstances, and she resolved to take the job.

Harris's firmness of purpose didn't last long. While she and Tarnower were on a Christmas visit to Arthur and Vivian Schulte at their place in West Palm Beach, she started having second thoughts about her decision. She felt distraught. She took a car and drove around aimlessly for a while. Then she stopped at a sporting-goods store and went in to buy a gun.

Suicide wasn't an entirely novel thought to her, as she would one day write in her autobiography. She'd toyed with the idea during the lowest moments of her marriage and occasionally in the years that followed. Maybe it was the answer now, she thought. Maybe she'd spend a last glorious week with Hi, then kill herself. But bureaucracy intervened: The store clerk wouldn't sell her a gun because she didn't have a Florida driver's license. Her Florida interlude over, she went home and prepared to start packing.

She wanted to make the move wearing her diamond ring. It was a sort of talisman, a proof of being loved; it seemed to give her confidence. Although she'd been wearing it off and on, usually she left it at Purchase in Tarnower's safe. Now she asked him for it, but weeks went by and he didn't give it to her. When she brought it up again, he confessed, "Look, I've sold it and I don't care to talk about it." The van der Vrekens filled her in: He'd sold it for $40,000 and given the money to Lynne Tryforos to help her pay a debt. For the moment, Harris swallowed this new and bitter betrayal and kept her peace.

In the summer heat, the moving van picked up Harris's furniture from Tarnower's basement, then swung into Manhattan for the boxes she'd packed at her little apartment. She headed south to Madeira's campus in McLean, Virginia, 400 lush, heavily wooded acres on the Potomac River, complete with ivy-covered Georgian buildings, horse barns, and playing fields. A feisty social reformer named Lucy Madeira had founded the school in 1906 and given it its motto: "Function in disaster, finish in style," a credo that Mildred Struven would doubtless have found congenial. Tuition at the school cost $5,100 a year, a hefty sum in those days, and Madeira educated many daughters of senators, diplomats, and other upper-crust governmental dignitaries.

Harris's new home was a two-story brick house called

The Hill, and she was alone in it. Both her boys were now out in the world. David, 27, was a banker in New York, and Jimmy, 25, had joined the Marine Corps. The house was pleasant, but she had no plans for spending all her free time in it. She'd made that clear to the search committee: "Please know that I will work hard for the girls and for the school," she'd told them. "But I will not marry Madeira. I will have a private life away from the school, a life that will refuel me."

Feeling less confident than such declarations sounded, a jittery but determined Harris got to work on the usual school problems. Things went pretty well her first year, though she began to develop a reputation for being prim, rigid, quick to anger, moody, and sometimes illogical. She ordered oranges as an alternative to sweets for on-campus snacks, but when peels appeared on the grounds, she banned the oranges. She spoke against short skirts, against no bras, and for the recitation of the Lord's Prayer. The more controversial she became, the more she felt that Madeira's board was being aloof and unsupportive. She felt isolated and lonely.

And less and less was Harris able to find safe haven with Hi Tarnower. Tension between her and Lynne Tryforos increased as the anonymous telephone calls continued. Harris was certain that it was her rival who was tormenting her. When Harris went up to Purchase that Christmas, 1977, she opened a dressing-room closet to find a blue nightgown of hers splashed with something like Mercurochrome. On Valentine's Day, 1978, back in Virginia, she received a card covered with typed obscenities. In March the doctor didn't invite her up for his birthday. She called a psychiatrist for help with a growing sense that she couldn't cope with anything anymore, but she lost her nerve, hung up, and invested in a mink hat instead.

As Harris was sinking, Tarnower was scaling new heights, turning out a diet book that would make him a household name in most of the Western world. For some 19 years he'd been handing out a one-page diet to overweight cardiac patients. It consisted of simple menus based on a fairly conventional high-protein, low-fat eating plan. His fellow doctors at the Scarsdale Medical Center handed out the plan, too. In April 1978, the *New York Times Sunday Magazine* mentioned Tarnower's diet. A patient—who happened to be president of

Bantam Books—urged him to turn his sheet into a book.

Former advertising writer Samm Sinclair Baker was engaged as coauthor for the project. He took Tarnower's basic plan and added more menus, some recipes, a little science, and lots of charts. When Baker turned in a draft of the first few chapters of *The Complete Scarsdale Medical Diet* that summer, Tarnower hated it—or so Jean Harris would later recall. He complained to her, and she, as always, was sympathetic. She thought a diet book was beneath him anyway.

Their conversation over the book came at a time of strained relations between the doctor and the headmistress. In midsummer Tarnower had banished her from Purchase for her calls to Tryforos, but he repealed the exile order after receiving this note: "Dear Hi, Your casual call cancelling a weekend with you that I have spent a summer of work looking forward to—like light at the end of a dark tunnel—is the kind of punishment I have not earned." In August she was allowed to visit.

While housekeeper Suzanne van der Vreken tried out diet recipes and Tryforos moved about with her orderly lists of chores, Harris sat at a card table outside the kitchen to rewrite Baker's draft. Baker got angry and rewrote her draft. The final manuscript was a team product whose authorship even the book's publisher couldn't identify. Perhaps on the off chance that Harris might take it into her head to sue for compensation for her work on the book, Tarnower offered her $4,000. The money made her angry; in a letter to Tarnower in September of 1978 she wrote: "Your voice sounded as though you were offering a little tip to a $2.00 whore. It was cold and utterly contemptuous." She'd only wanted his thanks.

Thanks, though hardly personal, came in the book's acknowledgments: "We are grateful to Jean Harris for her splendid assistance in the research and writing of this book." The chatty little book was worldly and amusing, and like most sensible diets, the one that it contained worked, at least temporarily, for a great many of its readers. Among Tarnower's intimates, the book served another purpose, eliciting a fond smile at the recipe for Borscht Suzanne and smirks at the Baked Chicken Breasts Herman nestled next to the Spinach Delight à la Lynne.

In January 1979 *The Complete Scarsdale Medical Diet* was published and hit Number One on the *New York Times* Best-Seller List, to stay there 31 weeks; the paperback version released a year later occupied the top spot for 40 weeks. Speaker of the House Tip O'Neill went on the diet, as did feminist writer Gloria Steinem and, it was rumored, England's Queen Elizabeth II. The most fashionable restaurants offered its dishes. By the end of 1980, the book had reaped an astonishing $11 million and sold close to five million copies.

Basking as his fame spread and the money rolled in, Tarnower went on the talk-show circuit, often taking Tryforos with him. The diet book seemed to be making almost everybody happy, but there were exceptions. Tarnower's fellow doctors at the Scarsdale Medical Center clamored futilely for a share of the profits, contending that the diet was created at the medical group and therefore they should all get a cut. And Jean Harris was damaged by the book doubly, personally and professionally. The painful truth was that, in his burst of good fortune, her lover had given her only a few dollars while he shared his time and his glory with his younger mistress. Moreover, the Madeira Board was not pleased at finding the school's headmistress credited in, of all things, a diet book.

In fact, the Madeira Board was not particularly pleased with Jean Harris even before the diet book came out, although she could claim a number of successes during her tenure. She had gotten the school properly accredited, improved the staff, revamped the curriculum, and bettered the college admissions record. But she had never enjoyed the board's full support and participation, and now they complained that she was away weekends more often than they found acceptable. They also noted to themselves that she was becoming increasingly frazzled and exhausted. Harris sensed herself spiraling downward: The more taxing and oppressive her job became, the more frightened and isolated she felt, and the more she needed Tarnower, who, ironically, was still the only person in the world who could make her feel better. And the more she needed him, the less available he was.

In October 1978 she drove to a gun store and said she needed a handgun for self-defense. In November she picked up a .32-caliber Harrington & Richardson revolver. The salesman showed her how to open the cylin-

Lynne Tryforos, Tarnower's young assistant, navigates his cluttered office as the diet guru eats lunch in 1979 *(left)*. For several years Tarnower had romanced Tryforos and Jean Harris simultaneously, and both women helped with the diet book *(right)* —Tryforos with administrative duties and the recipe Spinach Delight à la Lynne, and Harris with writing, for which Tarnower sent her $4,000 and a cryptic note *(below)*. Later, he inscribed her book with kind, but hardly tender, words *(below, right)*.

LOSE UP TO 20 POUNDS IN 14 DAYS AND KEEP THEM OFF

THE COMPLETE SCARSDALE MEDICAL DIET

PLUS

Dr. TARNOWER'S LIFETIME KEEP-SLIM PROGRAM

For the first time— the total plan for the diet that's taking America by storm, explained in full by the noted doctor who created it.

Herman Tarnower, M.D. & Samm Sinclair Baker

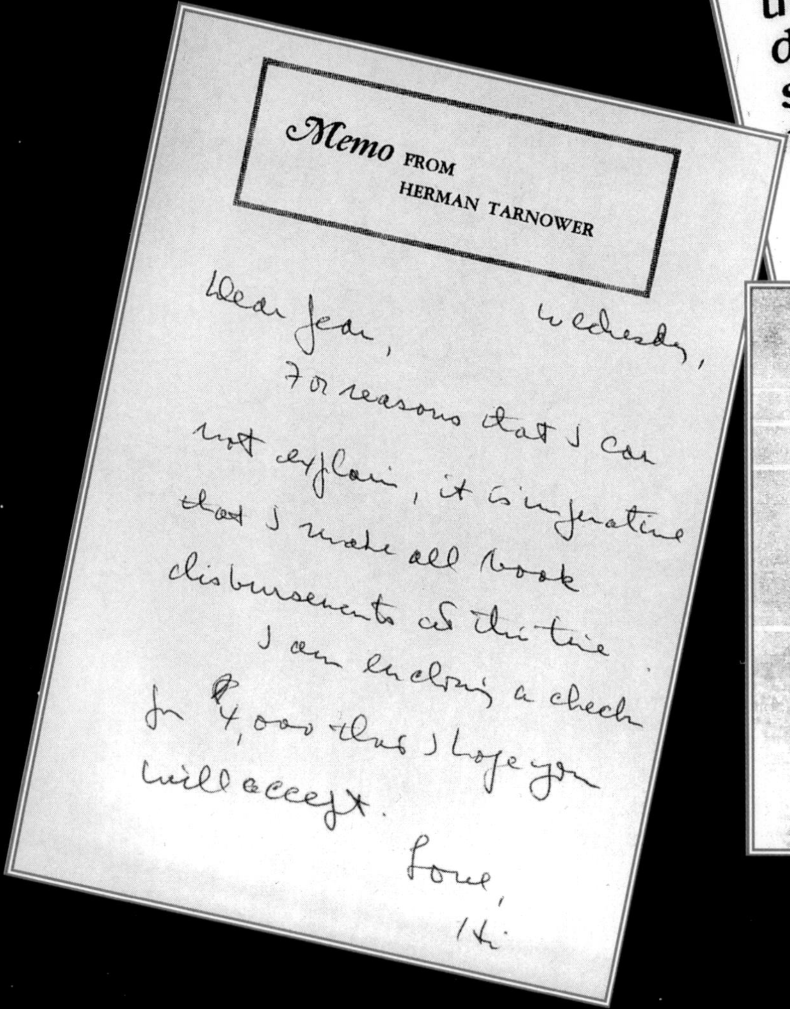

Memo FROM
HERMAN TARNOWER

Dear Jean,   Wednesday,

For reasons that I can
not explain, it is imperative
that I make all book
disbursements at this time
    I am enclosing a check
for $4,000 that I hope you
will accept.

                Love,
                Hi

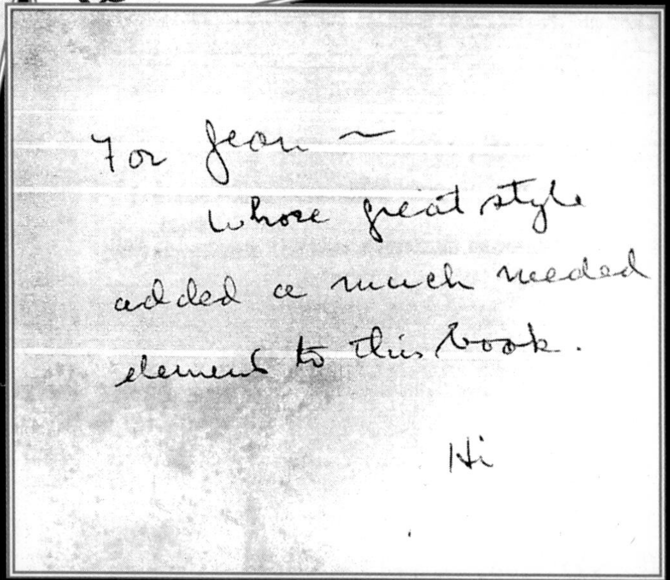

For Jean —
    whose great style
added a much needed
element to this book.

                Hi

25

Offended by what seemed like a payoff for her work on Tarnower's book, Harris wrote a long letter, four pages of which appear below, berating him for tipping her like "a $2.00 whore."

---

der and load it. She didn't buy bullets then. She put the gun on the top shelf of her closet. It made her feel safe. "I felt if I couldn't function anymore, I could handle it," she would say later, "and I didn't have to worry as much about becoming helpless."

Tarnower still did occasionally toss his longtime mistress a crumb of affection. In 1978 she went with him on two trips that had become almost annual events for them, a Thanksgiving visit to the John Loebs on Lyford Cay in the Bahamas and a Christmas trip to West Palm Beach to see the Schultes. When Harris was at Purchase packing for the Christmas flight, she found a yellow silk dress that she'd left in a downstairs guest closet wadded into a ball. She unrolled it and discovered that someone had smeared it with feces. Not wanting to shadow the trip, she said nothing to Tarnower.

After the holiday respite, Harris returned to Madeira to a hellish new year. A school appraisal commissioned by the Madeira Board recommended in May that the headmistress be fired. The report said that Harris was controversial, outspoken, and irrational in words if not in acts. What little confidence Harris had managed to hang on to evaporated. She went to her lover for comfort, but Tarnower, now relishing his new status as famous author and talk-show guest, had little to offer. "Hell," he said, "They won't fire you. They don't want the trouble of looking for someone else." If tactless, he was also apparently correct. The board rejected the report's recommendation and voted to keep her—though from that point on she felt that she was only camping out at The Hill.

Harris's visits to Tarnower now were a far cry from what they'd been when she was the light of his life, or even his mistress of choice. By 1979 Suzanne van der Vreken had gotten lax about cleaning up after the doctor's bedmates, so Harris would often spend the first 15 minutes or so of her weekend stay in Purchase putting into bureaus any evidence of Tryforos: a nightgown,

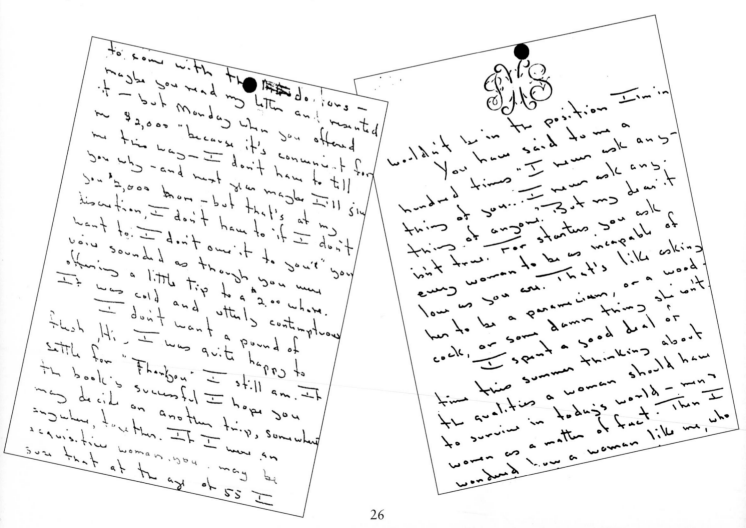

some pink electric curlers. At Madeira's spring break in March 1979 Harris flew to the Bahamas with Tarnower. When she returned she found all the clothes she'd left in his downstairs guest closet cut and ripped. Suzanne said that nobody had been in the house, except Tryforos, who'd slipped in for a few minutes the day before.

That summer Harris hardly saw her now-famous doctor. He refused to take her calls during the dinner hour or when Tryforos was in the house. He told the van der Vrekens to say he wasn't there. In response to the growing despair and anxiety that she expressed when they did talk, he increased her Desoxyn to 7.5 milligrams a day. The doctor had little regard for mental health specialists and never once suggested that Harris might benefit from counseling.

When school started up again, a second Madeira report vindicated Harris, and she got a commendation and a raise. But the good news raised her spirits scarcely at all. Not long after the second report, she told Jean Gisriel—the dean of students and Harris's second in command—that if anything happened to her, her two sons were to have equal shares of her estate. It seemed that thoughts of suicide pressed ever more insistently into her consciousness. She began to reread Tarnower's old love letters.

At Thanksgiving she and the doctor flew to Lyford Cay again, but there she mocked the diet book so waspishly that John Loeb told her to stop. During Christmas with the Schultes in West Palm Beach, Tarnower largely ignored her, though he did laugh at a poem she'd written for him, a parody of "A Visit from Saint Nicholas":

Twas the night before Christmas,
When in part of the house
Arthur was snuggling with Vivian, his spouse.
In the guest-room lay Herman, who, trying to sleep,
Was counting the broads in his life—'sted of sheep!

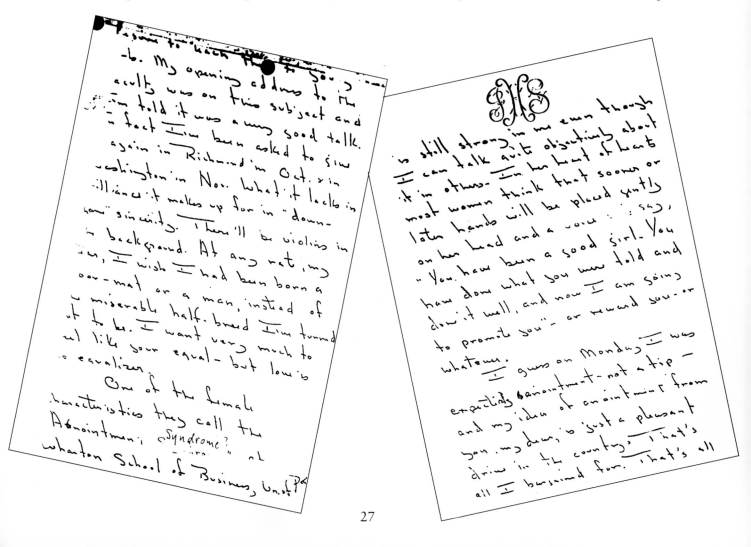

Harris was taunted by evidence of Tarnower's philandering on the front page of the *New York Times* on January 1, 1980, where a message from Tryforos (*circled*) wished "Hi T." a Happy New Year.

Besides the powerful stimulant Desoxyn, which Tarnower prescribed for Harris's chronic fatigue, he also gave her prescriptions for Percobarb, a depressant; Nembutal, a barbiturate; and Valium, a tranquilizer.

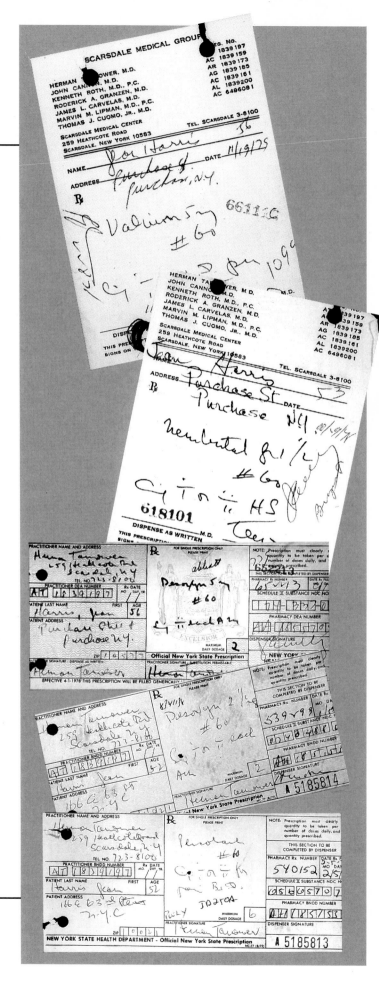

On Hilda, on Sigrid, on Jinx, on Racquel;
Brunhilde, Veronica, Gretel, Michelle;
Now Tania, Rapunzel, Electra, Adele;
Now Susie, Anita—keep trucking Giselle.
There were ingénues, Dashers, and Dancers and Vixons,
I believe there was even one Cupid—one Blitzen!

The poem went on cleverly in that vein, but a sensitive eye might have seen that the lacquer of Harris's wit was wearing thin; the pain was showing through.

The couple was still at the Schulte's when the 1980s began with one of the little dustups that had become typical of their relationship. On New Year's Day, a tiny advertisement appeared across the bottom of the front page of the *New York Times,* the customary place for expensive personals. It read: "Happy New Year Hi T. Love Always Lynne." Harris suggested tartly that Tryforos use the Goodyear blimp next time. Her depression during the holidays was obvious enough to alarm even the usually oblivious Tarnower, who responded by upping her Desoxyn to 10 milligrams. Lynne Tryforos apparently said later that he expressed to her his concern that Harris might be suicidal.

Whatever fears the doctor might have felt for his one-time fiancée, he put them out of his head in January. Tarnower traveled with Tryforos to Jamaica that month, and he also signed a new will. He bequeathed the bulk of his $5 million estate to relatives: the house and grounds to his sister Billie and cash bequests to various young nieces and nephews. He left $2,000 each to Suzanne and Henri van der Vreken for every year they'd worked for him—16 years at the time. Lynne Tryforos's two daughters would receive $20,000 each for college. He left $220,000 to Jean Harris, $200,000 to Lynne Tryforos, and $10,000 to Gerda Stedman.

Late in January at Madeira, Harris received an anonymous letter containing a copy of part of Tarnower's will. Her name had been scratched out and, in what looked like the doctor's handwriting, the name of Lynne Tryforos was penned in. She mailed this to Tarnower, as she'd done with all other anonymous material.

The doctor made no response. He was feeling a bit blue at the thought of turning 70 that spring, although he was cheered somewhat by the fine show of affection from his closest friends. They were arranging an April 19 celebration to honor him for a lifetime's contribution to medicine, and to commemorate the naming of a new cardiovascular research lab after him. And another happy event was on the nearer horizon, the wedding of Jean Harris's son, David.

Tarnower was not especially fond of children, but over the years he'd grown fond of Harris's boys, and on a mid-February weekend he gave a rehearsal dinner at his home in Purchase, for David and his bride, Kathleen. In a gesture of dubious taste, the doctor presented the young women taking part in the ceremony with inscribed copies of the newly published paperback edition of his diet book; he tucked a check for $1,000 into David's pocket. Harris was thrilled at this show of familial warmth, and she was also comforted when Tarnower made love to her that weekend. It was almost like old times. It almost made up for the news, delivered before she left on Sunday, that Lynne Tryforos had worked so hard on his upcoming banquet that he felt he had to invite her.

The banquet had taken on a symbolic significance that grew as the days passed. At the memorial intended to mark the zenith of his life and career, Tarnower was supposed to have one woman as his date. The one he chose to stand beside him on that night of nights would be tacitly acknowledged as the most important woman in his life. Harris realized this, and so, probably, did Lynne Tryforos. The news that Tryforos would be at the dinner wasn't especially unsettling to Harris, however; Tarnower hadn't made it sound as though the younger woman would be his special guest.

Harris left Purchase carrying the opening chapters of the doctor's new book, one on aging, and feeling that, on the whole, the weekend had been a success. As it turned out, those days would seem in retrospect the last flare of tenderness in a doomed affair. Not long after she left, Tarnower apparently indicated to a friend that he and the headmistress were through.

Shortly after David's wedding in February, Harris collapsed in San Francisco during a taxing 10-day fundraising trip. She wrote to her mother from bed, saying she'd been thinking of looking for easier and less lonely work. Flying home, she dreaded the spring break coming up in two days—she had no plans to go to Purchase.

She was met at the airport on Wednesday, March 5, by Jean Gisriel, and a long, terrible few days began.

Gisriel told her there'd been rumors of pot parties among students in South Dorm, and Harris ordered her to search for evidence the next day. Back at The Hill, she called Tarnower but he wasn't in. She had run out of Desoxyn. Withdrawal from the drug, especially for longtime users like Harris, can induce extreme fatigue, agitation, self-hatred, feelings of helplessness, suicidal depression, and a loss of touch with reality.

On Thursday, Harris managed to reach Tarnower, who promised more Desoxyn. He also passed along his decision about his dinner partner at the April 19 banquet: He wouldn't have one. Harris would sit with friends at one table and Tryforos with friends at another. Devastated, Harris hung up. She understood all too well. There was no way that she could hang on any longer to her threadbare fiction of being the Number One woman in Herman Tarnower's life.

She was struggling with her agonizing dual withdrawal—from her drugs and her fantasy—when Gisriel called to say that she'd found bongs in a laundry basket and marijuana seeds and stems in a bureau drawer at South Dorm. Harris called an evening meeting at The Hill of available Student Council members and on-campus faculty to hear from the accused—four students, all campus leaders, all seniors within a few months of graduation. The four denied smoking pot on campus, but there was considerable evidence against them. The upshot of the hours-long meeting was a unanimous vote for expulsion. Harris told the four girls to call their parents and pack. She didn't sleep at all that night. In the morning, parents, board members, and illustrious alumnae began ringing up to object to the expulsions.

On Friday, irate parents arrived to pick up their expelled daughters, and other students began to leave on spring break—but not before holding a rally protesting the headmistress's ruling. Harris was furious, but she also felt betrayed, beset on all sides. It was her third day without Desoxyn. She was coming apart. She called Tarnower, she got Henri: The doctor was out. She kept calling throughout the weekend, but she couldn't reach him. As it happened Tarnower was squiring Lynne Tryforos around Manhattan, to the 21 Club on Friday night and to a formal gala on Saturday. Moreover, Tryforos was staying at his house, and he'd told the servants that he wasn't taking unnecessary calls.

On Saturday, as more students left Madeira on break, some let air out of staff tires. A panicky Harris tried to get her life in order. She couldn't figure out how to hang up a dress. She didn't know if she could get through the day. Clothes, papers, confusion. She sat down to write a new will now that David was married. Students interrupted and she couldn't remember where she'd left it. In her frenzy and despair, unable to reach Tarnower by phone, she started writing him a long, jumbled letter.

In it, all the bitterness, pain, and rage that she'd dammed up for years behind forced good nature and brittle wit came pouring out in a great, anguished wail: "I am distraught as I write this—your phone call to tell me you preferred the company of a vicious, adulterous psychotic was topped by a call from the Dean of Students 10 minutes later and has kept me awake for almost 36 hours.... Let me say first that I will be with you on the 19th of April because it is right that I should be ... even if the slut comes—indeed I don't care if she pops naked out of a cake with her tits frosted with chocolate!... all I ever asked for was to be with you—and when I left you to know when we would see each other again so there was something in life to look forward to. Now you are taking that away from me too and I am unable to cope—I can hear you saying 'Look, Jean—it's your problem—I don't want to hear about it.'... 'Stupid' is certainly not the word for Lynn. In that I was totally wrong. 'Dishonest, ignorant and tasteless' but God knows not stupid. It would have been heartbreaking for me to have to see less and less of you even if it had been a decent woman who took my place. Going through the hell of the past few years has been bearable only because you were still there and I could be with you whenever I could get away from work, which seemed to be less and less. To be jeered at, and called 'old and pathetic' made me seriously consider borrowing $5,000 just before I left N. York and telling a doctor to make me young again— to do anything but make me not feel like discarded trash—I lost my nerve because there was always the chance I'd end up uglier than before....You keep me in control by threatening me with banishment ... and so I

stay home alone while you make love to someone who has almost totally destroyed me. I have been publicly humiliated again and again but not on the 19th of April. It is the apex of your career and I believe I have earned the right to watch it—if only from a dark corner near the kitchen.... I always thought that taking me out of your will would be the final threat. On that I believed you would be completely honest.... The gulf between us seems wide on the phone but the moment I see you it's as though we had been together forever.... I wish 14 years of making love to one another and sharing so much happiness had left enough of a mark that you couldn't have casually scratched my name out of a will and written in Lynn's instead. But for God's sake don't translate that into begging for money. I would far rather be saved the trial of living without you than have the option of living with your money. Give her all the money she wants, Hi—but give me time with you and the privilege of sharing with you April 19th."

By Sunday the campus was almost empty, and Harris had to face herself alone. She kept adding to the letter, which grew to nearly a dozen pages. A student staying over break went to The Hill and saw through a yawning door the headmistress's clothes strewn all over the floor, the kitchen a mess.

On Monday morning, March 10, Harris mailed the letter, certified—so often, it seemed to her, the doctor didn't receive her notes. Now he'd know what she'd borne all alone. But once the letter was in the mail, she changed her mind. He wouldn't like it! She must be jolly, not a whiner! She must be worldly and sophisticated about his other women! In an about-face, she rang up Tarnower at his office just before 10 a.m. and told him to toss out the letter, not to read it.

During their talk, according to Harris, Tarnower invited her up for April 5 and asked whom she wanted as dinner guests. But the true nature of the conversation might never be known for certain: Did she ask about the banquet again, or complain about Tryforos, or mention the will? A patient who claimed to have overheard Tarnower's end of the dialogue would quote him as shouting, "Goddammit, Jean. I want you to

Goddammit, Jean, I want you to stop bothering me!

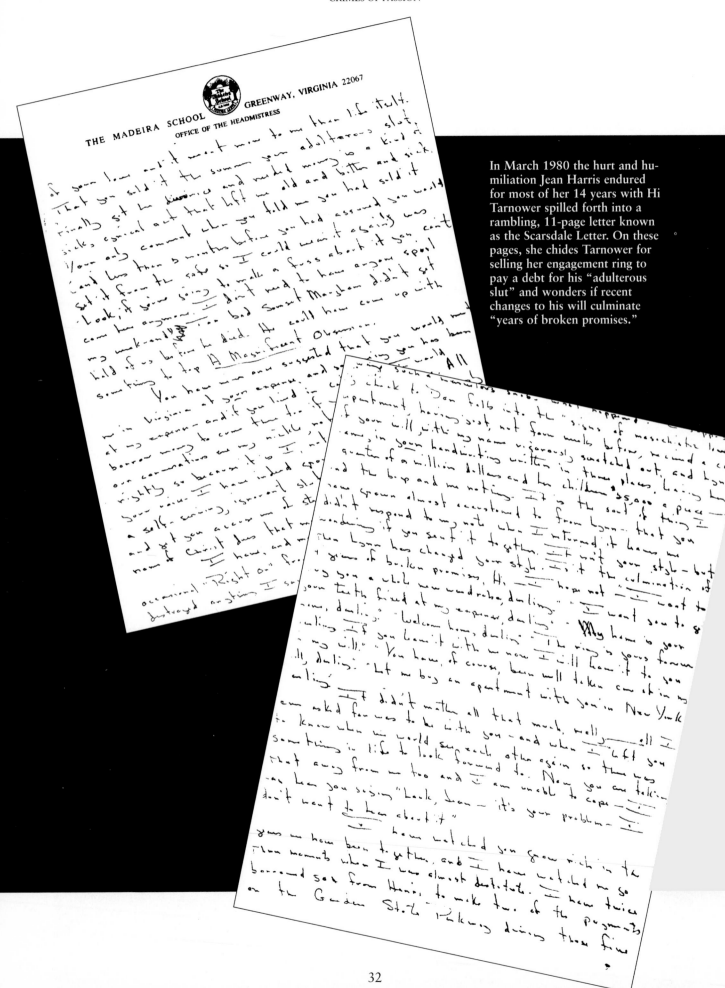

In March 1980 the hurt and humiliation Jean Harris endured for most of her 14 years with Hi Tarnower spilled forth into a rambling, 11-page letter known as the Scarsdale Letter. On these pages, she chides Tarnower for selling her engagement ring to pay a debt for his "adulterous slut" and wonders if recent changes to his will culminate "years of broken promises."

stop bothering me!" And "You've lied and you've cheated." And "Well, you're going to inherit $240,000."

If the telephone call was, in fact, unpleasant, Harris hung up clinging to the notion that at least she'd see him on April 5. So profound was her relief that she was able to turn to meetings, to the work on her desk. But then, in the 11 a.m. mail she received a letter from her pet student, a girl who'd suffered facial burns in an accident and whom Harris had taken under her wing. The letter criticized the expulsions, saying that lots of students smoked pot, and that it was hypocritical of Harris to punish just four of the girls. This last betrayal, as Harris saw it, sent her spiraling back toward the abyss. She decided to kill herself.

Not on campus, she thought. She wouldn't spook Madeira for all eternity. No, she must go home, to Hi. She'd do it there, down by the pond. It wouldn't especially bother him, she mused bitterly. It wouldn't even ruin his day. But it was all-important for her to see him one last time, to talk calmly, just to spend a little peaceful time, feeling safe again. Then she'd walk to the pond. Then she'd be dead.

About 3:30 Monday afternoon, Harris said to her secretary, "I'm leaving, Carol, I've had enough." The secretary would testify later that during this period her boss was acting like a person with "one foot in the grave and the other on a banana peel." Harris wrote a new will to replace the lost one and got it notarized. She put the will and some other financial papers for David and Jimmy on a chair in her front hall. She wrote two "to whom it may concern" letters with instructions on what to do with her remains. One said, "I wish to be immediately CREMATED AND THROWN AWAY." She put that one in her purse. She wrote a farewell note to her sister Mary Margaret saying, "I am so desolately lonely, Mary." She wrote to Madeira Board Chair Alice Faulkner, complaining of having had "so many enemies and so few friends." She concluded with, "I was a person, and no one ever knew."

At 5:16 she called Tarnower at home. She told him she'd had a bad few weeks. She'd like to drive up and talk to him for a few minutes. No, he said, his niece Debbie was coming for supper. But, Harris argued, Debbie always left early, and she wouldn't even be there till 10:30. No, he said, Tuesday is better. Not for her, she replied, she wouldn't be able to talk by Tuesday. "Hi, please just this once let me say when," she pleaded tiredly. "Suit yourself," he said.

She hung up. She got the gun from her closet, along with a box of bullets she'd picked up sometime after she bought the gun. She opened the box and took out a bullet and loaded it. She walked onto her terrace. What sound would it make? Left-handed, she pointed the gun at trees. She pulled the trigger. It clicked. Again. Another pull, and bang! So loud! Birds flew out of the trees. She mustn't have empty chambers when she shot herself. She opened the gun to remove the shell, but it didn't come out. She'd never asked anybody how to unload. Months later she'd find out that the gun had a rod for use in ejecting shells. In the kitchen, she poked it out with an ice pick. She loaded the gun and dropped some extra bullets into her jacket pocket.

She zippered the gun into her pocketbook and walked to the car. There was a bouquet of a dozen daisies on the front seat, left there by a staff member. While she was getting gas, she read the accompanying note of cheer.

Then she started the five-hour drive. At first she felt bad about not showing up for a scheduled supper in Washington, but if she telephoned, she reasoned, she might start crying. Almost everything seemed to bring on waterworks these days. Then as she drove, she simply tuned out. Peace enveloped her. She knew what was going to happen. She wasn't afraid to die. But, she asked herself as she crossed the George Washington Bridge, what if he were nice to her? Would that weaken her resolve? No, she wouldn't stay long enough to change her mind or lose her nerve. Just a few minutes. She drove undisturbed through a thunderstorm. She usually filled her gas tank for the return trip at a station just across the bridge, but tonight there was no need.

Here is what Jean Harris would say she remembered from that point on:

She pulled into the circular drive at Hi's house and was disappointed to find the house dark. He hadn't left a light for her. Carrying her purse and the daisies, she walked up the steps to the front door, but it was locked. She walked back down and through the garage to a door that was always left open. Up the spiral stairs, past the living room, on up she climbed, calling "Hi? Hi?" She reached his bedroom. He was just awakening.

She walked past Tarnower and sat on "her" bed to turn on the light. She said brightly, "Hi, it's black as pitch out there! I thought you would leave a lamp in the window."

"Jesus," Tarnower complained. "It's the middle of the night."

"It's not really that late and I'm not going to stay very long."

"Well, I'm not going to talk to anybody in the middle of the night." He lay there, hugging a pillow, and shut his eyes again.

Those moments of peace she'd wanted—how to get them? Finally, she said "I brought you some flowers."

He just lay there, with his eyes closed.

She tried a conversational gambit: "Have you written any more on the book?"

"Jesus, Jean, shut up and go to bed!"

"I can't go to bed, dear, I'm not going to stay that long, I'm just going to be a little while." No answer. "Won't you really talk to me for just a little while?"

Nothing.

She got up and went around the far side of her bed, past the ornate divider, planning to retrieve a shawl she'd left at the house. It would be a nice gift for her daughter-in-law, she thought absently. She placed the shawl on the bed and then walked into "her" bathroom. There she saw a teal satin negligee that wasn't hers. She took it off the hook, walked back to the bedroom, and threw it on the floor. No response from Hi.

Things weren't working out as she'd imagined. She went back to the bathroom and picked up a box of pink

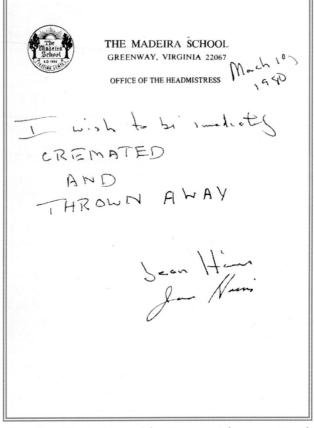

When Jean Harris departed for Tarnower's home on March 10, she left behind a new will, a letter of resignation, and a farewell letter to her sister. A desperate note *(above)* that she tucked into her purse and later gave to police said as much about her state of mind as her last wishes.

electric curlers. She threw them hard into the dressing area and heard glass break. She started back toward the bedroom. But there he was in the doorway, blocking her way. He hit her across the face. He'd never done that before.

She reached for a jewelry box and hurled it at her cosmetic mirror, which broke. He hit her again. With that, she felt calm.

There wouldn't be any pleasant talk, any peace or feeling safe. All right. Then just get the dying over with. She rounded the divider and sat calmly on her bed. She pushed her hair behind her ears. She raised her face to him and said, "Hit me again, Hi. Make it hard enough to kill." She closed her eyes and waited.

She heard him walk away, and then say, "Get out of here. You're crazy." She opened her eyes and sat there. The room was wholly silent, except for the rain on the balcony. She'd go now. She stood, facing the sliding doors at the front of the house, reached for her purse, felt its weight. She unzipped it and took out the gun.

"Never mind," she said. "I'll do it myself." Her romantic notion of dying by the pond now seemed pointless. The place didn't much matter anymore. She stood there, raised the gun to her head, and was pulling the trigger when he appeared from behind to push the gun down. It fired.

They both jumped back, and Hi held up his hand. It was bleeding. "Jesus Christ," he said, "look what you did." She stared. Hi walked around his bed and behind the divider to his bathroom. She started to follow, to help, but stopped. Now was the time. She'd act fast, while the water was running in his sink. But the gun was nowhere in sight. She fell to her knees between the two beds, found it under hers, and pulled it out. Suddenly Tarnower was back, jumping over the bottom of his bed, grabbing her left arm so tightly that she had to drop the gun. He picked it up in his bloody right hand and sat on his bed. He pressed the buzzer on the ledge of the divider to call the servants; pressed it again, again. She knelt by him. Any second, Henri or Suzanne would pick up the telephone in the kitchen and talk to him over the dial tone. "Hi, please give me the gun, please give me the gun, or shoot me yourself, but for Christ's sake let me die," she pleaded.

"Jesus, Jean, you're crazy," he said again, "get out of here." He reached for the telephone to be ready for Henri or Suzanne.

Harris pulled herself up on Tarnower's knees and grabbed the gun out of his lap. He dropped the phone and grabbed her wrist. She pulled back as in a tug of war. He let go, and she fell back onto the other bed. He lunged forward to tackle her, putting his hands around her waist. She felt what she thought was the muzzle of the gun in her own stomach. She pulled the trigger. "My God," she thought, "that didn't hurt at all. I should have done it a long time ago."

He fell back onto his knees between the beds. She got up and ran from him, but he wasn't following. At the other side of his bed near the divider, she stood and put the gun to her head. She took a deep breath and pulled the trigger. It clicked. She lowered the gun to examine it and pulled the trigger again. It fired, and the bullet went off into space. She put the gun to her head and shot and shot and shot and shot: click, click, click, click.

She had to be dead before Suzanne and Henri got upstairs! Maybe she needed more bullets from her jacket. She picked it up, went into the bathroom, and opened the gun, but once again she couldn't get the spent shells out. She banged the gun on the tub, harder and harder until it flew out of her hand. When she pulled it out of the tub, it was broken. She didn't know what to do.

She went back into the bedroom. Hi dropped the phone and was pulling himself up from between the beds. He looked exhausted. She picked the phone up but heard no sounds.

"Hi, it's broken. I think it's dead."

"You're probably right."

He leaned on her and she helped him onto his bed. His hands went out to either side. They looked at each other sadly. There was blood on her clothing. She didn't think she'd shot him anywhere but in the hand, yet he certainly looked as if he needed help.

She ran down the stairs. The dining room lights were on in the other side of the house, and she could hear Suzanne. She called out, "Somebody turn on the goddamn lights! I'm going for help!"

She put the gun on the front seat and drove toward the Community Center where she knew there was a working phone in a booth. Before she got there, she saw a police car approaching with its lights flashing. Good. Someone had reached them. She made a U-turn and pulled out in front of the police car to lead it back to the house, turning into the driveway with the car behind her. Henri was standing at the front door screaming, "She's the one! She did it!"

She and Suzanne and a policeman ran up the tricky spiral stairs. Now Hi was on his knees between the beds. He must have fallen while trying to phone again—the receiver was dangling off the shelf. The policeman ran back to his car for oxygen equipment. Suzanne knelt between the beds and held the doctor's hand, and Harris lay across his bed. She leaned over to caress his face, saying, "Oh, Hi, why didn't you kill *me?*"

Then there were policemen swarming all around. One of them asked her what happened.

"The doctor has been shot."

"Who did it?"

"I did."

Detective Arthur Siciliano asked, "Where is the gun?"

"In the car." She took him outside and showed him the gun on the car's front seat. Back in the foyer, she explained to the officers how she'd come up to Purchase to kill herself. She showed them the next-of-kin note in her purse and said there were more in Virginia. She said she'd been through hell with Tarnower and that she loved him very much. As Siciliano testified at the trial, she exclaimed, "He slept with every woman he could, and I'd *had it!*"

Harris begged to see Tarnower. Upstairs, police had tried resuscitation on the doctor, then strapped him to a flexible stretcher, and now they were maneuvering him down the spiral stairs the only way he'd fit, head first. Harris saw his face, his arm flopping. She collapsed into Siciliano's arms.

The police told her they were taking her to the station. First, she could call a lawyer. She rang up Leslie Jacobson from the van der Vreken's bedroom where—unbeknown to her—a separate phone line had been installed: "Leslie," she said, "I think I've killed Hi."

At the Harrison Police Station she was booked for aggravated assault. The sergeant had barely finished the entry when the telephone rang at 11:58. Tarnower had been pronounced dead. Hearing that, Harris collapsed, sobbing. The sergeant changed the charge to murder.

Jacobson arrived and called Alice Faulkner in Virginia; he needed her to fly him the documents Harris had left at The Hill. The sergeant telephoned the Virginia police with the same request, wrongly advising them that Harris had confessed to murder. A matron let Harris wash her bloody nylon blouse. With her fur jacket on over her bra, she was taken to the county jail in Valhalla. When they tried to shut the door to her cell, she screamed and screamed.

Doctors at St. Agnes Hospital had used a defibrillator to try to restart Herman Tarnower's heart and had drawn 1,500 cubic centimeters of blood from his chest cavity. Most of the bleeding had been internal. The autopsy revealed four bullet holes; three bullets were still in the body. One had entered the right chest and fallen into the chest cavity. One had entered the right rear shoulder and made a downward track to the kidney, breaking three ribs and piercing the diaphragm on the way. Another bullet had pierced muscle and bone in the right arm and lodged near the armpit. The fourth struck the palm of his right hand and went through the webbing at the base of the thumb.

A report by a ballistics expert would make clear that with firm pressure on the trigger, Harris's gun could fire without being manually cocked. The report also showed that five of the gun's six chambers had been recently discharged, but that the two o'clock chamber had not been loaded. An expert witness for the defense testified that four of the five spent shells had been double struck, meaning that Harris had pulled the trigger a second time on chambers that held empty shells. He concluded that the gun was fired in the following sequence: bang, bang,

Harris parked in the circular drive and entered Tarnower's darkened house (below) through the garage, where a set of spiral stairs led to his second-floor balconied bedroom.

In a rage, Harris threw a set of Lynne Tryforos's electric curlers out of the bathroom and broke this window in the dressing area. On the sill are items Tarnower was assembling for an upcoming trip with Tryforos.

After the shooting, police used string to try to determine the trajectory of the bullet that went through the balcony door *(inset)* in Tarnower's bedroom.

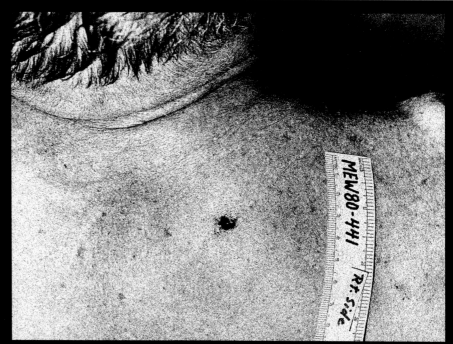

One of the four bullets that killed Herman Tarnower entered his back *(above)* and traveled downward, fracturing three ribs, penetrating the diaphragm, and coming to rest in the right kidney. In her haste to reload the gun *(below, inset)*, Harris groped in her coat pocket for more ammunition, scattering coins and bullets across the bathroom floor *(below)*. She was uncertain of how to eject spent shells from the gun and claimed that during an earlier test firing she used an ice pick like the one in the inset to remove them.

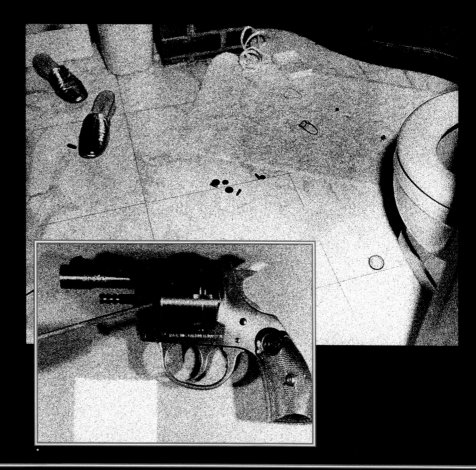

bang, bang, click, bang, click, click, click, click. This was exactly the sequence that Harris remembered—except for two missing bangs.

Jean Harris was freed on March 12, 1980, on $40,000 bail raised by her brother and sisters. On March 15, she signed into the United Hospital of Port Chester for psychiatric evaluation and therapy. She was found to be suicidal and sustaining a brain dysfunction later tied by psychiatrist Abraham Halpern to withdrawal from Desoxyn. Under Halpern's care, Harris resumed taking the drug; her upcoming trial was not the time for her to be going through detoxification, the doctor reasoned.

Ten days later, on March 25, Harris was released from the hospital, and a grand jury indicted her for second-degree murder; conviction would carry a mandatory minimum prison sentence of 15 years. The next day, at her arraignment, Harris entered a plea of not guilty.

Using statements from preliminary hearings, eager reporters presented Harris as an aging woman who had been jilted for a younger one by a famous doctor: Either she'd driven up there in the dark to shoot him or she'd driven up and begged him to kill her—and when he wouldn't, she shot him. Given the status of both the deceased and the accused, the story was inescapably sensational. Overnight, Harris became, as she would put it, a "cottage industry."

After her arraignment, Harris moved into a room offered by a local woman. Several times she visited the cemetery where Herman Tarnower was buried, and twice she ran into Lynne Tryforos at the grave. The first time neither woman spoke; at the next meeting, Harris noticed that Tryforos had planted pink and white petunias on the grave. "Now you've made even his grave cheap!" she spat.

In September, Herbert MacDonell, an expert who had reconstructed the crime scenes in the Robert F. Kennedy and Martin Luther King, Jr., assassinations, took Harris back to Tarnower's bedroom. He was impressed with her accurate recall of the events of that night and how perfectly her description fit the evidence.

Pretrial hearings began in October 1980, and 1,000 possible jurors were impaneled. Under questioning, Judge Russell R. Leggett found that a good number of

them had been on the Scarsdale diet; he did not consider that grounds to excuse them from serving, however. The final jury was made up of four men and eight women, most from middle-class backgrounds.

The People of New York v. Jean Harris opened to a crowded courtroom on November 21, 1980. The trial would last 14 weeks, until February 24, 1981, becoming one of the longest in state history. The courtroom could seat 150 packed close, and it wasn't long before spectators—mostly women—began to line up at dawn for the 70 seats available to the public. At front left, in their allocated seats, sat Harris's family; at front right sat Tarnower's family. Harris wore tweeds and a tortoise-shell headband. Her legs were crossed, and one foot jiggled constantly up and down, a gesture that denoted tension and stress.

Cool behind his steel-rimmed glasses, 34-year-old Assistant District Attorney George Bolen opened: An aging Jean Harris left Virginia with a gun containing five bullets to kill Dr. Herman Tarnower because she was being displaced by a younger rival, he said. She climbed the stairs in the dark and fired at the doctor in his bed. Defense attorney Joel Aurnou countered: Harris was a woman so upset by career problems, by the end of her role as an active mother, and by an overwhelming depression that she'd wanted to kill herself. Killing Tarnower was an accident.

Dr. Louis Roh, Deputy Medical Examiner of Westchester County, described Tarnower's wounds as those of a man taken by surprise. Suzanne van der Vreken explained why the doctor's telephone hadn't worked. When she heard the doctor's buzzer, she testified, she went into the kitchen to pick up his line, heard a shot, placed the phone on the counter, and wakened her husband in his room. He told her to call the police, but when she tried, there was no dial tone. She called 911 from the new phone in her room and reported the incident. Henri went out to look around. She described the condition of the bedroom: It was a shambles, the glass door to the balcony cracked by a bullet hole, the doctor's bed and blankets "really bloody," the tub in the guest bath chipped.

Police photographs taken a few days after the death confirmed the chaos, but as more information about the crime scene came out, it appeared there had been a dis-

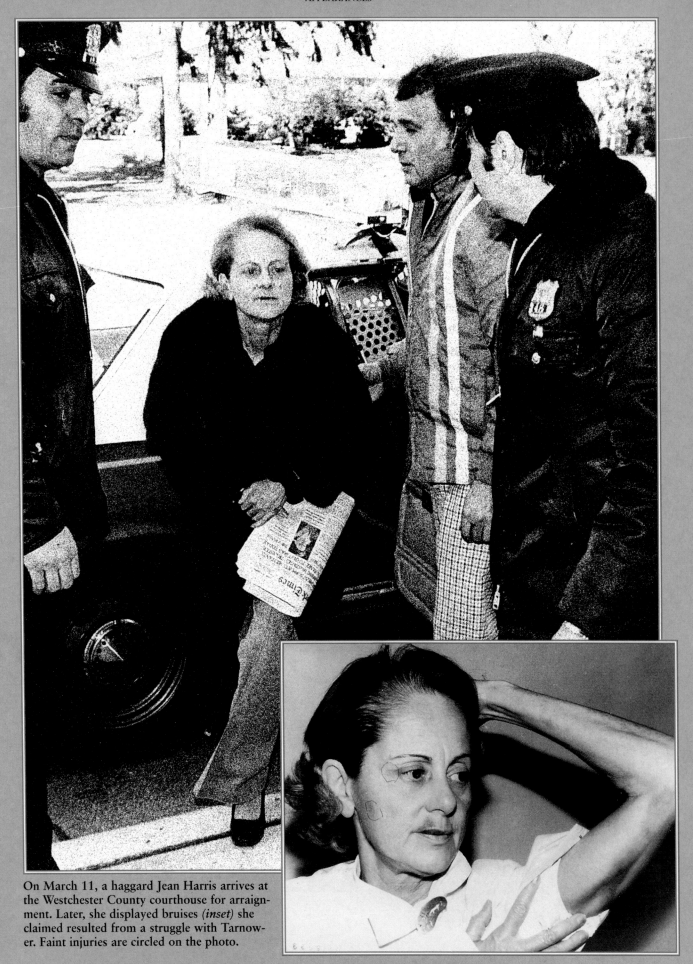

On March 11, a haggard Jean Harris arrives at the Westchester County courthouse for arraignment. Later, she displayed bruises *(inset)* she claimed resulted from a struggle with Tarnower. Faint injuries are circled on the photo.

tinct messiness in police procedure. A number of people had handled Harris's gun before it was dusted for fingerprints, the same for Tarnower's telephone. Early reports from police officers on the scene didn't mention much blood in the room, but later reports by the same officers emphasized that point. Bloody bedclothes with their telltale splatter patterns had been thrown into unmarked bags, and a blood-spotted rug that was photographed by the police was later thrown away by the van der Vrekens, with the consent of their lawyer. And the police surgeon was of the opinion that Tarnower might have lived had anyone realized he had a chest wound and rushed him in right away for treatment.

Throughout the testimony, Harris alienated the court by speaking out of turn. When Aurnou floundered, she took charge of him. When Bolen—or anyone on the stand—misrepresented a word or action, in her opinion, she scoffed or grimaced. When Judge Leggett refused a rereading of the pretrial transcript to show how testimonies had changed, Harris read a passage aloud at recess to reporters. She often came across as imperious and mean. And like most people numbed by tragedy, she cried not at the devastation of an autopsy report but at small kindnesses.

Major courtroom debate centered on bullets. Five had been fired, but only three had been taken from the body.

Jean Harris discusses her defense with lawyers Joel Aurnou and Bonnie Steingart in Aurnou's White Plains office. Her retriever, Cider, lies by her side.

One was found deep in the divider behind the doctor's bed, having penetrated at a downward angle. There was, at first, no fifth bullet.

Bolen argued that one of the three bullets in the body had gone through Tarnower's palm into his chest as he held his hand up in defense. Bolen's expert witnesses found "palm tissue" in the chest wound. Aurnou's expert witness, Dr. A. Bernard Ackerman, argued this down tiresomely with blackboard and chalk. One of the cells in question was actually cartilage, he determined, and while the other two samples couldn't be pinned down, he knew they weren't from the hand. Two other skin pathologists confirmed these findings.

Herbert MacDonell, another expert witness for the defense, testified that he had found a fragment of a fifth bullet in a post on the balcony—in line with what appeared to be a ricochet mark on the balcony floor. He spoke for nearly four days in a monotone, demonstrating with string and mathematics exactly how Harris's first shot had passed through Tarnower's palm, the double glass doors, and into the post. The court was bored but impressed. Had the trial ended there, Harris might have been acquitted, since her version of events clearly squared with the physical evidence.

But she took the stand. Drawn and pale in a brown and mauve suit with long pearls, she began eight days of testimony on January 27, 1981. In her wry way, she made clear to the jury that she'd never wanted to be part of Tarnower's gold cuff link collection. When she got

emotional, she put on her dark glasses. Sometimes she seemed smug, sometimes she appeared to be about a millimeter short of hysteria. When Aurnou inquired how she'd reacted to Lynne Tryforos's New Year's Day ad in the *New York Times* a year earlier, she repeated her Goodyear blimp quip. Everybody roared into laughter, so dangerous in court.

Harris simply could not remember more than three shots—one into the doctor's hand, one into her stomach, or so she thought, and one into space. Dr. John Train, a psychoanalyst who had examined Harris and was familiar with such reactions, was prepared to describe her amnesia as common shell shock, as the army used to call it, from extreme stress, but, by Aurnou's decree, no such psychiatric testimony was summoned. The defense attorney thought Harris's case would be weakened if that door was opened: The prosecution's psychiatrists would be allowed to evaluate Harris—and, he feared, victimize her.

At times Harris's testimony was wrenching. When Aurnou asked her what she'd meant when she had written to Alice Faulkner that she "was a person, and no one ever knew," she sobbed out her reply. She'd meant she was a woman "who had worked a long time and had done the things a man does to support his family, but still a woman, and I always felt that when I was in Westchester I was a woman in a pretty dress and went to a dinner party with Dr. Tarnower, and in Washington I was a woman in a pretty dress and the headmistress.... I was a person sitting in an empty chair." Harris wept, and Aurnou joined her.

When Bolen took up the cross-examination, he admitted into evidence the certified letter that Harris had written to Tarnower. Aurnou thought the letter would reveal Tarnower's cruelty in a way that Harris had made her attorney promise not to. In fact, however, the soon-to-be-famous "Scarsdale Letter" was about to seal Jean Harris's fate. When Bolen read the letter aloud in the courtroom, members of the jury gasped. What it revealed to them was the humiliation and jealousy that Harris had continually denied on the stand. No longer the gentlewoman driven toward suicide by job stress and a soured love affair, she seemed in the Scarsdale Letter a profane harridan, hounded by jealousy, angry enough to kill.

Triumphant, Bolen asked Harris if Tarnower had ever said to her "Goddammit, Jean. I want you to stop bothering me." Or "You've lied." Or "You've cheated." Or "You're going to inherit $240,000." No, she shouted each time. Soon Bolen summoned Juanita Edwards, the patient who'd overheard the telephone call from Harris to Tarnower nearly a year before. Edwards testified to hearing the doctor saying those very things.

In summing up, Aurnou used Herbert Mac-Donell's guess at when the two forgotten bullets had been fired—during the tug of war between the beds. As for prosecutor Bolen, he was now prepared to believe that Harris had been suicidal, but he maintained that one look at the teal negligee had fueled a murderous rage. Both sides rested, and Bolen asked Judge Leggett to allow the jury to consider, as an alternative to the murder charge, manslaughter in the first degree based on an intent to cause serious injury. If the jury couldn't find Harris guilty of murder, he wanted another shot at conviction. Aurnou and Judge Leggett refused, agreeing that no evidence had been presented to support such intent.

Bolen next offered manslaughter in the second degree, which is defined as recklessly causing the death of another and carries a maximum sentence of 15 years. The judge agreed to allow this charge for the jury's consideration as well as a proposal from Aurnou for negligent homicide, a lesser charge defined as killing someone through negligent actions and carrying a four-year maximum sentence. Neither of these charges required intent on the part of the accused.

The judge and other legal experts later expressed surprise that Aurnou did not put forward a defense based on extreme emotional disturbance—EED—which means that the accused intentionally killed the victim but did so without premeditation—in the heat of the moment, in other words. EED automatically reduces the charge to manslaughter in the first degree, which carries a minimum mandatory sentence of two to six years. Aurnou claims Harris would not permit him to use this defense because she believed it required

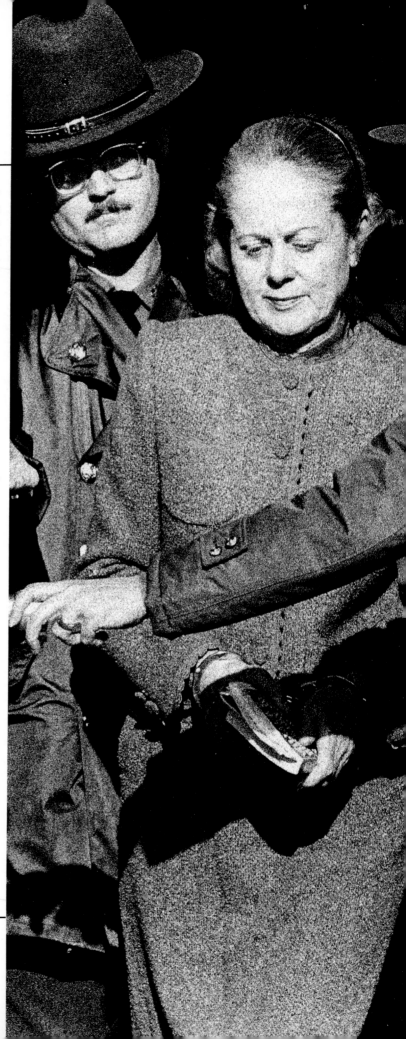

her to say she intended to harm Tarnower, which she strenuously denied. In fact, the law would have allowed her to maintain that the killing was accidental. Harris claims that this distinction was not clearly explained to her by Aurnou.

As the jury began deliberating, it became clear that the jurors had been sympathetic toward Harris until she took the stand. Some were worried by the anger she constantly expressed, others by the obscenities in the letter—perhaps Harris wasn't the lady she appeared to be. In addition, they couldn't reenact Harris's scenario, and they came to believe that the intent to kill entered her head sometime after she arrived at Tarnower's, perhaps even a split second before she fired.

On February 24, 1981, Judge Leggett called the court back. One by one the jurors pronounced Jean Harris guilty of intended murder. Aurnou stared straight ahead; numb and sedated, Harris whispered, "I can't sit in jail."

A woman police officer guided her through the ensuing pandemonium into a winter night, and into the backseat of a police car. She sat impassively, flashbulbs glinting off her headband. She was delivered to a cell at the county jail and put on suicide watch for the 24 days until sentencing.

When Judge Leggett called the court to order on March 20, 1981, Harris's hair didn't shine anymore, her skin was no longer translucent, nor her figure appealing. She now weighed 98 pounds. The judge asked her if she wished to be heard.

"Yes, I do." Trembling, she rose: "I want to say that I did not murder Dr. Herman Tarnower, that I loved him very much and I never wished him ill, and I am innocent as I stand here. For you or for Mr. Bolen to arrange my life so that I will be in a cage for the rest of it, and that every time I walk outside I will have iron around my wrists, is not justice; it is a travesty of justice." She went on to say that no one felt the loss of Herman Tarnower more keenly than she, and she concluded, "I am not guilty, your honor."

The audience broke into applause, which the judge silenced. Leggett pronounced the 15-year minimum mandatory sentence, to be served at the Bedford Hills Correctional Facility in Westchester County. The judge added, "I found you to be a brilliant, brilliant woman, and I am going to ask this: In regard to Mrs. Harris in

Following sentencing, Harris was taken to Bedford Hills Correctional Facility—located just 15 miles from Herman Tarnower's home.

Bedford Hills, my feeling is that she can be a most useful person in that facility and help other people."

As a matter of fact, Jean Harris, as prisoner #81-G98, did help other people in Bedford Hills. Off Desoxyn and onto the anti-depressant Elavil, she took stock of her new environment and concluded that her new companions—most of them younger women, poor, ill-educated, often abused—could benefit from things she could teach them. She tutored inmates to help them get high-school-graduate equivalent degrees. She helped a nun, Sister Elaine Roulet, with a parenting center where inmates with children could learn how to better care for them. She also helped Sister Elaine develop a summer camp for inmates' children, and she edited a book of letters written by children to inmate mothers. She also wrote three books, including her autobiography.

Harris was by now a symbol of woman wronged for untold numbers of American women, but she seemed destined to grow old in jail. Appeals for a new trial were rejected. In September 1984 she suffered a heart attack; when she experienced another a few months later, she was so horrified at the prospect of being taken to the hospital in chains again that she didn't report it. Governor Mario Cuomo rejected three pleas for clemency. Finally, on December 29, 1992, as Harris was being prepped for quadruple bypass heart surgery, he pardoned her. She was just a few months shy of 70, about the same age that Herman Tarnower was when he died.

Two years after the doctor's death, Harris had given a jailhouse interview to Barbara Walters for the ABC television magazine *20/20*. At that time Harris still appeared to be a woman distraught, dissolving into tears when asked about Tarnower, sobbing, "I think about him constantly. It's one of the reasons I don't care if I get out, actually, I can't imagine what it would be like out there without him."

In March of 1993, newly free after a dozen years in prison, a very different Jean Harris spoke with Walters again. Years and illness had taken their toll; she was no longer the handsome headmistress who'd caught Herman Tarnower's eye, or even the killer/victim whose fading loveliness and lovelorn tale had struck a chord with an aging generation of women who knew what it meant to define themselves wholly by the men in their lives. But, if no longer pretty, Harris looked, at last, at peace. She looked like a woman who'd gone far beyond appearances, and she sounded like one who'd rediscovered strengths once lost and found some new ones as well.

"I don't get angry about what went before," Harris told Walters, "because you know, I don't have that many years left to live, and I'm not going to spend them worrying about all the mistakes of yesterday, mine and other people's too. I've paid heavily for them, and I don't feel that I owe anybody any more thinking about those things. I have to go on, and I'm going on."

Her plan was to live in a cabin in New Hampshire, where she'd work to raise money for private schooling for the children of Bedford's inmates. She talked about a book she liked, Michael Drury's *Advice to a Young Wife from an Old Mistress*, wherein, Harris recalled, a man tells a woman, "Tell me that you're happy, but don't tell me I make you happy."

"I thought of that line so many times," Jean Harris said, "and thought, 'Listen, if you're happy, that's great, and you're ahead of the game, but don't sit around waiting for somebody else to make you happy.' And I never will again." ◆

Harris, pictured here with a fellow inmate's child, spent most of her 12 years at Bedford Hills volunteering in the parenting center, reading, and writing.

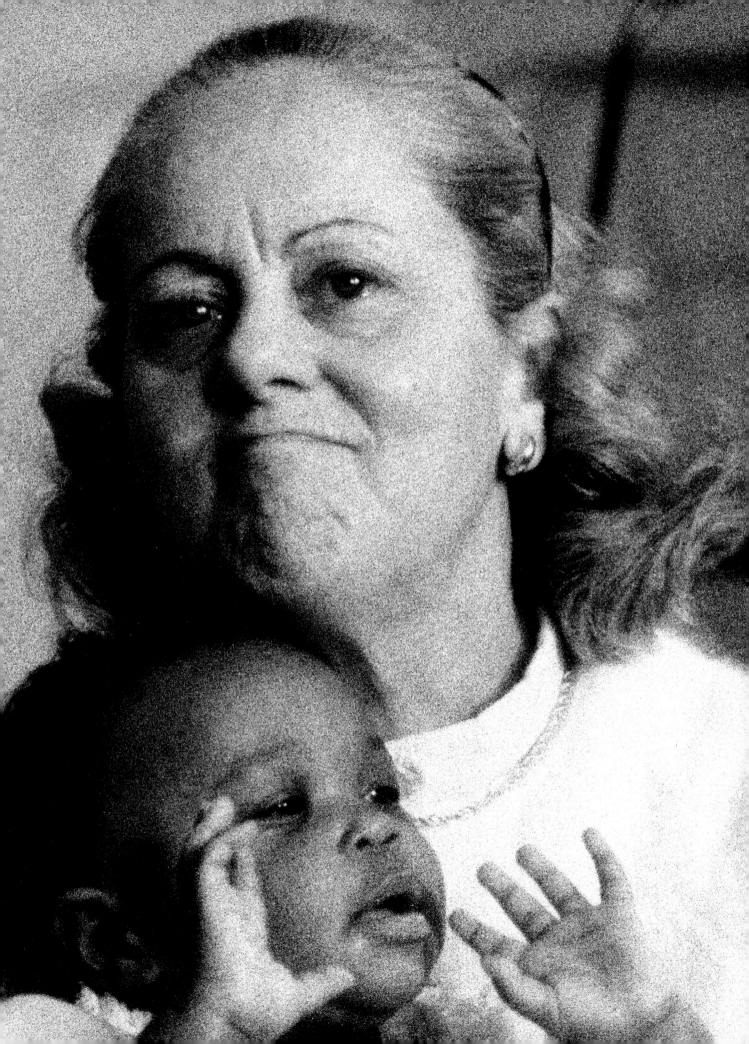

P*lease bury me in a very cute and sexy outfit.*

CAROLYN WARMUS

2

Femme Fatale

In the yearbook portrait taken during her senior year at Seaholm High School in the wealthy Detroit suburb of Birmingham, Carolyn Warmus looks like the all-American girl—confident, pretty, enthusiastic, bright, at the center of things; possibly the prom queen, or at least a contender. Her wide smile seems spontaneous and warm, the smile of a happy, well-loved girl—a golden girl, with everything going for her.

The people who knew Carolyn could tell you that she did have many things going for her, much to be happy about. She was a child of privilege, the eldest daughter of an insurance magnate whose family lived a life of yachts, private jets, expensive clothes, vacation houses, elaborate parties. And Carolyn could look forward to a future of lavish living, since she was endowed with a $12-million trust fund.

In fact the future looked bleak to her, and the lovely image of the golden girl was pure illusion. Warmus was lonely, empty, desperate for love. It seemed as if she would die if she didn't get it, and she would try everything—money, sex, tears, bullying, threats—to win the love she craved. But it kept slipping through her fingers. The day would come when there'd be only one alternative left. The golden girl turned into a femme fatale. She killed for love.

If there was ever a happy time in Carolyn Warmus's life, it ended very early, for most of her childhood years were lived on a marital battleground. Born January 8, 1964, she was the eldest of Thomas and Elizabeth Warmus's three children; her sister, Tracey, followed not quite a year later, and Thomas junior was born in 1968. Carolyn was six years old when her mother filed for divorce and requested custody of the children. Charging that Tom had been cruel to her, Elizabeth also attacked him for having no time for the children; he was too busy building his business empire. The couple traded charges of infidelity, apparently with good cause on both sides.

Nor was that the end of it, for Tom also accused Elizabeth of having a drinking problem, while she claimed in her suit that he was trying to do her out of her fair share of his financial holdings.

Warmth and affection may have been in short supply in the Warmus household in 1970, but money was not: High-school dropout Tom Warmus, the son of an illiterate coal miner, was on his way to becoming one of the richest men in Michigan. He had started out with a tool-and-die business, then founded an insurance company that specialized in credit policies, which insured loans on newly purchased automobiles. Perhaps the privation of his early life fueled his consuming ambition; a friend would later say of Tom Warmus that his prime goal was to make money. "What was missing was any kind of deep human feeling," the friend observed. "His philosophy is 'get what you want, and do whatever you have to do to get it.'"

Self-absorbed and demanding, Tom Warmus was as determined to get what he wanted in his personal life as he was in the professional arena, even if it upset his children—especially Carolyn, who seemed to take the family uproar much harder than her brother and sister did. The three of them stayed on with Elizabeth Warmus in the family home in Troy after Tom bought himself another place and moved out. On a number of occasions, though, he appeared in Troy unannounced and, over his wife's strenuous objections, spent the night at the house. Once he even turned her out of the bedroom they'd shared and said he was moving back in—she'd have to find somewhere else to sleep. When he took the children to his home for visits, Tom would sometimes keep them overnight without informing Elizabeth, who was expecting them back by bedtime. And at least once, on a Sunday evening in June 1972, he turned violent. After a day spent with the children, he told Elizabeth that he was going to keep Tom junior, then almost four years old, for the rest of the summer; it didn't matter to War-

mus that his wife had been granted custody of the children. The quarrel that ensued turned into a physical struggle, and as Carolyn, Tracey, and little Tom watched, their father threw their mother down on the cement driveway in front of the house. He then grabbed his son and drove off with him.

The bitter fighting didn't let up, even after the divorce became final in 1972. Two years later, Tom went to court to demand custody of his children, charging that his ex-wife had a live-in lover who was living off Tom's alimony and child-support payments. Denying any sexual misbehavior, Elizabeth countered that Tom Warmus was living with a "female companion" who often went on vacations with him and Carolyn, Tracey, and Tom junior. Although Elizabeth won that round, the court was so concerned about the effect the parents' continuing hostility was having on the children that the judge ordered psychological counseling for them. But that didn't stop the Warmuses from squaring off in court again, in 1976, because Tom had fallen some $35,000 behind in child-support payments. Since his income had been rising handsomely, he couldn't plead financial hardship and was ordered to pay up.

In and out of court, Tom and Elizabeth sniped at each other for three more years. Carolyn's sense of self may

At the age of 15, Carolyn Warmus went to live with her father in the lavish six-bedroom home he built for his second wife.

already have been fragile when, in 1979, her life once again underwent a drastic change: Elizabeth Warmus remarried, relinquished custody of the children to Tom, and moved out of state with her new husband. From that time on, she had only limited contact with her children.

Perhaps feeling abandoned and betrayed by her mother, Carolyn, along with Tracey and Tom junior, moved to the exclusive Detroit suburb of Franklin to live with their father and Nancy Dailey, his second wife. Years younger than Tom, Dailey had been his secretary before being appointed a vice president of his insurance company, which by now was the most successful of its kind in Michigan. Superficially at least, Nancy and Tom were birds of a feather. Her origins were as humble as his, and her ambitions for wealth just as great. They also shared a taste for ostentatious display. The house he built for her in Franklin was a lavishly decorated, three-story, six-bedroom affair with its own tennis court and swimming pool. Tom would later add a 13-car garage for his luxurious fleet of automobiles, which included a Lamborghini, a 1957 Thunderbird, and several Ferraris. When neighbors tried to block construction of the huge garage, he threatened to take advantage of an anachronistic law that permitted pig farming in Franklin. He got his way.

Millionaire Tom Warmus enjoys a speedboat outing on a Florida waterway, near one of the family's four vacation homes.

In Franklin, Carolyn and her sister and brother lived far more opulently than they had before their mother went away. A woman who knew the family thought Tom Warmus was generous to appease his conscience, for he remained as remote and cold a figure as ever. According to one of Carolyn's childhood friends, he was a dictator, alternately ordering his eldest daughter around and ignoring her. Such treatment resembled his behavior at the office, where Warmus required his underlings to toe the line, issuing written instructions on how to position his office window blinds and where to set his soda can on his desk. At the Oakland-Pontiac Airport, where he kept his eight private jets, Warmus strolled through his airplane hangar with a grease pencil in his hand, circling oil spots and scuff marks he wanted scrubbed clean. At home, Warmus provided Carolyn with a beautiful bedroom that was complete with its own giant-screen television, but the room didn't really belong to her. Her father wouldn't let her add so much as a rock poster on the wall.

Nancy Dailey wasn't the forbidding person her husband was, but when she tried to make friends with Carolyn she got nowhere. "Carolyn was very abrupt with her," recalled one of the young girl's friends. Like many other teenage girls confronted with a stepmother, Carolyn may have viewed Nancy as an interloper and a rival for her father's affections—and a formidable rival at that.

When Carolyn went to live with Nancy and Tom she was a vulnerable 15-year-old, "sort of plain and overweight," a classmate would recall later. She was also quiet and not especially popular with other kids. Nancy, by contrast, seemed full of self-confidence and ready to flaunt her assets, both physical and financial. A woman in Nancy's social circle remarked, "She'd dress Hollywood-style with her bosom sticking out of strapless sequined dresses and floor-length mink coats."

However much Carolyn may have disliked her stepmother, the attention Nancy paid to her appearance may have rubbed off on the teenager. Carolyn was soon cultivating a new look, losing weight, and spending a lot of money on her wardrobe. Not that her style mimicked Nancy's. It was more in keeping with the monogrammed preppy look favored by the popular crowd at school, although in winter Carolyn would often top off her outfits with a fur coat—a flashy touch borrowed from Nancy and intended to show off her wealth. Carolyn also took advantage of frequent trips to the family's vacation house in Pompano Beach, Florida, to maintain a perennial tan—an enviable possession in the long, gray Michigan winters.

Using money or belongings as a lure, Carolyn spent her high-school years feverishly angling for friends and popularity. It must have seemed unfair that both came so naturally to her sister, Tracey, who was prettier to boot. Tracey loved throwing parties, but not Carolyn; the prospect of being a hostess filled her with anxiety. She worried that nobody would come, or at least not the people she wanted to hang out with, unless she did something special to attract them, something extravagant, such as hiring a rock band for the evening. She also tried to buy people's affection with gifts and invitations to fly to Florida in her father's private jet for a holiday. "She'd say, 'I'll pay for your trip,' " remembered one young man who dated Carolyn. "She was 17 and she'd take whoever would go. Even people she barely knew." On one occasion she even resorted to paying someone $100 to fix her up with a boy she liked. Describing Carolyn as "a little unbalanced," a classmate commented, "She seemed to have the attitude that if she wanted something she'd just go out and buy it. 'I can get anything I want.' " The classmate could have been talking about Tom Warmus.

When she failed to get what—or who—she wanted, Carolyn took it hard. During a stay in Florida, she and two other girls went into a bar where she noticed an attractive guy. When he didn't respond to her flirtatious overture, she stormed out of the bar alone and didn't come home until the following morning. One of Carolyn's childhood friends would observe later, "She was very nice, but she didn't take rejection well." The older she got, the more rejection upset her. And her wounds didn't heal any faster; they lingered, ready to open up with every new rejection.

Though she couldn't override her pain, Carolyn understood where it had come from. In a devastating summation, she told a schoolmate that she had "no father, no love, no affection." Once, Tom Warmus kicked her out of the house and she remained away for a week; her father made no effort to contact her, she said. At times she was so depressed that she would talk about committing suicide, to almost anyone who would listen. Carolyn's contemporaries didn't know how to respond, and her deep unhappiness made them shy away from her. Money couldn't always draw them back. After taking her out several more times, Carolyn's $100 date backed

off. "I was glad to get her out of my life," he said later. But he also felt some sympathy and commented, "She was a very, very unhappy person." Doug Levine, who went to school with Carolyn from their elementary-school years onward, disapproved of the way she tried to manipulate people with money, but he, too, felt sorry for her: "She could never get enough attention. She was always looking for friends." Remembered another acquaintance from Carolyn's school days, "People used to go out with her to drive her fancy cars." She had a Jeep Cherokee of her own and access to her father's fleet of classic automobiles.

Not everything was black during Carolyn's high-school years, however. A good athlete, she won a spot on the girls' basketball team, and she made straight A's with a minimum of work, graduating with honors in 1981. That fall Carolyn entered the University of Michigan in Ann Arbor, only an hour or so from Franklin. In college she kept up her big-spending ways. She was always expensively turned out and eager to treat classmates to trips and other extravagances. When one man who'd known her at Michigan was asked to describe what Carolyn had been like in college he answered with one word: "Rich."

At the beginning of her sophomore year in college, Warmus pledged Pi Beta Phi sorority. For a time it seemed that she had finally found the circle of friends she'd never had in high school. As it happened, the Pi Phis she identified with most closely were Jewish, and they regularly went to parties with the members of Zeta Beta Tau, a largely Jewish fraternity. Warmus became one of the regulars herself, and most of the men she dated were ZBTs. Soon Warmus, who'd been raised a Catholic, was telling her sorority sisters she hoped to marry a Jewish man.

In 1983 Warmus met that man, or so she thought. His name was Paul Laven, and he was a member of ZBT and a graduate student in the psychology department. They began dating in June, and Warmus could hardly talk about anything or anyone except him. Her sorority sisters couldn't understand why she'd become so obsessed with Laven; they thought he was arrogant, aloof, and domineering. Nevertheless, Carolyn's whole life seemed to revolve around him, down to buying shoes only if she thought that he'd like them. She started wearing a gold

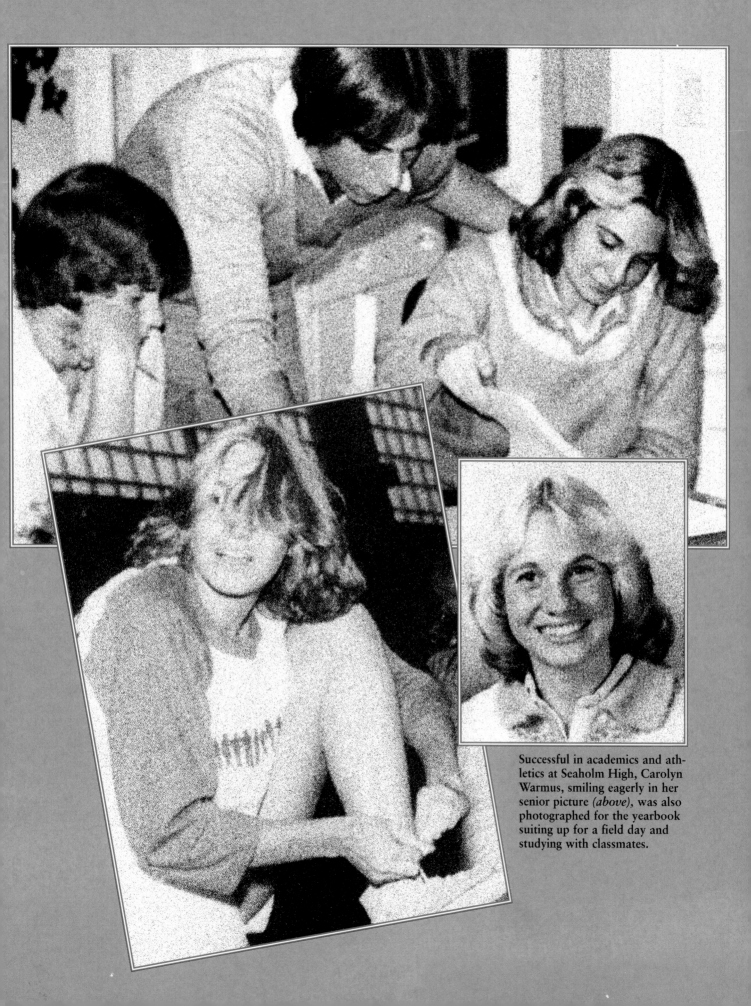

Successful in academics and athletics at Seaholm High, Carolyn Warmus, smiling eagerly in her senior picture *(above)*, was also photographed for the yearbook suiting up for a field day and studying with classmates.

Star of David around her neck and, with the thought of converting, attended classes in Judaism at the Jewish center on campus.

Warmus was so preoccupied with Laven that she had less and less time for her sorority sisters and began skipping meetings and other Pi Phi activities. In their opinion, she was making a fool of herself. She talked and acted as if her relationship with Laven was a serious one, but everyone—including Carolyn—knew he was dating other women. Perhaps she hoped that if she kept behaving like a fiancée, he'd come to see things her way. But that never happened. In December 1983, after six months of dating, Laven stopped seeing Warmus. He'd fallen in love with someone else—a Jewish woman named Wendy Siegel.

Warmus plunged into a terrible state, alarming her friends and family with her fits of weeping, outbursts of anger, and threats of suicide. Soon after the breakup, she called the Pi Phi house in tears. She was at home in Franklin. "I'm going to kill myself," she sobbed. "I'm taking a hotel room because I don't want anyone to find me." She also said something about driving up to a vacation home that her family owned in northern Michigan, and when Warmus suddenly slammed down the telephone, a quick-thinking sorority sister notified the state police. When a trooper caught up with Warmus, heading north in her father's red Ferrari, she was on the verge of hysteria.

Already fed up with her for neglecting the sorority, the Pi Phis wondered whether they might be held responsible if Warmus did something rash. They decided the risk wasn't worth it and expelled her from the group. It must have been a painful and humiliating blow. Carolyn Warmus was alone again.

And she was behaving like a woman possessed. Throughout the winter of 1984 she stalked Laven on campus and bombarded him with letters and telephone calls that alternated between vague threats and pleas to see him. But nothing swayed Laven, and by spring he and Siegel had become engaged and were sharing an apartment. On April 10 Warmus showed up at their place, screaming hysterically and pounding on the door until the police arrived and forced her to leave.

Paul Laven and Wendy Siegel had a respite from harassment while Warmus spent a week at her family's house in Florida during spring break. She announced her return by sending Siegel an overwrought, misspelled letter: "I really hope you enjoyed this past week of not being bothered by me, because now that Im back from vacation you can start worrying all over again," Warmus wrote. "And lit me tell you, with the tan I have now, you've got even more to compete with! Of coarse with a body like mine, I'm sure you relized what tough competetion you were up against even before I went to Florida. In fact, your just about out of the running compltly now!" Several weeks later Laven found a note on his car windshield: "P.—I'm 2½ months pregnant. CALL ME!!! PLEASE! Love, C."

Warmus was lying, but she nevertheless spread the tale of her pregnancy all over campus in an apparent bid for sympathy at the way Laven was mistreating her. The ploy did not have the intended effect on Laven and Siegel. Angry and deeply worried that Warmus wasn't going to let up, the couple swore out a complaint against her. In the words of their lawyer, her harassment had brought them to a "state of mind that they imminently fear for their own personal safety."

With innocent outrage, Carolyn Warmus asked a former sorority sister: "What does Paul think I'm going to do, show up at his wedding?" The young woman explained later: "That's the way she would act. She'd tell you a story indicating that she would never do anything like that. But you sensed there was something she'd done to make them believe that she would. You couldn't believe everything she said. Carolyn sometimes scared the hell out of me."

Perhaps at her father's insistence, Warmus signed a permanent restraining order in which she agreed never to contact Laven and Siegel again. The marriage took place without incident. Warmus's reasons for sticking to the terms of the order may have included the fact that she'd had a serious brush with the law several months earlier. She had stolen $7,000 worth of Nancy Dailey's jewelry and pawned it in Oak Park for $3,000 on February 5. Suspicious, the pawnbroker called the police, who in turn got in touch with Tom Warmus. He redeemed the jewelry and declined to press charges against his daughter. What prompted the theft—an odd undertaking for a wealthy young woman—was never explained. It may have been an oblique expression of hos-

tility toward her stepmother. Nancy had recently given birth to a daughter, an event that could have rocked Carolyn with an ungovernable surge of jealousy.

Losing Paul Laven gnawed at Warmus, and when her depression didn't lift her father insisted that she get some psychiatric treatment. That fall, when she went back to college, she resumed her instruction in Judaism, perhaps clinging to the hope that things would turn out all right with Laven. She told the rabbi who was instructing her that she was engaged to marry a Jewish man. It was customary for a couple to attend the classes together, and the rabbi wondered why Warmus always came alone. In June 1985, close to the time of her graduation from college, Warmus's ceremony of conversion to Judaism took place. Not a single friend or relative was there to celebrate what should have been a joyous occasion.

Back home in Franklin after graduating, she got a job as a barmaid and waitress at the Jukebox, a nightclub and pickup spot favored by college students and young professionals. The Jukebox had a fifties theme; the bar-

At the University of Michigan, Warmus dated—and later obsessively pursued—Paul Laven, pictured in 1983 with his Zeta Beta Tau fraternity brothers.

maids wore poodle skirts and bobbie socks and danced to vintage rock-'n'-roll atop the bar. Carolyn, with her big eyes, wide smile, and curvaceous figure, "was great," remembered the Jukebox's doorman. "She fit right into our carnival atmosphere. She never seemed to be in a bad mood." The hangout was a likely place to meet someone new, and Warmus behaved as though she'd gotten over Paul Laven. Still using her money to create the illusion of friendship, she would take her coworkers to dinner on their days off. She arranged for the manager of the Rickshaw Inn, a Chinese restaurant she frequented, to lay in a supply of top-of-the-line Dom Perignon champagne just for her and her companions.

It didn't take Warmus long to fix her sights on a Jukebox customer. Her new obsession was Brian "Buddy" Fetter, a young Jewish bachelor who worked in his millionaire father's carpet business. He and Warmus went out and went to bed. From their first night together, Warmus talked about marriage. But all Fetter wanted was some casual fun, and after three weeks of incessant

Wendy-

I really hope you enjoyed this past week of not being bothered by me, because now that Im back from vacation you can start worrying all over again, And lit me tell you, with the tan I have now, you've got even more to compete with! Of coarse with a body like mine, I'm sure you relized what tough competetion you were up against even before I went etto Florida. In fact, your just about out of the running completly now! I hope you enjoyed having Paul all to yourself this past week, because it will be a long time before if happens again. Of coarse, knowing Paul's devotion to me, he probably spent as little time as possible with you thes past week and weekend.
I guess as long as you keep letting him live in your apartment with you, he'll just continue to pretend to care about you. Go right on fooling yourself, Wendy--your just making Paul's job of fooling <u>you</u> even easier for him.

                                                        C---

When Paul Laven became engaged to a young woman named Wendy Siegel in the spring of 1984, Warmus desperately tried to win back her man by harassing the couple and writing an angry letter, full of misspellings *(above)*, to Siegel. "Your just about out of the running completly now!" Warmus taunted. A few weeks later, she falsely claimed in a note to Paul *(right)* that she was carrying his child.

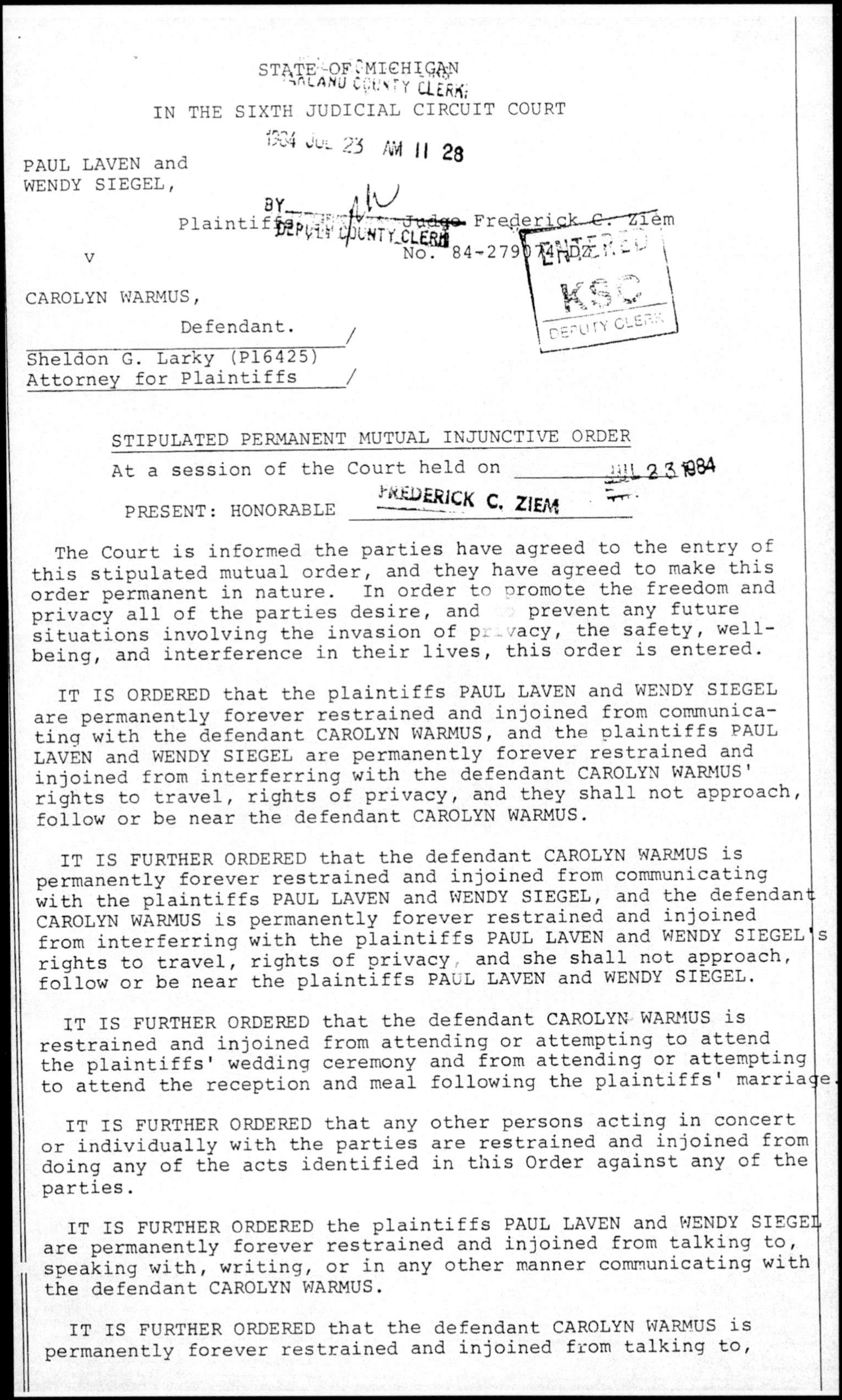

IN THE SIXTH JUDICIAL CIRCUIT COURT

1984 JUL 23 AM 11 28

PAUL LAVEN and
WENDY SIEGEL,

      BY_____
    Plaintiffs, DEPUTY COUNTY CLERK Judge Frederick C. Ziem

v   No. 84-2790 4-HD ENTERED

                            KSC

CAROLYN WARMUS,

      Defendant.   DEPUTY CLERK
_____/

Sheldon G. Larky (P16425)
Attorney for Plaintiffs   /

STIPULATED PERMANENT MUTUAL INJUNCTIVE ORDER

At a session of the Court held on _____ JUL 23 1984

    PRESENT: HONORABLE FREDERICK C. ZIEM

The Court is informed the parties have agreed to the entry of
this stipulated mutual order, and they have agreed to make this
order permanent in nature. In order to promote the freedom and
privacy all of the parties desire, and prevent any future
situations involving the invasion of privacy, the safety, well-
being, and interference in their lives, this order is entered.

IT IS ORDERED that the plaintiffs PAUL LAVEN and WENDY SIEGEL
are permanently forever restrained and injoined from communicating with the defendant CAROLYN WARMUS, and the plaintiffs PAUL
LAVEN and WENDY SIEGEL are permanently forever restrained and
injoined from interferring with the defendant CAROLYN WARMUS'
rights to travel, rights of privacy, and they shall not approach,
follow or be near the defendant CAROLYN WARMUS.

IT IS FURTHER ORDERED that the defendant CAROLYN WARMUS is
permanently forever restrained and injoined from communicating
with the plaintiffs PAUL LAVEN and WENDY SIEGEL, and the defendant
CAROLYN WARMUS is permanently forever restrained and injoined
from interferring with the plaintiffs PAUL LAVEN and WENDY SIEGEL's
rights to travel, rights of privacy, and she shall not approach,
follow or be near the plaintiffs PAUL LAVEN and WENDY SIEGEL.

IT IS FURTHER ORDERED that the defendant CAROLYN WARMUS is
restrained and injoined from attending or attempting to attend
the plaintiffs' wedding ceremony and from attending or attempting
to attend the reception and meal following the plaintiffs' marriage.

IT IS FURTHER ORDERED that any other persons acting in concert
or individually with the parties are restrained and injoined from
doing any of the acts identified in this Order against any of the
parties.

IT IS FURTHER ORDERED the plaintiffs PAUL LAVEN and WENDY SIEGEL
are permanently forever restrained and injoined from talking to,
speaking with, writing, or in any other manner communicating with
the defendant CAROLYN WARMUS.

IT IS FURTHER ORDERED that the defendant CAROLYN WARMUS is
permanently forever restrained and injoined from talking to,

A fearful Laven and Siegel secured a permanent restraining order barring any contact between them and Warmus.

telephone calls and unannounced visits he began avoiding her. She jammed his answering machine with long pleading speeches. She annoyed him at the club. Refusing to give up his favorite bar, Fetter bribed the doorman to tell him when Carolyn arrived so that he could creep out the back door. Fetter's ordeal lasted three months, until Carolyn's attention finally settled upon another man, a married friend of his, who also happened to be the manager of the Rickshaw Inn. He may have been the first married man with whom Warmus had an affair, but he wouldn't be the last.

What attracted Warmus to the manager initially may have been the fact that he and Fetter were friends, for she tried to enlist his help in rekindling Fetter's interest. Soon, however, it was the manager who was the target of her affection. For three months she hounded the man, once flying to another city and tracking him to a restaurant where he was doing business over dinner. "The maître d' came up to my table and told me that there was this drunk woman in the lobby looking for me," the man remembered later. "It was a nightmare."

By then Warmus had been fired from her job at the Jukebox by owner Mark Papazian. Customers had been complaining to him about getting monthly statements that included Jukebox charges they hadn't made, and an investigation showed that it had been Warmus who'd waited on all of the aggrieved customers. Papazian suspected that she'd been pocketing cash payments from customers and covering her theft by submitting fraudulent chits she'd run off from other customers' credit cards. When Papazian confronted Warmus, she denied that she was responsible. "She was very composed," he recalled later. "She said some other waitress was probably jealous of her and was blaming her." Papazian, who calculated that the false charges amounted to approximately $5,400, was convinced that Warmus was lying to him. He probably would have felt still more certain of her guilt if he'd known about the theft of her stepmoth-

er's jewelry the year before. Luckily for Carolyn, the Secret Service, the agency responsible for handling suspected credit-card fraud, didn't investigate cases that involved losses of less than $10,000. Papazian was left holding the bag.

Waitressing was only a stopgap occupation for Warmus anyway. She decided to be a schoolteacher, and in the spring of 1986 she moved to Manhattan to study for a master's degree at Columbia University's Teachers College. Taking an apartment at 210 East 22nd Street, near Gramercy Park, Warmus set out to explore the city. On her first New Year's Eve there, she went barhopping around Times Square and that night met the next object of her obsession, Matthew Nicolosi. Carolyn's new lover lived with his wife, Lisa, and their children in New Jersey, where he worked nights as a bartender at a Ramada Inn. Warmus would take a room at the Ramada, then go to the bar for a drink and discreetly slip her key to Nicolosi beneath a cocktail napkin. She'd be waiting in the room for him when his shift ended.

Expelled from her sorority because of her erratic behavior and still smarting from Laven's rejection, Carolyn Warmus was not the cheerful senior she appeared to be in her 1985 University of Michigan yearbook photograph.

The affair was scarcely off the ground when Warmus started lobbying for marriage, undaunted by the fact that Nicolosi had told her his wife was pregnant again. Desperate to please her lover, Warmus acquiesced to whatever he wanted sexually; she even agreed to a threesome when Nicolosi brought another girlfriend to one of their trysts.

Nicolosi made no move toward divorcing his wife—in fact, had no intention of seeking a divorce—so it was up to Warmus to remove Lisa Nicolosi from the picture. By February 1987, not two months after she'd met Nicolosi, Warmus mentioned a possible way out of her difficulty to Laurie Delaney, a Michigan friend who'd come to New York for a visit. She later recalled Warmus's confiding that "she could get someone to arrange for a hit on Lisa for $10,000. With Lisa out of the way she could be with Matt." Delaney thought her friend might be joking, but she couldn't be sure. Warmus had never minded spending money to get what she wanted.

Instead of a hit man, however, Warmus hired Vincent Parco, a 36-year-old private investigator whose name she picked at random from the Manhattan yellow pages. On her first visit to his office, in June 1987, she wore a white tennis outfit that showed off her long, nicely tanned legs. Parco sat up and took notice. Warmus told him she wanted a surveillance carried out of her lover, who was being slow to get a divorce as he'd promised her he would. If the lover's wife was confronted with something compromising—photographs, perhaps—she might demand a divorce herself.

Parco struck a deal with Warmus, even though she made him bend his profession's rules and let her go along on the surveillance. He assigned the job to his assistant James Russo, and that same day Russo and Warmus drove out to New Jersey. During the drive she chatted about herself and her romances. She'd been terribly broken up after a boyfriend back in Michigan married someone else, she confessed, but Nicolosi had made life worth living again.

The first stop in New Jersey was the Nicolosi home. Finding it was no trouble, for Warmus had followed her lover on a number of occasions and knew where he lived. After Russo photographed the house, they moved on to the Ramada Inn. Warmus spotted Nicolosi's car in the parking lot, and Russo told her to wait while he went into the bar to take some surreptitious shots. He was soon back. The bar was empty, he said, and his camera would have been far too conspicuous. They decided to wait in the parking lot until the end of Nicolosi's shift. When he finally came out, Russo succeeded in getting several photographs.

None of the photos looked at all incriminating, but Parco had an idea: They'd concoct something compromising by superimposing suggestive photographs of Warmus on the ones Russo had taken of Nicolosi outside the Ramada Inn.

Russo's photo session with Warmus took place at her apartment two days after their foray into New Jersey. No longer the sporty-looking tennis player, she was heavily made up and wore a pink wig. She smiled seductively at Russo and laughed and joked as she struck poses in several different costumes, including lacy lingerie, a transparent black body stocking, and a blue teddy. "She took almost everything off," Russo reminisced later. "Stuck out her tongue, lay on the carpet, held her breasts and seemed to be enjoying herself." Warmus was, he said admiringly, "in very good shape." After the last shot, she drew close to him and asked whether she had excited him. When he said no, she snapped angrily, "Maybe this will help," and kneed him in the groin. Russo left quickly.

Several days later Russo saw the developed photos on Parco's desk, cut into pieces and mixed with the pictures of Nicolosi. That was the last Russo saw of them. He assumed that Parco's cut-and-paste efforts were too amateurish to fool Lisa Nicolosi.

It didn't seem to disturb Warmus that Parco had failed to deliver. From then on the two of them became intimate friends. She took to stopping in at the office, going to lunch or a movie with Parco, and he sometimes took her along on a job for the fun of it. Some of Parco's business associates speculated that Warmus and Parco, who was a married man, were lovers.

Perhaps her budding relationship with Parco helped distract Warmus from her obsession with Matthew Nicolosi, because soon he didn't matter anymore. She was making a lot of changes in her life: She'd finished her master's degree at Columbia, moved into a new apartment on Manhattan's Upper East Side, and found a new job teaching computer science at Greenville Elementary

School, in a Westchester County suburb about 45 minutes from the city. Most important of all, there was a new man on the horizon.

Paul Solomon taught sixth grade at Greenville, and his classroom was diagonally across the hall from the computer room. A short, stocky man with dark, curly hair, the 39-year-old Solomon liked being in charge, and some people described him as domineering and arrogant—words that easily could have been applied to Tom Warmus. Even if he did rub some people the wrong way, Solomon was a devoted teacher and very good at his job. It didn't pay a lot, but between his salary and what his wife, Betty Jeanne, made as an account executive at a collection agency, they were comfortable enough. The couple had recently been able to swing the purchase of a modest but pleasant condominium at the Scarsdale Ridge Apartments near the school in Greenburgh. Married for 17 years, Paul and Betty Jeanne had a 13-year-old daughter, Kristan.

Paul and Betty Jeanne Solomon were college sweethearts. They had met at the State University of New York in New Paltz, in the spring of 1967. Betty Jeanne, then known as B. J., was a petite brunette, vivacious and sweet. Friends described her as sometimes stubborn and overdramatic but naive—a young woman, her sister Joyce Green said, "who assumed the best about people and then found out the truth when it was too late."

B. J.'s friends and family didn't much care for Paul Solomon. "Paul had a Svengali-like effect on her," Betty Jeanne's freshman-year roommate, JoAnn Frisina, remembered. "He was very possessive and domineering and jealous of her. He wouldn't let her cut her hair or wear makeup or skirts above the knee. He made her wear her glasses at all times. And he didn't want us to call her B. J. anymore. She became quiet and reclusive." Another classmate recalled, "B. J. was a sweet person, and he was not. He wasn't exactly . . . nice. He was rude to her. He was short, and I guess he was compensating."

The couple were married in 1970, and four years later Paul began teaching at Greenville Elementary, which was in one of the best school districts in the United States. Life among the well-to-do was expensive, especially for a couple with a young child. "So many of Kristan's friends came from wealthy families, it was difficult at times—Betty Jeanne had to tell her she couldn't have the designer jeans or whatever," remembered Joyce Green. Betty Jeanne worked as a teller with the National Bank of Westchester. She was bright, responsible, and hard-working, and by 1984, she had become branch manager. She soon moved on to a better-paying job with a collection agency, and the Solomons moved into their condo. Everything seemed right on track.

Everything but the marriage, which had gotten a little stale. Like many couples, the Solomons lived together, entertained together, raised their child together, but by

New to teaching and to Greenville Elementary *(below)* in 1987, Warmus found a mentor in 39-year-old fellow teacher—and married man—Paul Solomon.

the late 1980s, their lives overlapped very little. Joyce Green recalled that Paul "was always off either teaching something or coaching something or playing something, or having meetings about one of the three." They ate microwaved dinners on the go between work, meetings, and games. They also juggled extramarital affairs. Paul had had two liaisons, and for nine years Betty Jeanne had been seeing a man she'd once worked for. Paul wouldn't learn about her affair—or perhaps wouldn't admit it to himself—until much later, when it hardly mattered anymore.

Carolyn Warmus wasted little time in cultivating a relationship with Paul Solomon. She started dropping by his classroom to chat about her students and to ask his advice. It flattered him to be treated like a mentor, and he didn't discourage her when she started coming to practices of the girls' basketball team he coached at Greenville High School, where his daughter, Kristan, was on the varsity team. Warmus would sometimes join the girls on the court to show off the ball-handling skills she'd acquired in high school. And she made it a point to ingratiate herself with Kristan.

Betty Jeanne Solomon, shown here in a family snapshot, was suspicious of Warmus's frequent visits to the Solomons' Greenburgh, New York, condo.

ing around her school in Pleasantville. And Warmus said that she knew who this dangerous person was—a former mistress of her father's, bent on revenge. Her name was "Jeanne" or "Betty Jeanne."

Russo thought Warmus's story sounded fishy, and he said he couldn't do anything for her unless she could document the incidents with newspaper articles or police reports. That was the last he heard from Warmus. "I knew she was going to kill someone," he claimed later.

Parco, on the other hand, was beginning to soften. He and Warmus had been seeing a lot of each other, and, he later confessed, she knew how to push "the right buttons." Thus he remembered her calling on the spur of the moment to invite him over to her apartment for an intimate dinner for two. "I'm in black, sexy lingerie," Warmus breathed.

He claimed he turned down that particular invitation. In time, however, the button-pushing worked. Parco agreed to sell Warmus the gun, and he arranged for a machinist friend of his, George Peters of Brooklyn, to make a silencer for the Beretta out of stove insulation and two pieces of scrap metal. After test-firing the gun and silencer at his shop, Peters handed them over to Parco and received $1,000 for his handiwork.

On January 8, 1989, the day Warmus turned 25, Parco brought the Beretta and the silencer to her apartment. She paid him $2,500 cash.

For the second year in a row Paul Solomon was with his family instead of with Warmus on her birthday, even though he'd promised to take her out to dinner that night. He didn't even call to wish her a happy birthday. It was painfully obvious to Warmus that unless she took matters into her own hands, Paul Solomon would always belong to Betty Jeanne.

The Solomons' phone rang at 1:37 p.m. on Sunday, January 15. Paul and Betty Jeanne were at home alone that day; Kristan was away on a ski trip. The couple had slept late, then awakened to make love for the first time in a long time. After coffee and a mushroom omelet, Betty Jeanne stretched out on the living room sofa with a novel, and Paul sat across from her, browsing through the newspaper and glancing at the TV now and then.

He took the call in the den. It was Carolyn, gently but firmly reminding him that he'd missed her birthday the week before, that they hadn't seen each other since December. She got to the point: She wanted to see him that evening. At first he demurred. He'd had a touch of flu and was also tired because he'd been out late the night before at a party. "With your wife?" Carolyn asked curtly, with an edge in her voice. "That's what wives do," Paul replied.

Fresh from making love to Betty Jeanne, Paul nevertheless found himself thinking about sex with Carolyn, and he changed his mind about seeing her that evening. The conversation went on for 55 minutes as they talked about this and that. Carolyn asked about Kristan, and Paul told her about the ski trip and mentioned that she'd be gone until the following morning. They hung up after making a date to meet at 7:30 p.m. at one of their haunts, the Treetops Restaurant at the Yonkers Holiday Inn. Carolyn was happy.

Paul had a ready-made excuse for going out that night, since his bowling league met on Sundays. Betty Jeanne thought he should stay home and rest since he was a little under the weather, but he insisted it would do him good to get out for a while. Paul left about 6:30 p.m. and, to make his story good, drove to the bowling alley in the nearby town of Yonkers, 10 minutes or so from home. He chatted for about a half-hour with several different teammates, then slipped away to rendezvous with Warmus at the restaurant.

While Paul was busy establishing his presence at the bowling alley, Betty Jeanne's television watching was interrupted at 6:51 p.m. by the first of two telephone calls from a family friend, Josette Tilden. The two women discussed the plans their husbands and children had made to attend a New York Knicks basketball game. The phone rang again at 7:09, and Josette and Betty Jeanne had another quick talk about the outing. Seven minutes later, at 7:16, someone dialed 911 from the Solomons' telephone. The operator who answered the emergency call wasn't sure whether the first word

the hysterical voice at the other end of the line screamed was "he" or "she," but what followed was clear—"is trying to kill me."

Then the connection was broken. The operator immediately rang back, but no one picked up the phone. What followed was a tragic muddle. Mistakenly thinking that the call had come from Scarsdale, the operator called the police there. The error was compounded when the Scarsdale officer used an out-of-date directory to find the address the call had come from. The Solomons had gotten a new telephone number only a few weeks earlier, and what the officer found was the address of a customer named Berman who'd previously had that number. When officers arrived at the Berman apartment around 7:35 p.m., no one was home, and the landlord told them he hadn't heard anything unusual.

At 7:25 p.m., while the operator and the police were bungling the emergency call, Paul Solomon arrived at the Treetops Restaurant, took a seat at the bar, and ordered a vodka collins. Warmus was late. When she walked in around 7:45 p.m., there was a wide, happy smile on her face, and she was wearing a blouse buttoned low enough to attract the attention of several male customers. Warmus ordered champagne—a choice suggesting she might have something to celebrate.

She and Solomon lingered for more than two hours at the restaurant, holding hands, talking, and drinking and eating. He ordered oysters and teased her when she ignored fancier items on the menu and asked for a hamburger and french fries to go with her expensive champagne. She later described his demeanor in a 1993 television interview: "He was kissing me. He had his hands on me. He was very affectionate in public, which was not his norm."

Inevitably, the subject of their relationship and its future came up. According to Solomon, he told Warmus he thought she should see other men. "I'd be so happy to dance at your wedding and see you happy," he told her. "What about your happiness, Paul?" she replied. "Don't you deserve to be happy?" Betty Jeanne's name surfaced in a question Carolyn put to Paul: If his marriage ended, what did he think he would do? He answered that if anything were to happen to him and Betty Jeanne, he doubted he would marry again. It wasn't at all what she'd wanted to hear.

At 10:30 p.m. Solomon and Warmus left the restaurant and spent another hour together making love in the parking lot, in the backseat of her red Hyundai. Ten minutes after pulling out of the Holiday Inn lot, Solomon was home. When he opened his front door, the living room lights were off but the TV was playing; in its flickering glow he could make out his wife lying on the floor, facedown. Thinking she'd fallen asleep, he said, "Wake up. It's time to wake up and go to bed." She didn't stir. Solomon turned on a light and touched her. She was very cold, and when he turned her over he saw the blood. He put his head to her chest but heard no heartbeat. Crying hysterically, he dialed 911. When the first officers pulled up, he shouted to them, "Hurry, she can't be dead!"

Detectives summoned to the scene saw that Betty Jeanne Solomon had been shot at least eight times, and possibly nine, and had also been struck hard on the back of the head. Six .25-caliber shell casings littered the floor; perhaps the killer had picked up the others before running away. There wasn't any sign of forced entry, nor had anything been stolen. It appeared that the killer had had a key or had been let in by the victim herself—was someone Betty Jeanne knew. The neighbors hadn't heard any shots or other unusual sounds.

The obvious suspect was Paul Solomon. Taken to the Greenburgh police station for questioning, for three hours he insisted doggedly that he'd been bowling all evening. At last he broke down and, blushing deeply, began to describe his affair with Carolyn Warmus, the evening they'd just spent at the Treetops Restaurant, and their sexual encounter in the little Hyundai afterward. The story he told suggested that he had murdered his wife because their marriage had gone bad, and he'd fallen for another woman.

Two Greenburgh detectives rang the doorbell of Warmus's Manhattan apartment at 5 a.m. on Monday, the morning after the murder, and she smilingly agreed to go with them to the police station to make a statement about her Sunday evening date with Paul. Her story and his tallied well, down to having sex in the car, although she claimed he was the one who'd suggested they see each other that night.

Later that day Warmus phoned Vincent Parco to break the date they'd made for Monday evening. She told him she'd been questioned by the police about a colleague's wife being murdered—stabbed or bludgeoned, she said, eight or nine times. It was making her nervous to have the Beretta in her apartment, she said, and she wanted him to come by her apartment the next day and get it. On Tuesday, Warmus called again to say he needn't bother; she'd already gotten rid of the gun herself, throwing it out her car window along the parkway she traveled to and from work.

Besides disposing of a damning piece of evidence, there was something else Warmus saw to right away. Perhaps prompted by the possibility that she'd need legal help—or the chance that her name would crop up in a news story about the murder—she telephoned her father. Whatever Tom Warmus thought or said when she told him about her affair with Paul Solomon and Betty Jeanne Solomon's murder, his checkbook was open, and he instructed his lawyer to take care of Carolyn.

Not that the Greenburgh police were fixed on her then; it was Paul Solomon who interested them. Investigators soon had to admit, however, that his alibi was a good one. Several friends who'd been at the bowling alley on the night of the murder backed up his account, as had witnesses at the Treetops Restaurant. Moreover, however many times he was questioned, Solomon's story didn't change in any important details—a sign of truthfulness, since not even an accomplished liar with a first-rate memory was likely to be so consistent.

And then there was the surprising discovery made by the ballistics experts who examined the shell casings: The murder weapon had been equipped with a silencer, a device seldom used by any gunman other than a professional hit man. Although Richard Constantino, the lead detective on the case, wouldn't rule it out, he couldn't see Solomon using a hired killer: People seldom went to such expense unless they stood to make money from a murder, and Solomon apparently had nothing to gain from his wife's death except a modest amount of life insurance.

Warmus, on the other hand, had a great deal to gain from the murder, and that was Paul Solomon. Apparently not caring how it looked, she joined the mourners at the memorial service for Betty Jeanne Solomon and dismayed the widower by giving him a hug and a kiss. And, as she'd done five years earlier with Paul Laven, Warmus

Carolyn Warmus and Paul Solomon met at the Treetops Restaurant at the Holiday Inn in Yonkers the evening Betty Jeanne was murdered.

Struck in the head by a blunt object and riddled by nine bullets that penetrated her chest, back, arm, and leg, Betty Jeanne Solomon lies dead on her living room floor. Police noted that the victim's arms were positioned as if to ward off an attack.

started hounding Paul Solomon with telephone calls and letters, some of them 15 and 20 pages long. In a letter dated February 9, scarcely three weeks after the murder, she wrote, "You are the most important thing in my life. And I don't ever want to lose your friendship." There was sometimes a hint of impatience as Solomon kept turning down her pleas to see him. "When are you going to start living your life again, and include me in it?" she asked in a letter. Besides writing and calling, Warmus would stop by to tape notes to the Solomons' front door or leave presents for Kristan and Paul, including a sweater she'd knit for him and a Jack Nicklaus videotape entitled "Golf My Way."

The constant reminders that Warmus was waiting in the wings made Solomon uncomfortable, but he was too weak or too ambivalent to reject his lover altogether. He could have hung up when she called and he could have returned her letters unopened. He did neither, however, and she probably took heart from his mixed signals.

Warmus kept tabs on Solomon, and in June she spotted him with the same young woman several times. Noting the license

number of the woman's car when it was parked outside his condominium, Warmus asked Vincent Parco to find out the name of the owner. The car belonged to Barbara Ballor, a 28-year-old teacher at Greenville Elementary School. The possibility that Solomon might be sleeping with Ballor was intolerable to Warmus, filling her with jealousy and rage.

Then, on an afternoon in late July, Solomon went into Manhattan to play basketball with some friends. When the game was over, he decided on impulse to stop by to see Warmus. She wasn't home, so he went to a bar near her apartment to kill a little time before trying again. He'd just rung her bell when Warmus walked into the lobby wearing a sweatsuit—she'd been taking a golf lesson in Westchester County. She was ecstatic that Solomon was there and threw her arms around him. At his suggestion, they went back to the bar and settled into a booth. They talked as if they were still lovers, and Solomon let her know how much he'd missed her. Then without warning, Solomon shattered the intimate mood with the question that had been on his mind for months: "Did you have anything to do with Betty Jeanne's death?" The question must have been a nasty surprise, but she replied calmly, "Paul, I'm so glad you feel comfortable enough to ask me that. No, I would never do anything to hurt you or Kristan." For the moment at least, Solomon believed her, and he was extremely relieved. When she suggested that they go to her apartment—she said she wanted him to see the redecorating she'd done since he was there last—he agreed. It would be their last intimate encounter.

The thrill of being with Solomon quickly dissipated for Carolyn. Apparently regretting his impulsive visit, he refused to see her again. Already depressed at his having slipped through her fingers, Warmus got some very unsettling news from Vincent Parco—two Greenburgh detectives had been around to ask questions about her. His number had cropped up in Warmus's telephone records, which the police had reviewed in order to verify the call she'd made to Paul Solomon on the day of the murder. Curious as to why Warmus would need a private investigator, Detective Constantino had gone to see Parco. Volunteering nothing about the gun he'd sold Warmus, Parco claimed he'd had little to do with her beyond arranging the surveillance of Matthew Nicolosi and sent

In the summer of 1989, Paul Solomon was seeing a young woman named Barbara Ballor, who vacationed with him at the Condado Plaza Hotel in San Juan, Puerto Rico *(below)*. An angry, unbalanced Warmus followed the couple there.

the detectives on to talk to James Russo, the investigator who'd actually carried out the surveillance. Warmus had to wonder what else the police might have found out about her besides her affair with Nicolosi.

At the end of the month, she went back home to Michigan for a visit. Warmus seemed so close to the breaking point that her family was afraid she might attempt suicide or take out her anger and hurt on someone else—possibly Paul Solomon. After the disastrous Paul Laven affair in 1984 Carolyn had seen a psychiatrist, and Tom Warmus felt she should see one again. But father and daughter had a violent argument, and she went back to New York without getting any counseling.

In the following days Carolyn continued her emotional downward spiral, and she sounded so disturbed in several telephone conversations that Tom Warmus delegated his other two children, 20-year-old Tom junior and 24-year-old Tracey, to go to New York to check on their sister and report back to him. Apparently Tom senior couldn't spare the time to tend to his daughter's deepening crisis himself.

Carolyn went wild when Tracey and Tom junior showed up at her apartment on August 8. Her life was nobody's business, she screamed, and she railed against Tom Warmus for being a terrible father. She sobbed, said she'd kill herself, knocked over furniture, and threw things as her brother and sister tried to calm her and angry neighbors pounded on the wall to protest the noise. Frightened and desperate for help, Tom dialed 911 to summon an ambulance, and Carolyn burst into wordless screams of rage. She had to be strapped down for the trip to Metropolitan Hospital, where she spent the next week in the psychiatric ward.

While she was in the hospital, there was yet another downward turn for Warmus. In the interview he'd had with police the month before, investigator James Russo had described the excursion he and Warmus had made to New Jersey to dig up dirt on Nicolosi as well as the *Playboy*-style photo session at her apartment. On August 9, after a second interview with Detectives Constantino and Sullivan, Russo wrote out a four-page statement containing information that was far more incriminating. It was an account of the day Warmus had come to see him in the summer of 1988 asking to buy a

gun with a silencer, supposedly as protection against her father's vengeful ex-mistress, Betty Jeanne. At the time the police weren't sure what to make of the incident, but it would soon make a great deal of sense.

When Warmus was released from the hospital on August 15, Paul Solomon and interloper Barbara Ballor were uppermost in her mind. From a telephone conversation she'd had with Paul in early August, she knew he should now be on vacation in Puerto Rico. And the infuriating probability was that Ballor was with him. Her suspicions were confirmed when she called Ballor's apartment and, claiming to be a friend of Ballor's, wormed the information out of the young teacher's roommate, Tammy Rogers. Rogers, who felt somehow uneasy about the caller, said she didn't know the name of Solomon and Ballor's hotel when in fact she did. Warmus put in a call for help to Vincent Parco. Using the tricks of the private investigator's trade, he found out that the pair had a reservation at the Condado Plaza Hotel in San Juan. By the next morning Warmus was on a flight to Puerto Rico.

After checking into her room at the Caribe Hilton in San Juan, Warmus had lunch, then turned to getting in touch with Solomon. But she went about it in a curiously indirect way. Instead of telephoning the Condado Plaza or summoning a taxi, she dialed Barbara Ballor's apartment. Tammy Rogers answered. The woman on the other end of the line said she was a desk clerk at the Condado Plaza and began asking questions about Paul Solomon and Barbara Ballor's reservation. Rogers instantly recognized the voice—it was the woman she'd talked to the day before. Rogers didn't know what was going on, but she didn't like it and hung up.

Warmus spent the next several hours telephoning the Condado Plaza over and over. Every time there was no answer in Solomon's room Warmus's frustration mounted; she was especially irate with the desk clerk when he refused to tell her the room number. Her angry persistence worried the desk clerk, so the hotel security chief, Ali Baez, stepped in to take her calls. She was just as snappish with him, and in exasperation he finally hung up on her.

Tired of telephoning and leaving messages, Warmus took a cab to the Condado Plaza late that afternoon. There, she buttonholed a male guest and sweet-talked him into delivering an envelope to the front desk and calling Solomon to ask him to pick the envelope up in person. Warmus found a seat in the cocktail lounge from which she could watch the desk and waited, nursing a drink, for Paul to appear.

The call about the envelope puzzled Solomon, who'd just returned to the room after a lazy afternoon at the hotel pool with Ballor. Only a few friends knew where he was vacationing, and he couldn't think why any of them would have something delivered to him in San Juan. Minutes later, the phone rang again. It was a worried Tammy Rogers. As Solomon listened to her describe the disturbing telephone calls she'd fielded, he was flooded by anxiety. He'd scarcely said good-bye when the phone rang for a third time. It was security chief Baez informing him about the afternoon's barrage of telephone calls from an agitated Carolyn Warmus.

It was appalling to Solomon to think that she would stalk him and Ballor all the way to San Juan. Worse than appalling—it struck Solomon for the first time that she was a thoroughly dangerous woman. He didn't know exactly where she was at that moment, but he was suddenly afraid for himself and for Barbara Ballor. A terrible question had occurred to him: He asked himself why Carolyn had been so late for their date at the Treetops Restaurant on the night Betty Jeanne was murdered. He was afraid he knew the answer.

At the front desk, Solomon collected the waiting envelope and a telephone message. "Call me," the message read. "I'm here just as we planned. Caribe Hilton, Room 1574. Love C." In the envelope was a key to her hotel room. It was the last thing in the world Paul Solomon wanted.

From the cocktail lounge Warmus watched him read the note and open the envelope. He didn't see her, and apparently she didn't want him to—not just then. She went back to the Caribe Hilton to wait for Paul Solomon. She had no doubt he would come.

When Paul Solomon and Barbara Ballor flew back to New York that same night, her mind was reeling from the shocking things she'd heard about Carolyn Warmus in the last few hours. When the two of them walked into his apartment, the light on the answering machine was blinking. "Hello, it's Carolyn calling." Her voice was testy, annoyed. "I mean, I don't know what's going on. But I am down in Puerto Rico now, not pleased, is the fact that I'm down here, supposedly to be seeing you and you are nowhere around." Rambling on in a disjointed, manic vein, the message filled Solomon with dread. In a trembling voice he said to Ballor, "This is madness." Ballor had already heard more than enough. Their relationship was finished.

When Paul didn't come to her room at the Caribe Hilton, Warmus called the Condado Plaza and discovered that he and Ballor had checked out. Thinking they'd simply moved to another hotel, Warmus stayed on in San Juan for a day or two trying to hunt them down. Before she gave up and returned to New York, she heartlessly dragged Barbara Ballor's parents into her war against their daughter. With some help from Vincent Parco, Warmus had gotten the telephone number of the senior Ballors, and she now dialed their home in Michigan. Claiming to be a detective with the Greenburgh, New York, police department, Warmus described Paul Solomon to Mrs. Ballor as the prime suspect in the murder of his wife and added that the victim had been shot about eight times with a small-caliber gun equipped with a silencer. It would be in Barbara's own self-interest, she went on, to stop seeing him. Warmus was a good liar, and Mrs. Ballor was beside herself with worry until she was able to reach her daughter. When Barbara reported the incident to the Greenburgh police department, Detective Richard Constantino was sure that the phony detective had to be Warmus. At any rate, the caller had to be someone intimately familiar with the murder, for neither the number of times Betty Jeanne Solomon had been shot nor any information about the murder weapon had been made public.

Warmus snapped into focus as the prime suspect. And her bizarre odyssey to Puerto Rico didn't look like an isolated event but part of a pattern of romantic fixation that was emerging from information the police had already gathered about her. Paul Solomon had been complaining to them since May about Warmus's telephone calls and letters and gifts, and they'd learned about the curiously similar episode with Matthew Nicolosi from their interviews with Vincent Parco and James Russo.

The file on Warmus grew thicker as Greenburgh investigators made inquiries in Michigan and discovered that her history of romantic fixation stretched back at least to 1983, when she was making life miserable for Paul Laven. Even then, there'd been an undercurrent of violence that had frightened her victims.

To Richard Constantino, Carolyn Warmus looked more and more like Betty Jeanne Solomon's killer, and he collaborated with his partners to work out a plausible scenario for the evening of the murder. From her telephone conversation with Solomon early on the afternoon of January 15, Warmus could have realized that there'd be a window of opportunity for murder shortly after 7 p.m. that evening. Solomon had told her that Kristan would be gone until the next day, and he'd be on his way to the Treetops Restaurant for their date. Warmus went to the apartment and Betty Jeanne, though probably not pleased to see her, was polite enough to ask her in. As Betty Jeanne was walking ahead of her toward the living room, Warmus used the gun to strike her two quick blows on the back of the head. Betty Jeanne managed to fend off the attack long enough to dial 911 and scream for help before Warmus broke the connection and shot her a total of nine times. All told, perhaps 35 minutes elapsed between the time Warmus got to the Solomons' apartment and her arrival at the Treetops Restaurant around 7:45 p.m., some 15 minutes late.

Motive and opportunity seemed accounted for, but there was as yet no evidence linking Warmus to the shell casings found with the body, nor was there an eyewitness who'd seen her at the Scarsdale Ridge Apartments at the time of the murder. What finally made the case against Warmus was a tip the police got on November 9, 1989, from Rocco Lovetere, a former employee of Vincent Parco's. Lovetere, who'd gotten wind of the gossip circulating among private investigators that the police were looking into Parco's relationship with Warmus, told them that his ex-boss had sold her a .25-caliber Beretta Jetfire, along with a custom-made silencer he'd commissioned from machinist George Peters.

Armed with Lovetere's lead, Richard Constantino searched Peters's cluttered machine shop in Brooklyn and hit pay dirt. They found a two-by-four into which Peters had test-fired the pistol, and under a drill press they found a .25-caliber shell casing, which had lain on the floor since the day Peters had test-fired the gun and silencer, more than a year earlier. A microscopic exami-

Carolyn Warmus chats on a pay telephone near her Manhattan apartment shortly after her February 1990 arrest for Betty Jeanne Solomon's murder.

nation showed that the casing bore marks identical to the ones on the casings found near Betty Jeanne Solomon's body. The unavoidable conclusion was that the Beretta was the murder weapon. When Detective Constantino confronted Parco with Lovetere's story and the ballistics report, he stopped stonewalling and admitted that he'd sold the gun to Carolyn Warmus.

With the information provided by the three private investigators, the Greenburgh police were able to get a warrant to search Warmus's apartment. If they'd hoped to find incriminating items such as the Beretta, shell casings, or ammunition, they were disappointed. They did, however, come across some unmailed letters to Paul Solomon. In one, written close to the time she'd chased him and Ballor down in Puerto Rico, Warmus implied that Paul had killed his wife. To prove how much she loved him, she offered to sacrifice herself and confess to the murder, in order, she said, to "bring back some peace" into his life and Kristan's. And, with suicide in mind, Warmus had written out a list of instructions to be carried out after her death from an overdose of sleeping pills. "Please bury me in a very cute and sexy outfit," she wrote. "Something in pastel colors would be very nice. I'll try to choose a few options." She also listed the items she wanted buried with her in her casket: "My two favorite stuffed animals, Mortimer Alfonse and Little Fluff. All my pictures of Paul and Kristan that are in my apartment. All the notes and letters that Paul and Kristan have written me."

Warmus was arrested on February 5, 1990, and charged with second-degree murder. She denied that she was guilty and was released the next day on $250,000 bond put up by her father.

The case was a media sensation—"the ultimate soap opera," as *New York Times* reporter Lisa Foderaro called it, offering "sex, deceit, affairs, and murder." A Westchester woman following the story avidly explained its appeal: "Everybody knows that men cheat on their wives. But this is all so messy. It's the kind of thing you expect actors and musicians to do. Not nice people from Westchester." Reporters compared the case to *Fatal Attraction*, the 1987 movie in which actress Glenn Close played a murderous mistress hellbent on getting rid of the wife of her lover, actor Michael Douglas.

Movie production companies competed with one another to option Warmus's story, and *Penthouse* magazine made an unsuccessful bid to get her to pose for nude photographs. Nor was the bereaved Paul Solomon ignored in the furor. He sold the film rights to the story of his wife's murder to HBO for $175,000.

Warmus basked in the attention. Her clothes were carefully chosen to project the image of the femme fatale—sexy, glamorous, irresistible to men. When she arrived at the Westchester County courthouse for a pretrial hearing in June 1990, for instance, she was ready for the cameras. The skirt of her tight pink suit stopped at mid-thigh, and the jacket's plunging neckline revealed plenty of cleavage. To complete her costume she wore sheer black hose, black high-heeled shoes, and a wide-brimmed pink hat. Her eyes were hidden movie-star-style by an enormous pair of sunglasses. Facing reality had always been hard for Carolyn Warmus. She seemed to think she was a celebrated star playing a role rather than a woman accused of murder.

In the end, Warmus would be tried twice for Betty Jeanne Solomon's murder. When the first trial opened on January 14, 1991, the flashy femme fatale had been replaced by a prim-looking schoolteacher in bulky sweaters, turtlenecks, and long skirts—an image more likely to find favor with a jury. This new Warmus had lost her taste for media attention. She shrank from the gantlet of reporters and photographers confronting her at the beginning and end of each session, hiding behind umbrellas and obscuring her face with scarves. It was as if she wanted to be as invisible as possible, for at no point would she take the stand.

The prosecutor, 38-year-old assistant district attorney James McCarty, told the jury his case would be circumstantial. No gun had been recovered, and no one had seen Warmus, the defendant, enter or leave the Solomon condominium. But McCarty presented the testimony of more than 40 witnesses, and he laid out the story of Warmus's affair with Paul Solomon, their date on the night of the murder, and her relentless pursuit of him and its climax in Puerto Rico. He bore down on the fact that Warmus couldn't prove where she was at the time Betty Jeanne Solomon was killed, and he produced Warmus's telephone records, which, in addition to showing her call to the Solomon house that afternoon, showed

another call, made at 3:02 p.m. to Ray's Sport Shop.

McCarty called to the stand an employee of Ray's Sport Shop, who testified that a woman who bought 50 rounds of .25-caliber ammunition at Ray's that day—just hours before Solomon was killed with the same type of bullet—had presented as identification a driver's license bearing the name and photograph of Liisa Kittai. Kittai herself took the stand to dispel any confusion. A young woman bearing only a slight resemblance to Carolyn Warmus, she explained that her driver's license had disappeared from her purse during the summer of 1988, when she and Warmus were working together in the same department at the ROLM Company. Kittai swore she'd never been to Ray's Sport Shop.

McCarty entered into evidence the bullets recovered from the body and the shell casings recovered from the crime scene. As to the murder weapon, Vincent Parco recounted the history of the Beretta and the silencer, with Jimmy Russo as backup. A Greenville Elementary School nurse named Patricia January bolstered their contention that Warmus had had a gun. According to January, Warmus had told her only days before the murder that she'd gotten one, ostensibly to protect herself against burglars.

As the prosecuting attorney unfolded his case against Warmus, her fragile composure sometimes gave way. A week into the trial, after listening to the recording of Paul Solomon's frantic call to 911 after discovering his wife's body, she sobbed her way through an entire morning of testimony. On another day, Warmus was sternly rebuked by the judge for getting upset and storming out of the courtroom because the jurors were studying some of her letters to Paul Solomon.

Warmus's lawyer, David Lewis, 36, was the president of the New York Association of Criminal Defense Lawyers. His plan was to convince the jury that Carolyn Warmus had been framed for the murder of Betty Jeanne Solomon; that Paul, the unfaithful husband, and Vincent Parco, the sleazy private investigator who claimed to be Carolyn's friend, had orchestrated Betty Jeanne's death. Carolyn Warmus was guilty only of having an affair with a married man, her lawyer said. "We must be careful not to be swayed in our moral judgment by the sexual activity of a young girl in this day and age," Lewis intoned. "Carolyn was in love with Paul Solomon.

A seductively suited
Warmus exits a limo
for her pretrial hearing
at the Westchester
County courthouse.

Carolyn at times hoped he would marry her." And in a quiet voice, he added: "It's not such an odd dream for a young girl."

Even as Lewis presented her defense, Warmus showed little interest in the proceedings and would sit slumped in her chair staring blankly into space. The one seemingly bright moment in the long trial came when her father was called to the stand to testify on her behalf. He would be the only member of her family Carolyn would see during the entire trial; the rest stayed away. But Tom Warmus's appearance must have been small comfort. When he entered the courtroom he didn't acknowledge her little wave. He continued to ignore her completely while he testified, never glancing in her direction, even though she kept her eyes on his face, smiling fixedly. And, instead of staying on to spend time with his daughter, to comfort or encourage her, he left the courthouse without speaking a word to her and drove straight to the airport to catch his flight back home to Michigan.

The prosecution's case was good, but it took a hammering from David Lewis. His assault on the police investigation of the crime scene was especially damaging. Calling it sloppy and unprofessional, Lewis came down hard on an inexperienced young cop who admitted that he had allowed Paul Solomon to wash Betty Jeanne's blood off his hands before he was examined, perhaps washing away vital evidence. Then Lewis showed the court a photograph that Detective Richard Constantino had taken of Betty Jeanne Solomon's body and demanded to know what had become of the black glove seen lying near one of her hands. A woman's glove to all appearances, it had short fingers and long wristlets and was made for the left hand. An embarrassed Constantino admitted that the glove had simply disappeared, and no one had any idea where it was. He testified that a forensic expert had carried out a test for blood on the glove at the scene of the crime. The test was negative, and neither Constantino nor anyone else had thought to keep the glove as possible evidence. It was a major gaffe, for the glove might be a physical link, perhaps the only one, between the murderer and the crime.

After 14 weeks the trial ended in a deadlocked jury, with eight votes to four in favor of conviction. The judge declared a mistrial, and Warmus, still free on the bail her father had posted, moved in with her new lover, Victor

Distraught after a day of testimony in which jurors read her love letters to Paul Solomon, a now camera-shy Warmus, swaddled in coat, scarf, and dark glasses, slips out an emergency exit at the Westchester County courthouse.

Warmus's case was damaged by
the admissions of detectives
Vincent Parco *(top)* and James
Russo *(above)*, whom she approached about obtaining a gun.

Paul Solomon approaches the courtroom on
April 21, 1991, the fifth day of jury delibera-
tions. Granted immunity in exchange for testi-
fying against his former lover, he admitted on
the stand, "It's very hard to resist Carolyn."

Found at the murder
scene but misplaced un-
til the second trial in
January 1992, this
women's glove con-
vinced the jury of War-
mus's guilt.

Ruggiero. Recently separated from his wheelchair-bound wife, Ruggiero was a private investigator who'd served as Warmus's bodyguard during the trial. His neighbors in suburban Westchester County were scandalized when Warmus settled in, and her habit of sunbathing in the yard wearing a bikini made them even more indignant. "Can you believe the audacity of this woman?" one of Ruggiero's next-door neighbors said to Mike Gallagher, a newspaper reporter who later wrote a book about Warmus called *Lovers of Deceit*. "She snags another married man while she's awaiting trial for killing her other lover's wife, and she's walking around here half-naked like she owns the place! We want her the hell out of here!"

Prosecutor McCarty wanted the missing black glove before Warmus went on trial for a second time. At the very least, finding the glove would head off a repeat attack on the investigators' competence. Paul Solomon had searched his apartment for the glove before the first trial began, but McCarty asked him to do it again. On January 21, the day before the trial opened, Solomon found it in a cardboard box in the bottom of a bedroom closet. The missing glove, of black cashmere, was stuck to a piece of Velcro inside an old leather motorcycle glove of Paul's that he hadn't worn for years. Solomon and his daughter, Kristan, were certain the cashmere glove hadn't belonged to Betty Jeanne.

The glove was sent to a forensic laboratory for tests far more sophisticated than the one that had been done at the crime scene during the original investigation. An electron microscope, an instrument with enormous magnifying power, revealed faint bloodstains in the shape of fingertips on the back of the glove, as if a bloody hand had grasped it. Moreover, a match was made between the glove and fibers found under Betty Jeanne Solomon's fingernails.

The facts suggested that there'd been a struggle in which the already wounded, bleeding Solomon had grabbed hold of Warmus's hand and pulled off the black cashmere glove she was wearing. Still clutching the glove, Solomon fell to the floor, and Warmus shot her four more times as she lay facedown. The results of the tests were meaningless, however, unless the prosecution could demonstrate that the glove belonged to Warmus. Although the forensic experts found a single blond hair

on the glove, they could not compare that hair to Warmus's without her cooperation; she refused. McCarty's investigators then subpoenaed her American Express credit card records and found the information they were after: On November 9, 1987, more than a year before the murder, Warmus had bought a pair of gloves at a Westchester department store that proved a match to the mystery glove in material, style, and manufacturer. The only bit of information not included on the charge slip was the color of Warmus's gloves. Kristan Solomon's testimony helped overcome that uncertainty. The glove her father had found was, she said, "almost exactly like the pair" Warmus had lent her when they went skiing at Mount Snow, Vermont, in February 1988.

The glove tipped the balance against Warmus. This time around, the jury found her guilty of second-degree murder as charged. She showed no reaction at all when she heard the verdict. Her former lover, Paul Solomon, burst into tears. Her lawyer was kept on hold for five minutes when he telephoned Thomas Warmus to inform him of his daughter's fate.

On the day of her sentencing Carolyn Warmus was neither the femme fatale nor the prim schoolteacher. Dulled by sedatives, she shuffled into the courtroom wearing prison-issue slippers, blue jeans, and a sweatshirt from her alma mater, the University of Michigan, where romance had begun going so terribly awry for Carolyn Warmus. She stood unsteadily before the judge. Her voice was faint and quavering, and Judge Carey asked her to speak up. She spoke tearfully at first, then, her voice rising, almost hysterically. She was not responsible, she said. She was a victim.

"I had no knowledge of it, and I was not a participant, and I was nowhere near the apartment on that day. I am standing here before you, Judge Carey, devastated about being sentenced for a crime that I did not commit, and I can only ask you for leniency because I am innocent. If I am guilty of anything at all, it was simply being foolish enough to believe the lies and promises that Paul Solomon made to me and allow myself to be manipulated by him. That's all. Thank you."

The judge gave Carolyn Warmus 25 years to life for murdering Betty Jeanne Solomon. Paul Solomon was not in the courtroom when she was sentenced.◆

Lovelorn

Love is a risky business. There are no guarantees that it won't turn sour or die, nor is there any insurance to protect against cooling passion, broken vows, deceit, or desertion. Most people who have been rejected by a lover or spurned by a spouse weather their heartbreak and anger and humiliation and eventually get on with life. For a few, however, the injured lover's emotion turns itself inside out and takes on lethal proportions. The price exacted for betrayal is death, in some cases from a faithless partner, in others from a usurping rival. Whoever the victim, a crime of passion is a perverse act of devotion—a murderous testament to the killer's depth of feeling that is as powerful as any declaration of love.

Such a crime is peculiarly disturbing because the emotions that fuel it are ones that many men and women experience to some degree. As shown in the five stories that follow, apparently normal, law-abiding people can shock friends and neighbors by killing for love. It's almost too close for comfort.

French Twist

--- --- --- --- --- ---

Pierre Chevallier's relatives didn't welcome the news that he'd fallen in love. In their opinion, Yvonne Rousseau, a midwife who'd met the 30-year-old doctor at a hospital in Orléans, France, was no match for him: She was the 27-year-old daughter of peasants, while he belonged to an old, well-to-do Orléans family. When the couple wed in December 1939, none of the Chevallier clan was present.

The marriage took place while Pierre was home on leave from the French army. World War II had recently broken out, and he was serving at the front. He went on to become a hero, earning the gratitude of his fellow townspeople for leading the Resistance forces that drove the Germans out of Orléans in 1944, the year before the Allied victory. For his service he was elected the city's mayor that same year, and his rise to political stardom began.

Two years later Pierre Chevallier was elected a representative to France's parliament, the National Assembly. He began spending most of his time in Paris, about 70 miles from home. While he was there tending to the business of government, Yvonne remained in Orléans with their two small sons.

Because of her humble background, Yvonne was ill-equipped to follow her husband to his new and glamorous social heights. She felt timid and awkward at receptions and parties and constantly apologized to him for her lack of social graces. At a loss for small talk, she memorized parts of literary reviews and looked for opportunities to spout these borrowed opinions to her husband's

glittering associates. He began leaving her at home.

In 1950 Pierre found what he considered a more suitable social and romantic companion in the person of Jeanne Perreau, the wife of department store owner Léon Perreau, who accepted the affair with equanimity. The mother of four children, Jeanne was a vivacious redhead, poised and stylish where Yvonne was shy and dowdy. The women were slightly acquainted with each other, but virtually the only thing they had in common was Pierre.

Yvonne remained in the dark about her husband's affair for many months. Then, on June 13, 1951, when she was tending to Pierre's clothes, she found a note Jeanne Perreau had written to him. It closed with the devastating words, "I love you; I am yours." Yvonne took the marriage vows very seriously and considered this betrayal a sin. But when she tried to talk to Pierre, he brushed her off—he was up for reelection in four days and was too busy campaigning to be bothered. He won by an enormous margin. At his victory celebration he snubbed his wife and flirted openly with his mistress.

On June 29 Yvonne again confronted her husband about his unfaithfulness, and this time Pierre announced his intention to get a divorce and enjoy life with Jeanne. Yvonne wept and fell to her knees, begging him to relent. In response, he suggested she take a lover and remarked, "As far as I'm concerned, you're a free woman."

It had a terrible ring of finality. The miserable wife went away on a seaside holiday, but it did nothing to lift her spirits. Always a heavy smoker and coffee drinker, Yvonne began relying on barbiturates and stimulants as well. She brooded about suicide, and went so far as to ask her sons' doctor how many sleeping pills it would take to kill her.

Almost at the end of her rope, Yvonne

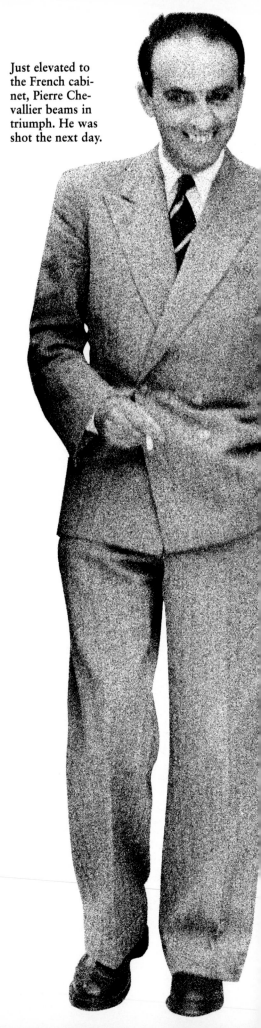

Just elevated to the French cabinet, Pierre Chevallier beams in triumph. He was shot the next day.

called on Léon Perreau to beg for his assistance in bringing the affair to an end. "If you don't do something, I will kill him, or kill myself," she threatened. "There is nothing to do," the worldly Léon replied. "They love each other." Depressed and despairing, Yvonne went back to Orléans and purchased a revolver.

As she plumbed the depths, her 42-year-old husband attained the pinnacle of his career. On Saturday, August 11, he was named a junior cabinet minister—Secretary of State for Technical Instruction, Youth and Sport. Yvonne learned of Pierre's appointment from a neighbor and sent him a telegram of congratulations.

That evening Pierre called her to say he planned to stop by the house the next morning to collect some clothes. She stayed up all night, drinking coffee, smoking, and taking stimulants. He was in a hurry when he arrived at 9:15 a.m. on August 12; his chauffeur was waiting outside their apartment building to drive him to an appointment. Yvonne followed him to the bedroom, crying and pleading with him not to leave her. "If you leave me, I'll kill myself," she sobbed. Yvonne would later testify to his cruel response: "It would be the best thing you could do with your life."

To prove she was deadly serious, Yvonne showed Pierre her gun. He reportedly said, "Well, for God's sake, kill yourself, but wait until I've gone!" And to drive home his indifference, he tossed off an obscene gesture. Yvonne pointed the loaded gun at her husband and shot him four times. At the noise, one of her sons ran into the room. She led him downstairs and left him with the concierge, then returned to the bedroom and fired a fifth shot into Pierre's lifeless body. Then Yvonne picked up the telephone and dialed the chief of police. "My husband wants you urgently," she told him. When he arrived, she

surrendered and readily confessed to the killing.

The death of the popular politician triggered a great outcry, and Yvonne Chevallier was denounced in the press as the "Assassin of Orléans." But as the details of Pierre Chevallier's private life began to surface, a groundswell of sympathy developed for his wife, and by the time her trial opened on November 5, 1952, it was Yvonne Chevallier, not her husband, who was viewed in many quarters as the victim.

After 15 months in prison, Chevallier arrived in court looking gaunt and ravaged, with dark circles under her eyes. Her hands trembled as she endlessly twisted a handkerchief, and she would faint twice during the two-day proceedings. But not because she was dealt with

During dramatic trial testimony, Yvonne Chevallier claimed she was not aiming at her husband but shooting randomly. He was hit five times.

harshly. Indeed, the judge was notably sympathetic. After Chevallier described how she had fallen to her knees and begged her husband not to seek a divorce, he chided her gently: "Did you not know, Madame, that you were wrong to abase yourself in this fashion, that it is not a good way to win back someone's heart?"

The spectators crowding the courtroom were eager to size up the other couple in the drama. They laughed when Léon Perreau explained that, although he had sent a previous lover of his wife's packing, he didn't interfere in her affair with Pierre Chevallier because "I found him a likeable chap." When Jeanne Perreau took the stand, however, the courtroom resounded with hisses rather than laughter.

Pierre Chevallier's mistress shared her husband's relaxed attitude toward the

Their marriage intact, Pierre Chevallier's mistress, Jeanne Perreau, and her husband, Léon, present a united front at the trial. Both gave evidence about Jeanne's affair with Chevallier.

bonds of matrimony. She called her husband "a good companion" and declared her intention to stay with him. Her liaison with Chevallier was, she said, "a private affair between myself and my conscience. I loved him and he loved me." The spectators applauded when the defense counsel suggested that Perreau should be deeply ashamed of her behavior, but she shrugged off his criticism. "Love does not make one ashamed," said the unrepentant Perreau. "I believe that for love one is never punished." Shocked by her attitude, the judge excused her from the court and forbade her to return.

At the conclusion of the testimony, the prosecutor called for a guilty verdict, although he recommended a sentence of only two years in prison, out of a possible 20. "Think of the repercussions of your decision," he urged the jury. "Will you put a gun in the hands of all those women who believe themselves wronged in their marriage, and promise them impunity?" Nonetheless, after deliberating for only 40 minutes, the jurors voted unanimously in favor of acquittal. The spectators erupted in applause and cheers.

The Bishop of Orléans extended the church's official absolution to Yvonne Chevallier, but she wasn't so quick to forgive herself. As a self-imposed penance, she took herself and her two sons off to the former penal colony of French Guiana, where she worked as a midwife among the poor. ◆

A combination of skill and shady business practices made horse trainer Buddy Jacobson a millionaire.

East Side Story

A slight, intense, untidy figure in torn jeans, with scraggly hair and brush mustache, Howard "Buddy" Jacobson retained a residue of celebrity in his corner of Manhattan. He'd once been the nation's best-known trainer of racehorses, and the winningest trainer three years in a row. He had never been very popular, however. Jacobson annoyed the racing establishment with his naked greed for money, his disregard for tradition in a sport that was built on it, and his rudeness in a world where manners were still important. He proclaimed racing "a business, not a sport," and the horses merely "machines, numbers, goods."

Jacobson's specialty was buying up thoroughbreds that had disappointed their owners, then running them in as many winnable small-purse races as they could stand. "He was a genius," observed one student of the Sport of Kings, "because he wasn't dealing with great horses—whether they won or lost depended on how he placed them, not how good they were." But Jacobson may have been too interested in winning for his own good. He was among the first to drug horses with steroids to help them win. That, plus violations of etiquette and an owner's accusation of theft, got him suspended by the state racing association.

Undeterred, Jacobson sold off his horses and plunged into buying property. By 1973 he'd become a budding real-estate mogul, dabbler in discotheques, partner in a Vermont ski lodge, and owner of a pair of apartment buildings on Manhattan's tony Upper East Side. He lived in apartment 7D, one of six units in the seventh-floor penthouse of his building at 155 East 84th Street.

The rest of his dwellings were turned into another kind of stable, stocked with young, new-to-New York flight attendants, models, and aspiring actresses, whom he resolutely coaxed onto his own sexual merry-go-round. With the aid of bugged telephone and intercom lines, he isolated his prey by intercepting the young women's calls, then invited the lonely renters out for giddy group dinners and, afterward, bed. He told everybody that he was in his late twenties; he was 43. He claimed that David and Douglas, two young men often on the premises, were his brothers; in fact, they were his sons from a marriage now over.

When 18-year-old cover girl Melanie Cain moved into apartment 7D with Jacobson in December 1973, she was a hot new property with Ford Models Inc., one of the city's top agencies. But being the wholesome face on the cover of *Seventeen* magazine wasn't enough—she craved high-fashion bookings as well. When Ford dropped her, she started her own agency, called My Fair Lady after her favorite musical. Jacobson did the paperwork—in his own shady fashion—out of an office on the ground floor of their building.

For a time, Cain was the agency's only asset, but a busy one. Her success lured other young women into the modeling game, and the persuasive Buddy made

JACK TUPPER

Melanie Cain *(top)*, a $100,000-a-year magazine cover girl, founded a modeling agency with Buddy Jacobson. His lover for five years, she broke off the relationship in 1978 after meeting bar owner and neighbor Jack Tupper *(above)*.

them want to stay. He was becoming, one of his pals would later say, "the East Coast Charles Manson," referring to the murderous California cult figure. His philosophy on spotting and grooming models had been learned at the track. "You've got to be nice to them—girls or horses," he said. "You've got to be their friends."

Jacobson's version of being nice was to strengthen his hold on the aspiring mannequins by sending them out on phony appointments with cronies who pretended to be ad executives, or with a photographer who'd shoot a lot of pictures—with an empty camera. Many of the models expressed their gratitude with their bodies. As for friendship, Jacobson was completely cynical. "Friendship does not exist," he told his son David. "There's only people using each other. And that's perfectly all right."

Despite such cynicism, Jacobson was careful to keep Cain near the center of his frenetic existence; she was the calm eye in his storm. She lived with him—except for a few spats—for nearly five years and rarely complained about his compulsive infidelities. After all, he seldom wanted to be with any of his other conquests more than once; among the models, he was known as the Minute Man. He was possessive toward Cain, but casually so. She didn't know that he had once pulled a gun on a rival and ordered him to stop seeing a woman. "She's my property," he'd declared.

In 1978, as the 22-year-old Cain began to see through Jacobson's manipulations, things changed at 155 East 84th. The tenant in 7C moved away, and a man named Jack Tupper picked up the lease. Tupper owned a neighborhood bar that Jacobson frequented. But he also had a secretive side—he would disappear from Manhattan for weeks at a time, on trips to South America, he said, to sell computers. But, to Melanie Cain, he seemed pleasingly different. Big and powerfully built, at 33 he was more easygoing, and more fun, than his scruffy little landlord. Cain went with Tupper for a weekend in Puerto Rico; when they came back, she'd shed her allegiance to Buddy. In July of 1978 she moved out of Jacobson's apartment and into Tupper's, across the hall.

Jacobson may have thought he loved Cain—at the very least, he wanted no one else to have her. For two weeks he went around loudly proclaiming that she was his wife. He protested that he was dying of cancer. He harassed the couple with loud noises and long interruptions in their hot water; he had them followed, and he tried to buy Tupper off, offering him $100,000 and his pick of the My Fair Lady models in exchange for Melanie's return. Tupper refused, and he and Cain went looking for another apartment to share. On Sunday morning, August 6, 1978, she went to sign a lease on their new place.

When Cain returned she had difficulty reaching their apartment; the elevator was out of commission, and the stairway door was blocked with bricks. Finally making her way to the seventh floor, she tried to tell Jacobson about the problems, but although she could hear something like furniture being moved in his apartment, he didn't come to the door. In 7C, she found Jack Tupper gone, although his keys and wallet were still there. Perhaps, she thought, he was out jogging.

Two hours later, as Cain's fears mounted, she looked out of the apartment door to see Jacobson and his son Douglas frantically ripping up the hall carpet and carting it away. On the pad she saw moist, reddish stains, and the elevator door had a russet palm print that might have been blood.

Later that same day, in the neighboring borough of the Bronx, Louis Carattini and his family came upon some suspicious activity at a dump—on their approach, two men leaped into a yellow Cadillac and, with a third man already in the car, hurried away, leaving behind a burning wooden crate the size of a coffin. Carattini alerted firemen to the crate, which, when cracked open, revealed a stabbed, bludgeoned, bullet-riddled body: Jack Tupper. He had been shot seven times. But Carattini's wife, Estella, had seen the intense, glaring face of Buddy Jacobson as the yellow Cadillac sped past them, and her husband had jotted down the license number. The firemen notified police, who picked up Jacobson, still in the car, and booked him for second-degree murder. They also brought in one accomplice who was later acquitted. The third man has never been identified.

Jacobson's trial began in January 1980, and Estella Carattini took the stand to help send him away, despite death threats against herself and her children, presumably relayed from Jacobson. Cain testified for nine days as the prosecution's key witness. Behind the scenes, Jacobson frantically yanked at any strings he could find. Some jurors received messages that $25,000 would appear on their doorsteps if they failed to reach a verdict.

The defense alleged that Jack Tupper had been a drug trafficker, killed by other dealers in an apartment where one of them lived, two doors down from Jacobson's, in apartment 7F. Cain, Jacobson's attorney contended, had been

dealing drugs too and had begged Jacobson to help her cover up the murder. Buddy said he'd taken the body to the dump because "I saw that helpless look in her eyes and realized I would do anything for her."

But the mauled and mutilated corpse bespoke an angry, panicked murder, not a gang-style execution in cold blood. The jury rejected the defensive tactic and, after a sensational 11-week trial—the longest, costliest trial Bronx County had seen—found Jacobson guilty of second-degree murder in April 1980.

Now Jacobson chose a desperate—but brilliant—gambit. In jail awaiting sentencing, he summoned a business associate who owed him a good deal of money. Jacobson forgave the debt, but he borrowed his visitor's identity. After shaving off his own bushy mustache and swapping clothes with the other man, Jacobson walked into the street, where his son David waited in a car a block away. A new girlfriend, 22-year-old Audrey Barrett, took the felon into exile.

But Barrett soon tired of the game and deserted Jacobson near Eureka, California, about a month after his escape. His sons also turned away from him. Douglas had steered clear of the murder altogether. David's defection was more pointed. Back in Brooklyn, he kept Jacobson talking on a pay phone in Manhattan Beach, California, until police could trace the call and pick him up. A sentence of 25 years to life awaited him back in New York, for the murder of Jack Tupper. Jacobson explained that he'd fled to gather evidence to prove his innocence. No one believed him.

Another of Jacobson's lies—the claim that he was dying of cancer—finally caught up with him a decade later, while he was still a prisoner in New York's maximum-security prison at Attica. Bone cancer actually began spreading through his body in 1988 and killed him in May 1989.◆

Church-woman

Candy Montgomery *(below)* and Betty Gore's husband, Allan, ended their affair eight months before Betty was killed.

Candy Montgomery and Betty Gore weren't very close, but they had a lot in common. Both were 30 years old, both were married to electronics executives, and both had two young children; in fact, their daughters were best friends. They lived in neighboring suburban towns about 25 miles northeast of Dallas, Texas—the Montgomerys in McKinney and the Gores in Wylie—and both attended the United Methodist Church in nearby Lucas. Both women sang in the church choir, and Candy Montgomery taught Sunday school. They socialized together and baby-sat each other's kids. And after nine years of marriage, each woman was faintly dissatisfied with her husband.

But the similarities ended there. Candy Montgomery was bubbly and outgoing, Betty Gore more serious, sometimes to the point of sourness or despondency. Montgomery was deeply involved in PTA and church activities, while Gore devoted herself to teaching fifth-grade reading and maintaining a spotless house. Gore was known to her students as a strict disciplinarian and to other adults as a moralist; Montgomery was more of a free spirit, who liked to gossip with her closest friends. In an effort to bolster her sagging marriage, Betty Gore had persuaded her husband, Allan, to attend a church-sponsored weekend workshop called Marriage Encounter. Candy Montgomery's solution to her own restlessness had been to have an affair with Betty Gore's husband.

The affair, which had lasted from December 1978 until October 1979, was long over by the morning of Friday, June 13, 1980, when Candy Montgomery, a vacation Bible school teacher, arrived at the Lucas church with her kids and five-year-old Alisa Gore. Montgomery read a parable to the assembled youngsters, then drove to the Gores' to pick up a swimsuit for Alisa. The child had slept over at the Montgomerys' the night before and was invited to stay again that night, but she needed her suit for a swimming lesson. Candy Montgomery was only a little late returning to the church to join the other Bible school teachers for lunch. She seemed her usual, cheerful self. No one noticed the cut on her forehead, near the hairline.

Late that night Allan Gore, who was out of town on business, called the neighbors and asked them to check his house; he had been trying to reach his wife all day and she wasn't answering the phone. Walking through the Gores' unlocked front door, the neighbors found Betty faceup in a pool of blood on the laundry-room floor, hacked beyond recognition with a three-foot ax the family kept in the garage for splitting firewood. The couple's younger daughter, 11-month-old Bethany, was screaming in her crib—cold, hungry and wet, but otherwise unharmed.

It was Wylie's first murder in more than 25 years and the police questioned every drifter and drug addict they could pick up. But the more they reviewed the evidence in the case, the more convinced investigators became that the killing had been done by a family member or a friend. There were no signs of forced entry, and money and jewelry were undisturbed. Small, bloody footprints found in the laundry room where Betty Gore died and in the bathroom where the killer apparently rinsed off the victim's blood, persuaded detectives that their quarry was not a man, but a woman or a youth. Then Allan Gore told them of his affair with Candy Montgomery.

The police interviewed and fingerprinted the Gores' circle of friends, including Montgomery, and on June 26, 1980, after a bloody thumbprint found on the freezer was matched with Montgomery's left thumb, police arrested her. Her minister expressed shocked disbelief, calling her a "very pleasant, very loving person," and an admiring friend told a reporter firmly, "Candy doesn't have a dark side."

In early July, the Dallas newspapers revealed the affair between Candy Montgomery and Allan Gore and trumpeted that during a lie-detector test arranged by her attorneys, the suspect had admitted killing Betty Gore. It seemed that the trial could contain no big surprises, but it did. On the witness stand, Montgomery acknowledged a second liaison after her affair with Allan Gore. And she pleaded not guilty by reason of self-defense.

On Montgomery's behalf, Dallas psychiatrist Maurice Green testified that Candy Montgomery had been in a "dreamlike" near-trance when she killed Betty Gore, and had maintained a "dissociative reaction" since that day. This accounted, he said, for her ability to act normal around family and friends after the killing; she felt as if someone else had done it. He compared the phenomenon to an electric circuit breaker, protecting Montgomery's mind from "her intense feelings of fear and rage." She was a "somewhat overcontrolled person," he said, and "angry and ashamed at the violence she discovered in herself" on June 13. In fact, she had succeeded so well in blotting out the events of that day that it had taken intensive work with a hypnotist to dredge them out of her memory.

On the stand, Montgomery testified that Betty Gore, with the family's firewood ax in her hands, had confronted her about the affair with Allan; that Betty had said, "You can't have him. I'm going to have a baby and you can't have him this time." Although Montgomery assured her that the affair was in the past, Gore was implacable: "I've got to kill you," she said, and the two women grappled for the ax. Gore, taller and some 30 pounds heavier, struck the first blow—opening the cut near Montgomery's hairline—but Montgomery, fighting for her life, struck the next one, splitting Gore's skull. They wrestled for the ax, kicking and falling on the blood-slick floor, until Montgomery pleaded with Gore, "Please let me go; I don't want Allan." Gore's response—an eerie, drawn-out "Shhhh," with one finger to her lips—triggered something elemental in her, Montgomery declared. With redoubled strength, she wrenched the ax out of Gore's hands and delivered a frenzy of hacks and chops—for a total of 41 wounds—before her rage was spent. Exhausted, Montgomery had stood fully clothed in the Gores' shower to rinse away the blood, then changed into dry clothes at home before returning to the Lucas United Methodist Church for lunch.

The hypnotist who was called into the case, psychiatrist Fred Fason of Houston, described an event from Montgomery's childhood that he believed explained the fury that she unleashed in her struggle against Betty Gore. Candy was only four years old, screaming in fear and anger as a doctor stitched up a gash on her face, when her mother admonished her, "Shhhh! What will they think of you in the waiting room?" From that moment, Fason testified, Montgomery had been unable to express those forbidden emotions of fear or anger until 26 years later, in the struggle with Betty Gore. "That explosion of violence," he said, "was a result of the violence that had been buried within her and blocked within her all these years." Montgomery had completely forgotten the incident in the emergency room, Fason said, and she was amazed to learn of it after the hypnotic session: "She said, 'My God! You mean I killed my mother, and not Betty Gore?'"

The jury found Montgomery not guilty of murder, by reason of self-defense. The verdict was controversial; critics asked how such an orgy of blows, some delivered after the victim was dead, could have been deemed defensive. Close to home, the members of the Lucas United Methodist Church seemed to absolve Montgomery of guilt in the death of Betty Gore, but they could not forgive her for the adulterous affairs. Hate mail poured into Montgomery's home, and her neighbors shunned her and stared at her when she ventured into the local supermarket. Her husband stuck by her, however, and in December of 1980, two months after the trial, the family moved away. Two weeks later, Allan Gore was quietly married to Elaine Williams, another parishioner at the local church, whom he had begun seeing within weeks of Betty's death; his two daughters went to live with their maternal grandparents in another state.◆

Killer Tycoon

Joseph Robb was a self-made man. The son of a Belfast, Ireland, plumber, he had risen from humble origins to head an international supermarket chain headquartered in Toronto, Canada. He worked long hours, then he faithfully headed home to his wife, Sheila, a public-relations executive, and their two teenagers. The Robbs lived in a million-dollar house in a Toronto suburb and spent weekends at their lakeside cottage. Neighbors thought they were "the normal, happy, average family." But then in May 1987 Joseph Robb, 41, learned that his wife was having an affair.

The signs had been there for some time, but he had missed them. That spring, after 22 years of marriage, 39-year-old Sheila had told him she no longer wanted to have sex with him; she had also become unreasonably critical, finding fault with his lack of knowledge about wines and his mundane taste in cars. When she announced she was going to move into an apartment in another part of Toronto, Robb blamed it on the pressures of her new job (she had recently joined Canada's Royal Trust Company) and the frequent travel it required. He tried spending less time at work and wooing her with flowers, but she accused him of "psychological warfare." The scales didn't fall from his eyes until he found the love letters. "I thought at first they were intended for me, because of their intimate nature," he later recalled. "But they were meant for Michael Horton."

Michael Horton, 41, had been Sheila Robb's boss from 1981 to 1985 at the Toronto office of Burson-Marsteller, a New York-based international advertising firm. He was now living in London, heading the firm's European operations. Joseph Robb suddenly understood that his wife's traveling enabled her to keep seeing Horton.

In Toronto, both of the Robbs had socialized with Horton and his wife, Margaret, and Robb considered Michael Horton a family friend. Urbane and charming, he was a dynamic salesman whose career included stints in Belgium and Argentina as well as in Canada, and he lived a glamorous, jet-setting life. Horton's sophistication made Robb's dogged work habits, devotion to his family, and suburban home seem stodgy.

Joseph Robb desperately wanted to keep his marriage together, so he decided to go to London to persuade Michael Horton to end the affair. Robb told his wife he was taking a business trip, bought her a gold necklace and a bou-

Joseph Robb, shown here three days after his violent showdown with rival Michael Horton, later testified that it was the first time he'd been in a fight since his school days.

quet of roses, and flew to London on May 23, 1987. En route, in an effort to apply his executive problem-solving skills to his love life, Robb wrote himself a memo on the purpose of the upcoming meeting. "Objective: Back off. Strategy: Surprise confrontation." No, that wasn't right; he crossed off that strategy and replaced it with another: "Communicate seriousness of my intention and resolve." Clearly he expected to persuade Horton to bow out; he made no notes on his wife's wishes in the matter.

Meanwhile Sheila Robb telephoned Horton, who told her that he had recently spoken to Robin, as her husband was known, and the two men planned to meet at Robb's London hotel. When Horton heard from Sheila that Robb knew of their affair, he asked whether her husband might turn violent. She assured him, "Absolutely not. Robin does not lose his temper, he is always a very rational, lucid person who approaches problems logically and calmly."

After an all-night flight, Robb checked into London's five-star Churchill Hotel and arranged for Horton to meet him there at six o'clock that evening. Convinced by Sheila that violence was not likely, Horton suggested that the two men talk in Robb's room, not in the lobby. When Robb asked him to end the affair, Horton seemed amused. "He chuckled slightly," Robb recalled: "He said that his feelings for Sheila and hers for him were a reality, and nothing could be done about it." Robb repeated his plea, a little louder this time, "because I felt he was not taking in what I was saying; he was so in-

different to what was so important to me." Minutes later, when Horton announced he was "off to dinner"—a business gathering at which he was to be the featured speaker—Robb grabbed him by the lapels and wrestled him back into the room. In the struggle, Robb picked up a bottle of mineral water and smashed it over Horton's head, then clubbed him with a bottle of gin. "Horton personified everything that had happened," he said later, "the deceit, the alienation, the fact that my wife had given me the cold shoulder, that she was leaving me. The man in front of me had been intimate with my wife. I just wanted to keep on hitting him."

As Horton tried to regain his feet, Robb, in what he later called a "blind rage," grabbed his open penknife, which he used for sharpening pencils, and stabbed at his rival's face and head; two of his 29 slashes struck Horton's jugular vein. When his frenzy subsided, Robb called an ambulance, sobbing into the telephone, "There's been a fight. I have just killed somebody." Horton was taken to a hospital and died of his wounds that night.

Dubbed the "killer tycoon" by the

British press, Robb and his trial were front-page news. He was cleared of murder charges but found guilty of manslaughter, and he was sentenced to three years in prison. Robb's sentence might have been harsher if not for a sympathetic judge whose own wife had left him, after 29 years of marriage, for one of his friends. From the bench, Judge Sir James Miskin commiserated with the defendant over the "disgusting affair" and his wife's "idiocy."

MICHAEL HORTON

The chairman of Joseph Robb's company announced that he would keep the executive's job open for him, but Sheila Robb, who did not attend her husband's trial, was not so forgiving—she advised the court that no reconciliation was possible. Meanwhile, Michael Horton's widow, shocked at her husband's death and at the revelation of his affair, suffered a nervous breakdown and was confined to a psychiatric clinic.◆

The Best
Laid Plans

Donald Weber appears
relaxed and untroubled
at a gathering in the
spring of 1990 in Robin-
son, Illinois. He had re-
cently returned to his
hometown after living in
New York for six years.

Donald Weber, Jr., was a young man who seemed destined to succeed, ordained by family and experience to thrive in the world of his ambitions. When he failed, Weber brought that world to a crashing end.

Growing up in the 1960s and 1970s, Dusty Weber, as he was known, was one of the golden boys of Robinson, Illinois, a town of about 7,000 located about 200 miles south of Chicago. His socialite mother, Shair, ran Weber Travel, booking cruises for the town's elite and treating them to prevacation dinners at the local country club; his father, Don senior, whom one family friend called "the best businessman in Crawford County," ran successful real-estate and insurance companies. The family lived on a picturesque 12-acre estate. The house was decorated with furniture and objects that Shair collected on her frequent trips to Africa and the Orient. An extensive gun collection, said to number more than 300 weapons, was displayed in the poolroom. The senior Weber enjoyed big-game-hunting expeditions, and the walls of his real-estate office were lined with trophy heads.

By all accounts, Don junior, eldest of the five Weber children, was expected to emulate his father's success, even surpass it. The father was a big fish in a small pond, but he wanted greater things for his son. Accordingly, he mapped out a shining path for Dusty to follow. After earning an accounting degree at the University of Illinois at Champaign-Urbana, the young man would attend a prestigious law school. The final stop on the path to success was Dusty's choice: A high-powered position in that biggest and toughest of ponds, New York City.

Donald Weber, Jr., had all the right qualifications. He was bright, handsome, and impeccably well-mannered.

And he embraced his father's vision, with its companion teaching that hard work and perseverance would yield success. In high school, Weber led Robinson to a state track-and-field championship. In one track meet, the young athlete lost a shoe at the start of a race but continued running. He crossed the finish line on a torn and bleeding foot, but he won. Dad's advice worked.

Right on schedule, Weber entered

LYNDA SINGSHINSUK

Champaign-Urbana and began his accounting studies. Then, in the summer of 1983, when he was a senior contemplating the next step in his life plan, Don met a hometown girl named Lynda.

Lynda Singshinsuk was the daughter of a well-to-do Robinson doctor and his wife. Like her parents and brother, Lynda was born in Thailand, and the family maintained close ties with relatives there. The Sings, as people in Robinson called them, knew the Webers through business dealings: Weber Realty owned the land on which the Singshinsuk's house had been built, Weber Insurance covered their cars, and Weber Travel booked their trips to Thailand. Lynda was a science whiz who planned to

study medicine, following in the footsteps of her radiologist father.

When Lynda Singshinsuk arrived at Champaign-Urbana, Weber offered to show her around. They grew close over Thai meals that Lynda's mother sent from home, and eventually they became lovers. They seemed to complement each other: He was gentlemanly but assertive; she was graceful but shy.

In the fall of 1984, Weber's agenda separated them when he went off to Fordham University Law School in New York. Nevertheless, they continued their relationship through visits, letters, and phone calls; she even sent his favorite Thai dinners, frozen, by overnight mail. She also mailed photos of herself in sexy lingerie, and some in the nude. In the summer of 1987, after Weber had finished his law degree, he accompanied Singshinsuk and her mother to Thailand so he could meet her relatives there—a signal that the relationship was serious.

Soon after they returned from Asia the couple separated again. Don often talked about coming home to be with Lynda, who entered medical school at Northwestern University in Chicago, but he did just the opposite. He took a job in New York with KPMG-Peat, Marwick, one of the nation's largest accounting firms. And although he promised in an October 1988 letter that he would return to Chicago in a few months, he enrolled in a two-year master's program in tax law to bolster his career credentials. These were expected steps for one who was so intent on succeeding, but they weren't the actions of someone as deeply in love as Weber claimed to be. Lynda was upset with Don's new plans and thought New York had changed him; "he'd become a hermit," she told a friend.

Singshinsuk began to slowly pull

away. The shy girl who entered the University of Illinois began medical school as a confident young woman. In Chicago she met dozens of interesting people, and she bubbled with enthusiasm when she told Weber about them.

Over a period of nearly two years, there was one name that came up with increasing frequency: that of Lynda's laboratory partner, Thad Stappenbeck. Thad was just a good friend, Lynda assured Don. Nevertheless, Weber began listening suspiciously to her words and scrutinizing her letters for signs of infidelity. He thought Singshinsuk sometimes lied to him about her

friends and how she was spending her time. He became convinced that her relationship with Stappenbeck exceeded simple friendship. But Lynda denied it, and the couple carried on.

In April 1989 Peat, Marwick fired Weber, saying he didn't "have the aptitude for the profession." Apparently he didn't look around him and see that he was only one of many who were similarly treated—all bright, all capable, and all routine casualties of the aggressive, competitive world of public accounting. Donald Weber, Jr., however, was stunned and humiliated. This wasn't part of his plan.

He lied about losing his job, telling Lynda and his family that he had quit to devote full time to his legal studies. Now, he wrote

Jay J. Armes, the private detective hired by the Singshinsuk family to investigate Lynda's disappearance, strikes a dramatic pose with a Mac-10 submachine gun equipped with a silencer. The detective lost his hands in an explosion when he was 11.

to Lynda, he could finish school and join her sooner.

From hundreds of miles away, perhaps Don could convince himself that at least he still had the perfect relationship—a bright, beautiful, adoring woman, loyally waiting for him to return. But that dream, too, was shattered. A week after he was fired, Lynda called and told him that she still loved him, but she "loved Thad, too."

If losing his job had derailed Weber's plan, Singshinsuk's rejection, equivocal as it was, demolished it. He couldn't concentrate on his studies. He attended his brother's medical-school graduation burdened with the feeling that he had let his parents down. He was too ashamed, though, to confide in them. In July, he traveled to Chicago to take the Illinois bar exam, but he doubted that he would pass. His world was crumbling. It could be repaired only if he could win Lynda back. He wrote her letters, sometimes two a day.

Lynda was indecisive. She had become attached to Stappenbeck, but she could not bring herself to break cleanly with Don. Weber had talked of killing himself, and she felt guilty. He blamed her for his life falling apart. In October he broke up with her, but they reconciled three days later when he told her, "I can't live without you." Shair Weber counseled Lynda to make up her mind: "You just don't know how to break up with a boy." His family urged him to get out of the relationship, but he could not let go. Home in Robinson for Thanksgiving, he told Lynda, "I'm just so frustrated, I could kill. I could kill your parents. I could kill Thad. I could kill you." Back in New York, he consulted a psychiatrist, who asked him whether he loved Lynda.

"I don't know," he said. "But I know I'm obsessed with getting her back. Is that love?"

In January 1990 Weber decided to move to Chicago. But a visit that month ended badly; he suspected that Lynda had been sleeping with Stappenbeck and angrily dumped his cologne over her sheets and pillows. Before leaving, a friend of Singshinsuk's remembered, Weber threatened to kill her and her parents. On the telephone later, he told her, "You haven't seen my rap yet. You know what I'm capable of." Lynda was alarmed and wanted to get a court order of protection, but an attorney talked her out of it.

When Lynda finally confessed, in early February, that she and Stappenbeck had been lovers for four months, the admission "really blew my world apart," Weber said later. He also considered it a blow to his career. "If she had told me when she started sleeping with Thad, it would've been fine by me, it would've been over, I could have studied."

Weber abandoned his life in New York and disposed of most of his possessions. Before he left the city to drive home to Robinson, he made copies of the nude photos Singshinsuk had sent him; to embarrass her, he mailed them to her parents and friends. By one account, he first tried to extort $20,000 from the Singshinsuks in return for not sending the pictures.

Weber's two brothers decided that he was mentally unstable and should be institutionalized, but before they could accomplish it, Don hopped a plane and went to Thailand for a vacation. It was the wrong destination—every young woman he saw there reminded him of his lost love.

In April, after staying in Thailand for six weeks, Weber returned home to his parents. He had no plans. He refused to confide in old friends who called him. "I'm in too deep to burden you guys," he said.

On Monday, April 16, 1990, almost a year after losing his job, Weber strained his back while working for his father. His mother gave him some Tylenol with codeine and he lay down for a rest. After 20 minutes, he opened his eyes with the conviction that Lynda Singshinsuk had to die. At least, that is one story he later told authorities. Another is that he learned that Lynda and her mother planned a trip to Thailand, with a stopover in Dallas. Thad Stappenbeck's parents lived in Houston, and ignoring the 240 miles separating the two cities, Weber decided that the intention was to pay a visit that would be a "formal prelude to marriage." The idea of Lynda married to his rival was unbearable.

That afternoon Weber gathered a .22-caliber handgun, some ammunition, and a rope, climbed into his mother's car, and drove to Chicago. On the way, he stopped for soft drinks and improvised a silencer for the .22 from two empty cans. He reached Lynda's door at 10:30 that night, wearing a black coat and hat. Singshinsuk was dressed in shorts and a light shirt. Their conversation was brief. "I can't live with what you've done," he told her. "You've ruined my life." Then he shot her six times in the chest; one bullet pierced her heart.

Despite the makeshift silencer, the noise of the rapid-fire shots seemed ear-splitting to Don. He expected a curious crowd to arrive at any moment, so he sat down to wait. When he was still alone with Lynda's body after an hour, he cleaned up the room, tied up her body, wrapped it in a sleeping bag, and loaded it into a laundry hamper that he found in the hallway. He dragged the hamper to the car, hoisted the 95-pound cargo into the trunk, and drove back to Robinson, where he buried Lynda Singshinsuk in a garbage dump.

Police in Chicago listed Lynda as a missing person, a possible suicide; without a body, there was no crime. They questioned Don several times but let him go when they couldn't place him at the scene of the murder. Five months went by, then, after reading that hunters sometimes found the remains of murder victims, Weber dug up Lynda's body, loaded it into the trunk of the car once again, and drove west. He paused in Las Vegas to pawn the jewelry Singshinsuk was wearing when he shot her, then doubled back to Arizona. There, in an isolated spot in Kaibab National Forest, about 60 miles south of the Grand Canyon, he reinterred his former lover.

Next, Weber fled to Thailand, where he rented a cheap room and got a job as a tutor. Thailand seemed the perfect place to go; although he later explained that he chose it because the country has no extradition treaty with the United States, perhaps his obsession with Lynda drew him there—his two previous visits had centered around her in one way or another. And it was Lynda's homeland.

Donald Weber, Jr., might have gotten away with murder. However, on Christmas Day, 1990, out of cash and despairing, he called the Singshinsuks collect and offered to reveal the whereabouts of their daughter's body in exchange for $50,000. The money would allow him "to put my life together," he said.

The family called the FBI. They also hired a private detective from El Paso, Texas—Jay J. Armes, who brandishes steel hooks in place of the hands he lost in a childhood accident. A colorful self-promoter who claims to have worked for such celebrities as Elvis Presley and J. Paul Getty, Armes tracked Weber to a girlfriend's home in Chiang Mai, Thai-

Lynda Singshinsuk's body was unearthed from this shallow grave in Arizona's Kaibab National Forest on January 26, 1991, nine months after her murder.

land's second-largest city, 363 miles north of Bangkok. The girlfriend, Armes said, bore a striking resemblance to Lynda Singshinsuk.

With help from four Thai bodyguards, Armes captured Weber and spent 22 hours grilling him about Lynda's murder. According to the detective, Weber confessed but showed no remorse. He drew a map of Lynda's grave site and later flew to Arizona to lead a private search party, organized by Armes and including his sons, to the spot. Armes lured Weber away from the relative safety of Thailand with a

promise and a threat. He told Weber that he wouldn't be arrested, that the family only wanted Lynda's body. If Weber did not come, Armes added, "I told him, 'You can get lost again. I would find you and be closer than your underwear for the rest of your life.'"

Armes lied. Police were hiding in the forest as Weber watched the detective's men uncover Lynda Singshinsuk's badly decomposed body, and the FBI arrested him on a charge of extortion. In March 1991, once the victim's remains had been identified, Weber was charged with murder, armed robbery, and concealing a homicide.

Weber told his lawyers he wanted the death penalty, but even that ambition was denied. Under Illinois law, the death penalty can be imposed only after a jury returns a guilty verdict. Weber pleaded

guilty to spare the Singshinsuk family the ordeal of a trial and was sentenced to 75 years in prison for murder, armed robbery, and concealing a homicide. He will be eligible for parole in 2027.

Weber has blamed his actions on depression, painkillers, and even Lynda Singshinsuk herself. But Thomas Epach, the Illinois Assistant State's Attorney who prosecuted the case, blames only Donald Weber, Jr. "He was the center of his universe, and you don't say no to Donald Weber."

Lynda Singshinsuk said no, and paid with her life. ◆

A prisoner at Illinois's Menard Correctional Center, onetime attorney Donald Weber was assigned a job in the law library.

Havent
you got the guts
to say goodbye to
my face?

RUTH ELLIS

3

Enemies

Who is that pompous little ass?" demanded Ruth Ellis, her reedy voice rising in pitch, as the slender young man made his way into the Carroll Club in London's West End one September evening in 1953. From her seat at the bar, Ruth had heard what the stranger called Carroll's as he stepped through the door—a "den of vice," he'd said to the friends accompanying him. That didn't sit at all well with Ruth, since she was employed by the club as a hostess. This new arrival was, she thought, "too hoity-toity by far," swaggering around in his properly ancient tweed jacket and baggy gray flannel trousers.

"Oh, that's David Blakely," answered one of the club regulars sitting with Ruth. "He's a racecar driver."

She watched Blakely cruise the room, leering at the women. "I suppose these are the so-called hostesses?" he remarked with a wide grin to one of his pals. Ellis stiffened and swept a wave of platinum blond hair away from eyebrows carefully plucked into dark auburn arcs. She was nearsighted without her glasses, but she was able to see that he was boyishly good-looking. And she could hear the benefit of breeding in the well-modulated tones of his upper-middle-class accent. Money there, too. That seemed obvious when he ordered double gins for the house—15 drinks in all.

Blakely sauntered over and studied the striking woman perched at the bar. Ruth's chalky complexion contrasted sharply with her blood red lips, half-pouting, half-parted in a tight smile. The vase of red carnations at her side cast a rosy blush on her slim white neck. Blakely chuckled—she looked like the photograph on the front of a cheap valentine with a naughty message inside. The clubs were full of such women, hustling drinks and turning tricks with the customers after hours. That was exactly what hostesses were hired to do at a drinking club like Carroll's—keep the boisterous, boozy members happy and coming back night after night. They were hardly an exclusive lot—virtually anybody who was willing to pay a drinking club's nominal dues was welcome.

Up close, Ruth could see Blakely's long, curly eyelashes; they seemed almost silky in their lushness. He looked more handsome and even younger than she first thought. He motioned toward the hostesses chatting and drinking with their customers. "I suppose you are another one of them?" he asked Ruth.

"No, as a matter of fact I'm an old has-been," she snapped. Ruth's answer hinted that she might be feeling her age, with her 27th birthday less than a month away. She'd been at this game for a long time.

Blakely let her retort pass without comment, downed his double gin, and turned his back to Ruth. "Come on boys, let's get out of this sink of iniquity," he said, waving them on to the next drinking spot. He didn't bother to bid Ruth good-night.

As Blakely departed, Ruth Ellis swung around on her stool and hissed to the barmaid, "I hope never to see that little shit again." But she would, before very long. And when she did, she'd change her mind about David Blakely. In the seamy clubs of London's West End, the city's theater and entertainment district, the two of them—the hard-used, peroxide-blond prostitute and the spoiled, upper-crust ne'er-do-well—would play out a drama of passion to a deadly end.

Born October 9, 1926, Ruth Hornby Neilson was the second daughter and the fourth child of Bertha and Arthur Hornby. He was a musician, an accomplished cellist who went by the stage name Neilson—it must have sounded more in keeping with the cello. He earned his living by playing in orchestras and jazz bands; when such work was scarce, he grudgingly joined the ensembles that provided background music for silent films in theaters. She was a French-Belgian orphan who'd been brought up by nuns in such rigid Roman Catholicism that she was unable to explain the simplest facts of modern life to her own girls. Ruth would ply her trade neither practicing contraception nor apparently worrying much about it.

At Ruth's birth, the family had just moved from Manchester in the industrial midlands to the Welsh resort town of Rhyl on the Irish Sea. Rhyl lay just west of Liverpool, the great port from which liners crossed the Atlantic and cruise ships departed for the Mediterranean, Africa, and the Canary Islands. The ships all had orchestras, and for much of Ruth's early life, her father was away at sea. From time to time as the years passed, a lonely Bertha would join her husband, leaving friends to look in on the children. Mainly, the couple's two boys learned to fend for themselves, while Ruth's sister, Muriel, older by five years, took care of little Ruth and generally made do.

In 1933, the family left Rhyl for the factory town of Basingstoke, 50 miles southwest of London. With the birth of two more daughters and the decline of cruise-ship business in the Depression-racked 1930s, Neilson desperately needed a full-time job and signed on to play in a movie theater. But he had always detested such mindless sawing away on the strings; it was beneath his talents. He vented his mounting frustrations on his family, shouting at Bertha and the kids and knocking them around. Ruth escaped the slaps and punches only because Muriel bravely placed herself between her father and her younger sisters. Even though Ruth was shielded from her father's blows, for the impressionable little girl such frightful violence came to represent a norm of sorts in male behavior.

Things got worse when Arthur Neilson lost his movie-theater job. The talkies were swiftly replacing silent films, and there was no further need for musicians in the wings. Neilson managed to find work as a hall porter in a mental hospital, but the pay was poor and the menial tasks an affront to his dignity. At home, the shouting and yelps of pain grew louder.

Overwhelmed by the turmoil, Bertha Neilson reverted to her convent days and did little except knit, crochet, and pray. When Muriel wasn't in class at Fairfields Senior Girls' School, where Ruth was also a student, she shouldered many of the household responsibilities. She didn't get much help from Ruth, who was getting to be a handful for her older sister. Impudent and resentful of discipline, she had a habit of disappearing for hours at a time, and no one could make her tell where she'd been.

In early adolescence Ruth Neilson wasn't a beauty, but she probably wasn't really "plain as hell," as she would later describe her 13-year-old self. Her nose was too big for true beauty; she was skinny; the blond hair of her childhood was beginning to darken to brunette; and she wore heavy, black-framed eyeglasses to correct her extreme nearsightedness. Nevertheless, she pretended to be gorgeous. And rich.

"Ruth hated us to be poor," her mother recalled years later. "She hated boys, too, at that time. That seems so strange now. But she always liked clothes, and she'd borrow mine and dress up in them." Yet when Ruth took off the costume jewelry and makeup, the party dresses and high heels, and looked away from the mirror, she saw her pile of hand-me-downs from Muriel and the dank little rooms of the rented house. She vowed to escape. As Bertha Neilson remembered, "She wasn't like my other children. She was so very ambitious for herself." Ruth was only a little girl when she told her mother with great conviction, "Mum, I'm going to make something of my life."

Ruth quit school at 14 and got a job as a waitress at a Lyons Corner House, one in a chain of modest restaurants. It was 1940, and World War II had enveloped Great Britain. The restaurant was always filled with servicemen ready to flirt with the waitresses. Ruth quickly learned that the tips would multiply for a girl who flirted back, and to make herself more attractive, she wore her eyeglasses at work only when she absolutely had to. Whether she learned about sex at the Lyons Corner House is unknown, but she definitely changed her ideas about boys. They'd change still more after she left Basingstoke for London.

Her father's insolence had cost him his job at the hospital, but with wartime shortages of labor, he was quickly able to find work as a chauffeur for a London limousine company. A two-room apartment came with the job. Originally, Arthur Neilson planned to live there alone, but Ruth pleaded with him to let her come along, and surprisingly, he gave in. Ruth was 15 when she arrived in London in 1941. With her came a girlfriend she called Mac, both of them more than ready for the excitement of the city.

You may be my older sister, but I'm 10 bloody years older than you in experience.

The arrangement didn't last long. One evening, Bertha Neilson showed up unexpectedly and found her husband in bed with young Mac. Bertha may have opted out of much that went on around her, but she had not opted out of marriage. Like a good Catholic wife, she hurled Mac's suitcase out the window and pushed Mac herself out the door. For once, Arthur kept his mouth shut. Then Bertha moved herself, her husband, and her daughters (the boys were fighting in the British army) into an apartment where Muriel could keep house and Bertha could keep an eye on Arthur.

The London blitz was then in full swing, the German bombs raining down night after night. Ruth thrived on the danger and excitement. "A short life and gay one," she liked to say. Taking to heart the conventional wisdom that gentlemen prefer blondes, Ruth treated her hair with peroxide until it was a gleaming platinum blond and whisked Muriel off to the bars and dance halls where the soldiers, sailors, and airmen awaited.

Ruth was so fine boned that a man could encircle her wrists and ankles with his thumb and forefinger, and that delicateness coupled with an enviable figure proved highly attractive to men. She was good fun, too—bright, laughing, confident, and very willing. Night after night, 20-year-old Muriel would wait patiently in the shadows while her younger sister bid a long, ardent good-bye to the friend of the evening in a doorway or a darkened alley. There were many nights when Ruth sent Muriel home, went off alone with a date, and didn't return until morning. When Muriel worriedly reproached her, Ruth would retort, "You may be my older sister, but I'm 10 bloody years older than you in experience."

Tragedy struck the Neilson family one night when a bomb leveled their apartment house, trapping Arthur in the rubble. Ruth arrived shortly after it happened. The German planes were still overhead, but she courageously disregarded the bombs and helped dig her father out of the wreckage. He survived, but the head injuries he suffered left him unable to hold down a full-time job for the rest of his life.

To help make ends meet, Ruth joined Muriel at a munitions factory. But there was no letup in her frenetic romantic life, and her health suffered. From March to May 1942 she underwent treatment for rheumatic fever at St. Giles Hospital in Camberwell. On her release, the doctors prescribed exercise, which Ruth happily interpreted to mean dancing. She wangled a job as a photographer's assistant at the jam-packed Lyceum Ballroom, where she danced with the customers and peddled the services of the resident photographer. One evening a woman friend arranged a blind date for Ruth with a soldier she knew. It took only one night for 16-year-old Ruth to decide that she was in love.

The man's name was Clare—Ruth would never reveal his last name, if she even knew it—and he was a French-Canadian soldier 10 years older than she. Darkly handsome, solidly built, confident, and charming, he looked wonderful to Ruth in his army uniform. And she never forgot how royally he treated her. On his Canadian pay, which was more generous than that of British soldiers, and with a favorable exchange rate, Clare could afford to woo Ruth with bottles of champagne at nightclubs in the glitzy West End district of London, gifts of jewelry and dresses, and fresh flowers, especially red carnations, which became her symbol of love. "We seemed like one person as we waltzed around the floor," Ruth later recalled. "I was dancing as I had dreamed, in the West End of London."

Inevitably, considering her lack of instruction or concern, Ruth became pregnant. She realized it shortly after the New Year of 1944. She had just turned 17, and it was the first of several such mishaps in her brief life. Clare acted the perfect gentleman. He offered to marry her; and to marry Ruth, he would even leave the wife and children in Canada that he had neglected to mention until now. But the staunchly Roman Catholic Bertha Neilson would not hear of that, though she would later wistfully remark: "I shall always think Ruth's life would have turned out differently, if the child's father had been able to marry her."

Clare Andrea Neilson was born on September 15, 1944. For a time the father helped support his infant son. Then, at the end of the war, on the day Clare boarded a ship for Canada, a letter and a bouquet of red carnations arrived at the Neilson home. It was the last Ruth ever heard from him.

Deserted by the man she adored, humiliated, and saddled with an unwanted child, Ruth steeled herself against further hurt. "I no longer felt any emotion about men," she once said. "Outwardly I was cheerful and gay. Inwardly I was cold and spent. Somehow, in my association with men, nothing touched me." But she was fooling herself. At heart, Ruth Neilson remained a romantic—and unfortunately, much more would touch her and hurt her in her relationships with men.

Ruth left Andy, as she called the child, with her mother in the working-class suburb of Brixton, where the Neilson family now lived. Since her father was partially disabled and her mother was incapable of holding down a job, Ruth bore responsibility not only for her son but also for part of her parents' support. She didn't have any choice; she had to get a job.

She spotted an advertisement for evening work: "Wanted. Model for Camera Club. Nude but artistic poses. No experience required. Highest references available. Confidential." That might be the ticket. She stripped for three club members and got the job. For a pound an hour, Ruth posed naked before as many as 20 amateur shutterbugs and other interested club members. It made little difference to her that some of the cameras contained no film. After work, members often took her out on the town, with dinner and dancing in the West End. It wasn't as much fun as it had been with Clare, but it was still the West End.

In late 1946, at the Court Club, a hangout for gamblers, dandies, unhappy demobilized soldiers, and hard drinkers of every stripe, Ruth met another man who would contribute to her fate. He was Morris Conley, the Court's fiftyish jowly owner, who'd once served a two-year jail sentence for bankruptcy, fraud, and illegal gambling. He stocked the Court and his three other drinking clubs with black-market liquor and employed young women to indulge whatever tastes a customer might bring with him.

Conley recognized a prime recruit when he saw one, and he zeroed in on Ruth Neilson the moment she entered the Court on the arm of one of her camera club friends. By the end of the evening, Conley had offered her a job as a hostess. It was a step up from nude modeling, and she accepted the offer.

In addition to a base salary of five pounds a week, Ruth was paid a 10 percent commission on the food and drink her customers bought. Under Morris Conley's tutelage, Ruth learned how to boost club profits by ordering champagne, for which the bartender poured carbonated cider, or a gin and tonic that contained not gin but water. A clever and popular hostess could at least triple her five-pound base pay with bar commissions, and Ruth got so good at it that she was soon taking home 20 pounds every week—not counting what customers paid for her sexual services. The more experienced hostesses at the club gave Ruth advice on how to fend off unwanted advances without alienating the customer, and how, when she chose, to negotiate an appropriate fee for lovemaking.

For an evening at the club, Ruth would wear one of the gowns that Morris Conley provided for her, as he did for all his hostesses. This was very important to Ruth, with her love of clothes. But there was a price. Conley supervised every fitting, and the intimacy he claimed as his right didn't stop there. Ruth knew that having sex with him was part of the deal. She'd be out of a job if she refused, and out of a wardrobe as well, for Conley retaliated against hostesses who resisted his advances by slashing their clothes.

Sex was the stock in trade at the Court Club, and Ruth had a coy routine for introducing it into conversation with a new customer. Almost inevitably the man would ask where she was from, and she would tell him that she was from Manchester—but only because she had been conceived there. By the time she got around to being born, she teasingly corrected herself, the family was living in Rhyl. This was considered risqué banter in the 1950s, and such an exchange marked her as a possibility for the man.

As the conversation progressed, with the man buying drinks for them both, Ruth would start salting her speech with four-letter obscenities. Many males got a kick out of hearing such talk from a woman, she'd observed. If her companion had a store of dirty jokes, Ruth would hang on every salacious word and laugh uproariously at the punch line.

The Court Club closed at 11 p.m., at which time Ruth and her friend for the evening, if they'd struck a sexual bargain, might go to one of the rooms Conley provided in his clubs for the hostesses and their customers. Naturally, he received his cut of the proceeds. If sex wasn't in the offing, the couple might join a group going on to the Hollywood, another of Conley's clubs, which remained open until 3 a.m.

Ruth was soon the envy of other hostesses on the club circuit. Whatever a customer desired, Ruth enthusiastically supplied. She performed alone or in tandem with other hostesses while the client watched or participated. Other times she donned the vestments of a client's fantasy—perhaps high-heeled boots and see-through plastic rainwear—and, if he wished, engaged in bondage games that called for whips, chains, and leather straps.

The kinky amusements aside, Ruth was widely admired for her mastery of lovemaking. "What an artist," marveled one satisfied gentleman. "She gave you the full treatment, and by the time you got through, you felt out of this world. She really developed her potentialities to the limit as a sex symbol."

The money Ruth brought home was more than welcome, and if her parents in Brixton suspected how she was earning it, they kept it to themselves. They saw next to nothing of their daughter. "We used to hear her coming in during the early hours of the morning and sleep until noon," recalled Bertha. "She began to change. She used a lot more make-up and had smart clothes of the sort other girls in the neighborhood never wore."

During the four years Ruth Neilson worked as a hostess at the Court Club, she would have been outraged had anyone called her a prostitute to her face. The men she had sex with were not common strangers, nothing like street-corner pickups. To her mind they were friends she came to know in the congenial confines of her club. Many of them were of a higher social class than she, and she counted it an honor to be an object of their desire. The wealthier ones occasionally invited her to weekend house parties in the country or took her on shopping expeditions where they spent lavishly.

By Ruth's moral lights, she was an enterprising modern woman, and she worked hard to please her admirers and remain in their favor. She read the news columns so she wouldn't appear stupid at the dinner table, and she studied the society pages in order to recognize the Middle Eastern prince, American industrialist, or Greek shipping tycoon she might encounter on an evening or at a weekend gathering.

In early 1950, Ruth got pregnant again. An abortion was quickly arranged, and she carried on as before at the club. But she was 23 years old now, and the episode may have started her thinking about family and future.

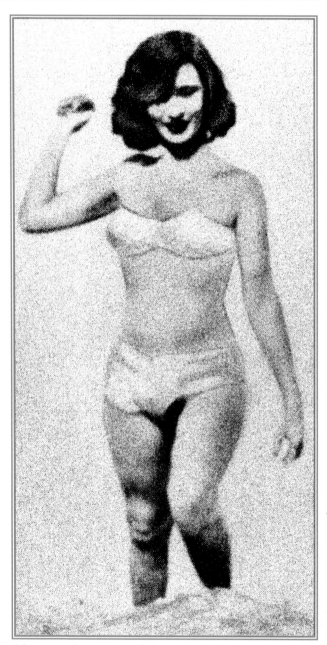

After several years as a platinum blonde, Ruth had returned to her natural brunette hair color when she posed for this 1950 snapshot at the shore. She soon went back to bleaching her hair.

George Ellis, a well-to-do dentist and drinking-club habitué, had been divorced shortly before he began courting Ruth Neilson. His alcoholism helped sour their marriage in less than a year.

Whatever the cause, she was heading toward her first serious involvement with a man since Clare, her Canadian lover, had vanished from her life.

The man was George Johnston Ellis, a recently divorced 41-year-old dentist who was known as one of the Court Club's most notorious sots. People called him the "mad dentist" and rolled their eyes at his wild, drunken stories. Lonely and craving companionship, Ellis was obsessed by Ruth from their first meeting, in June 1950. But while she let him buy her as much bogus champagne as he pleased, in the beginning she wouldn't go out with him, despite his repeated invitations. Then one night when he was pestering her again, she agreed to meet him later at the Hollywood Club—but only to shut him up; she had no intention of keeping the date. As Ellis patiently waited for Ruth outside the Hollywood, he was set upon by some toughs and so severely razor-slashed across the face that the wound required eight stitches.

The attack made Ruth feel so guilty that, when the persistent George asked her out again, she accepted his invitation and this time didn't stand him up. He hired a car and driver, took her to his posh golf club for drinks and dinner, then back to the West End to make the rounds of clubs. By the time they were ready to call it a night, both Ruth and George were very drunk. She woke up beside him in his elegant home in Sanderstead, a suburb just south of London. And in the weeks that followed, she discovered that the alcoholic dentist wanted nothing in this world so much as to lay his considerable bank account at her feet.

They dined in the finest restaurants, danced at the trendiest nightspots. Ellis bought her whatever caught her fancy and took her on a long holiday to a four-star seaside hotel in Cornwall, where their suite came to 100 pounds a week and room service brought champagne and caviar for breakfast. They went boating and flying; George was a pilot and insisted on flying Ruth over South London upside down in a rented biplane. She didn't care for that, but she was coming to care a great deal for George Ellis.

When people looked at them together—the florid, balding, middle-aged man and the young platinum blond woman—Ruth made a point of kissing him or putting her arms around him so everyone would know that it wasn't just some dirty assignation. She told her sister Muriel: "I do respect him and love him. It really is the real thing."

Whatever love is or is not, Ruth Neilson to the end of her days insisted, "I did not get fond of him only to the extent of what he could spend on me." Yet it is unquestionably true that George Ellis represented a major step upward for Ruth. He was a professional man, educated, cultivated, from a good family; he had a fine home, money, and the prospect of much more, for he had confided to Ruth that he expected a substantial inheritance when his nearly 70-year-old mother died.

I *did not get fond of him only to the extent of what he could spend on me.*

Ruth's son Andy, now six years old, lived sometimes with her parents and sometimes with Muriel, who was married and had children of her own. Ruth visited the boy every Sunday and paid for his support, but otherwise she had virtually no role in his upbringing. With George Ellis that could change. She could marry him, persuade him to stop drinking, and bring Andy to live with them. Perhaps more children would come along, and Ruth would take her position in society as a respectable wife and mother.

In September, Ruth moved into Ellis's home in Sanderstead with the mutual understanding that they would be married if all went well. To Ruth that meant principally one thing: George would have to control his drinking. But all did not go well. The condition she'd imposed had no effect on George's drinking habits. That began to anger Ruth; it was one thing for him to squander his money at the Court Club when he was single—and she the hostess profiting from his excessive spending—but now, with marriage in the offing, he was frittering away what would soon be her money as well.

At Ruth's insistence, Ellis checked into Warlingham Park Hospital near Sanderstead for treatment as an alcoholic. He spent two or three weeks drying out and emerged from the hospital declaring himself cured. Ruth was ecstatic. They were married in a private ceremony at the Registrar's Office in the town of Tonbridge on November 8, 1950. The following day, George Ellis got drunk again. A week later, he was back at Warlingham Park Hospital. Then he was out again, cured again, and then drunk again.

For a time Ruth tried as hard as she knew how to make the marriage work. Andy came to live with them, and she wrapped herself in the role of mother and housewife. She made sure she looked the part, tying her hair back in a ponytail, toning down her makeup, and dressing in tweeds and sensible flats.

Although it was probably an accident and not a deliberate attempt to further her dreams of a different life, Ruth got pregnant in January, scarcely two months after the wedding. George didn't want a child, but she didn't get an abortion, and as the months passed, her advancing pregnancy only exacerbated matters. Ruth's pleadings about his drinking became verbal assaults. She shrilled that he was a "drunken old has-been from a lu-

natic asylum." In reply he called her a "bloody bitch from Brixton" and snarled that he should never have married beneath him. Time and time again, Ruth stormed out of the house to seek refuge with her family, swearing that she would never return. But within a few days, she'd be back with Ellis again.

Things just got nastier. Sitting at home nights waiting for her drunken husband and watching the dinner get cold, her respectable life in shreds, she began to entertain the paranoid fantasy that her husband, who was working for another dentist, was carrying on with female patients, nurses, and the wives of other dentists. In her fury, Ruth literally spat in Ellis's face when he denied her accusations of infidelity. George retaliated by hitting her with his fists.

So it went all winter and spring. In April, Ellis was fired because of his drinking. In yet another attempt at sobriety, he returned to Warlingham Park Hospital. Four months pregnant, Ruth prowled the halls searching for evidence of her husband's infidelity. According to a male nurse, "Mrs. Ellis appeared to be on constant watch, continually checking on the staff, patients, even the visitors on the bus serving the hospital as to every movement of Dr. Ellis."

At one point, Ruth pointed to a woman patient with whom her husband was friendly and yelled: "So that's the old bag you're getting it with here." On another occasion, believing that George was involved with a female doctor, Ruth burst into the hospital shrieking obscenities. T. P. Rees, the physician who was attending Ellis, tried to calm her down, but Ruth had to be forcibly restrained from raging into George's room. Rees administered a sedative and later gave her a prescription for the drug. She would turn to it in times of stress for the rest of her life.

Ruth Ellis gave birth to a daughter on October 2, 1951, with her sister Muriel by her side. She named the baby Georgina after her husband, but he wanted no part of the child and instructed his attorney to advise Ruth to give the infant up for adoption. In November, a year after they'd married, Ellis filed a petition for divorce on grounds of mental cruelty, and Ruth did not seek a reconciliation. Under British law, it would be three years before the divorce became final.

The next step was foreordained. The delivery of her baby girl had been difficult and Ruth was still feeling poorly. But with two children to support, she had no other choice. In December, leaving Andy and Georgina in the care of her family, Ruth hurried back to the life she knew best, back to London's West End, and back to Morris Conley.

Delighted to see his star hostess again, he immediately installed her at Carroll's, formerly named the Court Club. A restaurant and a dance floor had been added, and the place was now open until 3 a.m. To top off Ruth's homecoming, Conley also furnished her with a two-bedroom apartment, rent-free, where she could entertain her men friends. Although the apartment was modest, it was located in Mayfair, a district known for its elegant homes and exclusive shops. To Ruth, so conscious of status, so anxious to climb, her address meant everything. She had arrived.

For 18 months Ruth Ellis swam along in her element. The men couldn't get enough of her, and her friendships expanded to include a monied international set: a banker from Iran, an oilman from Canada, a factory owner from Norway, a tycoon from Switzerland who signed his mash notes "your naughty Norbert."

Just before Christmas of 1952 Ruth had a bad scare. She started feeling ill, and when her regular doctor could not diagnose the malady, he sent her to Middlesex Hospital, where specialists determined that the problem was an ectopic pregnancy. In this condition, the fetus grows not in the uterus but in one of the fallopian tubes; without swift, expert treatment, it often proves fatal. Ruth spent two weeks in the hospital, then had to spend another four months recuperating.

She was back at Carroll's in April 1953 and performing with all her usual skill and gusto. The summer and early fall were boom times for 26-year-old Ruth Ellis. One of her devotees gave her a racehorse, which she immediately sold; another pressed 400 pounds into her hand and, according to Ellis, told her that sex with her was the "best he'd ever had."

With her double windfall, Ruth could afford to ease off pushing drinks at Carroll's for a little while, party wherever she pleased, and indulge her passion for clothes; always an easy touch, she also had the cash to lend to other hostesses who came up short.

By September, Ruth had gone through almost all of the money, and she was hard at work again. There was a new crowd for her to make friends with—racecar drivers. They'd show up at the Carroll Club after their favorite hangout, the Steering Wheel Club, closed for the night at 11 p.m. Young, sexy, and free-spending, they were led by Mike Hawthorne, a tall, blond, 23-year-old daredevil driver on his way to becoming a world champion. And among those who basked in Hawthorne's reflected glory was David Blakely.

Not many people ever had much use for Blakely, and that included Hawthorne himself. For among Blakely's numerous unattractive traits was an infantile sense of humor that knew no bounds when he was drunk, which was often. His fellow racecar drivers shuddered at the memory of the night David presumed to put ice down Mike Hawthorne's neck and followed that insult by soaking the world champion with squirts from a soda siphon. Hawthorne shot to his feet and went after Blakely in a fury. Another driver rescued the terrified Blakely, who was scrambling for cover and squealing for someone to help him.

Cliff Davis, the man who saved the situation, would later offer a devastating appraisal of Blakely. "David," he said, "was a good-looking, well-educated, smooth-talking supercilious shit." It was a state Blakely may have entered naturally. The traumas of his early childhood didn't seem excuse enough.

David Moffat Drummond Blakely was born on the 17th of June in 1929, the youngest of John and Annie Blakely's four children. The family's home was in Sheffield, a steel town in northern England, where "Dr. John" was a much-admired and well-to-do general practitioner. Annie was the smart, sophisticated daughter of a wealthy Irish horse dealer; she organized charity bazaars and spent most of her energy on her rich social life, while nannies took care of the children and servants managed the spacious Tudor-style home just outside town. All in all, it was a typical English upper-middle-class existence—until everything came apart on a chilly evening in February 1934.

That evening, an unemployed waitress named Phyllis Staton, 25, was deposited at her parents' back door, nearly dead from acute septicemia, or blood poisoning.

Andy Neilson, shown here with his mother at the age of eight, was taught to call Ruth's various lovers "uncles." A lax disciplinarian, Ruth was generous with pocket money and let Andy roam London on his own.

A car was seen driving away, and she told her parents that "the Doc" had brought her home. Staton died the following day. It was discovered that the fatal infection was the result of a botched abortion, and John Blakely was charged with murder.

At the inquest, the doctor admitted that he'd been having an affair with Staton, but he said that he was only one of many lovers. He also acknowledged that when the young woman had become pregnant, he had supplied her with a drug that could induce an abortion but denied performing an operation on her. Moreover, Blakely said, he didn't know whether Staton had taken the drug or not. The prosecution had little evidence to contradict him, and in the end the Sheffield magistrates dismissed all charges.

John Blakely's patients remained loyal, and his practice continued to flourish. His wife, however, never forgave him; she found the affair especially humiliating because Phyllis Staton had been socially inferior. There

followed six years of domestic upheaval until in 1940 Annie Blakely secured a divorce on grounds of adultery.

Custody of the four children went to the mother. Although David, then 11, sorely missed his father, he quickly adjusted when Annie remarried in 1941. In fact, he came to identify more closely with his stepfather than he did with his natural father.

Humphrey Wyndham Cook was the wealthy son of a London textile merchant and had in his youth been one of Britain's better-known racecar drivers. He offered Annie the monied life she required: jewels from Cartier, clothes by famous designers, and a large, luxurious apartment in Mayfair. And Cook transmitted to young David his passion for racecars. At boarding school, David skimped on his studies but spent long hours poring over *Autosport, The Motor,* and other racecar journals. During vacations he and Humphrey Cook would hit as many sports-car meets as they could.

After boarding school, David did a stint as an officer

Among the club patrons who accepted this invitation for the party Ruth Ellis threw on her 27th birthday were many members of the auto-racing set.

in the British army. When his military service was completed, his mother and stepfather settled him into a nice apartment near theirs and arranged for his old nanny to take care of him.

Besides furnishing David with a place to live, Cook used his connections to arrange a job for his stepson as a management trainee at the elegant Hyde Park Hotel. The salary for trainees was not much, less than three pounds a week, so the Cooks gave him an allowance of five pounds weekly. Then they waited for David to make his mark in the hotel business, and to find a debutante of his class to marry.

Ruth Ellis

invites you to her

Birthday Party

on Friday 9th. October 1953. at 7 p.m.

COCKTAILS & BUFFET

Carroll's Club, *58, Duke Street, W.1.*

But they had the boy all wrong. Blakely wasn't interested in working. What he really wanted to do was fiddle with cars and booze it up with the racecar crowd at the Steering Wheel Club. And he was no more interested in finding a suitable wife than he was in his job.

Blakely's mania for racing got even worse when his birthday rolled around and his stepfather gave him a secondhand H.R.G., a middling-fast sports car named after its designer, H. R. Godfrey. David paid even less at-

tention to the hotel; he thought of nothing but cars and he started to race.

At sports-car meets in those days, amateurs frequently competed in the various classes alongside professional drivers who were sponsored by the manufacturers. David Blakely aspired to being a professional, but he never made it past the amateur fringes. Nobody remembers him winning a race. He seems to have been more or less adequate technically, but he lacked a first-rate driver's courage and stamina. "He didn't have a lot of backbone," commented Cliff Davis, who once took Blakely aboard as codriver and navigator in a grueling rally. "David just flaked out after five or six hours. He was like a sack of potatoes in the passenger seat."

One of the few racecar people to have more than a casual acquaintance with Blakely was Anthony Findlater. Eight years older than David and married, Ant Findlater was of David's educational and social stratum, an automotive engineer by training and a racing buff by avocation. The two met in 1951, when Blakely came around to inspect an antique Alfa Romeo Findlater had advertised for sale. A few weeks later, David invited Ant to look at his H.R.G. They hit it off well enough to strike a deal whereby Findlater would keep the car in top condition and David would race it. What Findlater didn't realize was that Blakely wanted not only his mechanical expertise but Findlater's pretty, dark-haired, 27-year-old wife, Carole.

That spring and summer, Blakely was a constant visitor at the Findlater apartment. Carole, an editor with a woman's magazine, was Blakely's intellectual superior by far, but she was attracted by his good looks and easy charm. They began an affair, meeting evenings at a pub near the Hyde Park Hotel, Carole excusing her absences by telling Ant that she had to work late or go to meetings of the journalists' union.

In the fall, Blakely pleaded with her to elope with him. He adored her, he mooned; he couldn't live without her. She agreed to run off with him, but in the middle of packing her bags she thought better of it and called him to say she was not going away with him after all.

Several days later Carole and David met at the pub near the hotel to talk. "I hope you didn't tell Ant who you were going to run off with?" he asked. She replied that she had, and David exploded in anger. "You stupid bitch," he shouted. "Now look what you've done. Who the bloody hell will tune my car now?"

Amazingly, the Findlaters and David Blakely were able to smooth things over and remain friends. There was something about the impetuous young Blakely that made many women want to mother him, and perhaps Carole shared that impulse, even though his angry outburst had revealed how thoroughly selfish he was. As to Ant and David's relationship, their shared interest in cars kept the bond between them intact. The Findlaters would be there to see David's relationship with Ruth Ellis through to its tragic end.

Never inclined to earn his salary, Blakely became still more negligent of his job when his natural father died of a heart attack in February 1952, leaving 7,000 pounds to each of his four children. While not a fortune, it was a significant sum at that time, and it enabled David to start playing the big spender as soon as the drinking clubs opened at 3 p.m. His favorite, after the Steering Wheel, was one of Morris Conley's establishments called the Little Club, or "the Little," as regulars called it. He would slip out the side door of the hotel to spend the afternoon boozing and bragging about his fictitious racing exploits.

Finally fed up with Blakely's frequent absences, the Hyde Park Hotel management fired him in October 1952. The indulgent Humphrey Cook attributed the sacking to what he called "high spirits." Far from being punished, David was treated to a trip abroad in the company of his mother and stepfather. Upon their return early in 1953 the family moved from London to Penn, a village in Buckinghamshire 30 miles northwest of London where Cook had bought a mansion named the Old Park. Part of the house had been made over into an apartment with a separate entrance for David, and his nanny was there to look after him. He also had a place to stay in London, since the Cooks still maintained an apartment there.

David got a job at Silicon Pistons, an automobile parts manufacturer in Penn, and since it was much closer to his interests than the hotel had been, he more or less applied himself. To his family's delight, he was also seeing a suitable young woman. She was Mary Newton Dawson, the 21-year-old daughter of a rich woolen-goods manufacturer in northern England. They'd met when she was a guest at the Hyde Park Hotel.

Mary Dawson was perhaps a little horsy, hale, ruddy-complexioned, and big-boned. But she had money to burn, and David was impressed by one certain sign of affluence when he visited the Dawson estate: It boasted its own gasoline pump. Blakely squired Mary to sports-car rallies and, when she was in London, they made the rounds of nightclubs with the Findlaters. But if Mary thought David was in love with her, she had misread his feelings. Aside from her potential for money, Mary's function was to keep Blakely's mother and stepfather happy. At the same time that he was dating Mary, David was also involved with a pretty blond movie usher and an American model on assignment in London. And there was still another clandestine liaison, with a married woman he'd met playing darts at the Crown, a popular pub in Penn.

In the summer of 1953, when he was juggling his complicated romantic life, David hatched a scheme to build and race a sports car, using what was left of his inheritance to fund it. Ant Findlater eagerly accepted when David offered him a salary of 10 pounds a week to manage the project. They leased garage space and bought an H.R.G. body and a twin overhead-cam 1,500 cc. Singer-H.R.G. engine to power the Emperor, as the nascent sports car was christened.

That carved off a big chunk of Blakely's remaining capital. But when he turned to his stepfather with every expectation of getting more money, he received a nasty jolt. Humphrey Cook was a patient, big-hearted man, but he'd gotten wind of David's affair with the married woman from Penn and was upset about it. Although he didn't go so far as to cut off the allowance David had been receiving since his Hyde Park Hotel days, Cook refused to foot any bills for the Emperor.

But David was nothing if not resourceful when it came to getting his own way. On Wednesday, November 11, 1953, under "Forthcoming Marriages," *The Times* of London announced his engagement to Mary Dawson.

The Little Club was located upstairs from a handbag shop. As the manager of the club, Ruth Ellis had the use of a rent-free apartment on the floor above.

Annie Blakely Cook and her husband were overjoyed; the boy was obviously maturing and finding his place in life. Humphrey Cook was now more than happy to help out with the Emperor.

Within two weeks of his engagement announcement, 24-year-old David Blakely was living in an apartment over the Little Club with the establishment's new manager, Ruth Ellis.

Ruth's popularity at the Carroll Club had convinced Morris Conley to award her the management of her own place. He had just fired the manager of the Little Club, and he offered Ruth the job with a salary of 15 pounds a week, plus a 10-pound weekly entertainment allowance to spend on customers. In addition, she would have the use rent-free of a two-room apartment above the club. Conley's cut and his sexual attentions still went with the arrangement. But all in all, it was another advance. Ruth quickly accepted—and dived into dangerous new waters.

David Blakely had remained a regular at the Little Club, and in all likelihood he was one of the first customers Ruth Ellis served in her new capacity as manager. He must have reconsidered the woman he'd slighted only a few weeks before at the Carroll Club, for he started telling his friends about the "smashing blonde" who was running the Little. And he did his best to impress her.

For two weeks running, David showed up every day, spending freely and wearing his rich man's dark suit, with bowler and umbrella. David's efforts were impressive enough for Ruth to invite the "pompous little ass" to bed—for no charge. Soon he was living with her and encouraging friends to go with him to the Little Club to meet the woman he bragged was the best in bed in all of London.

In the first few

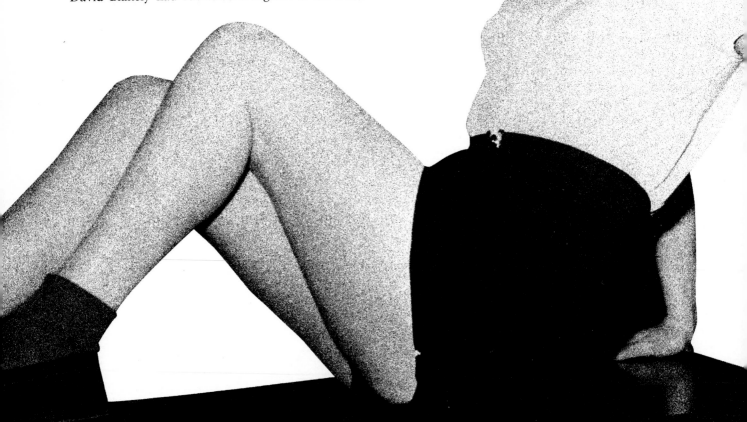

months of their relationship, Ruth was still practical enough to manage the Little efficiently and look after her finances. While saving her nights for David, she used the afternoons when he was at work in Penn to entertain clients in her apartment upstairs. By early 1954 Ruth was pregnant again. It was anybody's guess who the father was, but David had been living with her for four months, and she told him that he was responsible. He didn't offer to pay for the abortion, and she never asked him to. However, she later insisted that Blakely did offer to marry her. If there actually was a proposal it was a lame one at best, since he was engaged to Mary Dawson and Ruth was still officially married to George Ellis. But she used his discomfort to move herself out of the bedroom and in the direction of his social set.

After much nagging, Ruth prevailed and Blakely finally took her to a sports-car meet. The outing proved to be a disaster. Not knowing any better, she wore a white cocktail dress with a sweetheart neckline and matching high-heeled pumps to the track. Ruth realized her mistake the moment she arrived and saw that all the other women there were dressed in tweeds, plaid scarves, and leather boots or sturdy oxfords. It apparently hadn't occurred to Blakely to suggest that Ruth wear a more suitable outfit, and he was mortified when the other women distanced themselves from her. Ruth countered by focusing on the men, many of whom afterward told Blakely that she was "tremendous fun."

By the time the two got back to London, they both were furious. David accused Ruth of flirting as though she were "tarting around the bar," and she accused him of deliberately not informing her of the dress code "to make me feel socially inferior."

Ant Findlater was not among those who thought Ruth tremendous fun. He told Blakely that she didn't fit in with the racing crowd and in fact "stood out like a sore thumb." Carole Findlater liked David's new friend no better. She remembered meeting Ruth for the first time at her husband's birthday party in April of 1954. "She was wearing a black dress with a plunging neckline," recalled Carole. "She had a small bust, small wrists and ankles, the effect was shrimplike. She said 'Hello' to me in a tiny voice when we were introduced, and then ig-

nored me the rest of the evening. She spent all her time talking to every man at the party." Ruth's only comment about meeting Carole was that she "behaved like the Mother Superior herself."

As time went on, the tarty image of Ruth increasingly appeared to bother Blakely. He knew that she entertained other men in the apartment and complained sourly: "It's not what you do at night that worries me— it's what you do in the afternoon." At the club, he frequently said loudly to the patrons, "Look at her—flinging herself at any man." Ruth likewise began to find her lover something of a problem—and perhaps for a better reason. The supposedly well-off Blakely sponged off her shamelessly, mooching drinks and asking for money and whining that all his funds were tied up in building the Emperor. Worse, his drunken behavior was causing trouble at the Little.

David had learned nothing from the soda siphon episode with Mike Hawthorne. He so delighted in childishly squirting streams of water around the room that barmaid Jackie Dyer one evening picked up a siphon herself and hosed him down. He stood there stunned for an instant, then immediately raced upstairs to Ruth and demanded that Dyer be fired. Ruth reacted like a smart businesswoman and stood by her barmaid.

"I began to think that it was time that the affair ended," she later recalled. "We seemed to be getting too deeply involved, the business at the club was beginning to suffer and I was being monopolized." There was another problem, and that was Morris Conley. He had started charging Ruth Ellis rent for the apartment because he knew that David was living there and didn't like the arrangement.

Although she understood well the risks David posed to her livelihood, Ruth's sensible analysis gradually shriveled in the heat of her passion for him. Instead of giving David the boot, Ellis hit on a foolish scheme: she would take an alternate lover in hopes that it would somehow force Blakely into line. It did nothing of the sort; it only accelerated her rush toward tragedy.

The man Ruth Ellis chose as her second-string lover was Desmond Cussen, the wealthy, 33-year-old director of a family tobacco wholesale-retail house. He was a bachelor and a sports-car buff who often turned up at the Steering Wheel Club; he'd met Blakely there, and it

Recalling her stint as a teenage model for a photo club, Ellis strikes a seductive

was from him that Cussen had learned about the Little. Not a particularly attractive man, Cussen was reserved in manner, paunchy, and had slicked-down hair that gave him a slightly seal-like look. Stolid though he seemed, he was crazy about Ruth and had been from the moment he laid eyes on her. That was worth quite a lot to Ruth, particularly when she noticed how angry David got when she flirted with Desmond.

Desmond Cussen was as generous and undemanding as David Blakely was pinched and impossible. "Desmond was so restful after David," Ellis later said. Dog-like in his devotion, Cussen bought her perfume, clothes, and jewelry. He treated her like a lady and felt honored to be seen with her. He gave her cash to spend as she pleased while demanding nothing in return. He was very slow to make any sexual overtures, a fact that surprised and puzzled Ruth. Perhaps his reticence was one of the things that made Cussen so restful.

After they finally did become lovers, no great passion ever developed between them, at least not on her part. Some years after Ruth Ellis's story had run its course, Cussen described her to a biographer as "sexually very mechanical." That was extremely odd and was, wrote another biographer, "in stark contrast to the memories of many of her club friends, not least Cliff Davis," who recalled that the only time he and Ruth "hit it off" was a fabulous experience. She was, Davis exclaimed, an artist. In Ruth Ellis's world, Desmond Cussen was an old shoe, comfortable and dependable, but not very shiny. David Blakely continued to fill her dreams.

Two weeks before his 25th birthday, in the first week of June 1954, Blakely went to France to take part in one of the most important events in the sports-car calendar, the grueling 24-hour Le Mans competition. David's star seemed ascendant: He was to be a relief driver for the Bristol Works team. On Friday, the 11th of June, he mailed Ruth a postcard with the message, "Arrived O.K. Haven't had a drink for three days!!! Wish you

were here. Will probably see you Tuesday. Love David."

To celebrate both his birthday and his team's showing at Le Mans, Ruth organized a party at the Little for Thursday, June 17. But Thursday came and went without David. By the end of June, she hadn't seen him or heard from him again.

Angry and drinking heavily, Ruth took Desmond Cussen to bed; he had been patiently waiting for her to make the first move. "I'm not married to David and I can lead my own life," she told him.

In early July, Ruth received another postcard from Blakely and discovered that he'd stayed on in France for another race without letting her know. "Darling," the card read, "have arrived safely and am having quite a good time. The cars are going very well. Looking forward to seeing you. David." He added the postscript: "Love to Desmond!!!"

Blakely returned shortly afterward, and it seemed to Ruth that he'd missed her and was concerned about Cussen. It looked as if her ploy was working. "David was getting rather jealous," she remembered. "He asked me what I had been doing and all kinds of things like that, and, of course,

At his birthday party in April of 1954, a bearded Ant Findlater joins his wife, Carole *(far left)*, Ruth Ellis, and David Blakely for a photograph.

I did not tell him." She rescheduled the birthday party and ordered a cake decorated with a miniature racecar. Blakely arrived very late, around 11 p.m. He offered no apology and was somber and curt.

A few nights after the party, David told Ellis he'd been late because he was at the Hyde Park Hotel breaking his engagement to Mary Dawson. He didn't follow up with a declaration of love, instead remarking offhandedly, "You're not going to lose me after all."

It is entirely possible that it was Mary Dawson, and not David Blakely, who broke off the engagement. The young woman might well have gotten tired of being neglected, of David's continual drunkenness, and of his lack of character. Wounded pride at having been sent packing by his fiancée might have been the explanation for David's black mood on the night of the birthday party.

Ruth was ecstatic. She allowed herself to fantasize that there might still be a chance of

marriage, even though she could imagine how negatively his family would react to her. Blakely did nothing at the moment to disillusion her and was, for a time, much more attentive to her. "He literally adored me, my hands, my eyes, everything except my peroxided hair, which he always wanted to be brunette," she recalled. "Now he was free, I allowed myself to become very attached to him. I thought the world of him. I put him on the highest of high pedestals."

Just as she hoped he would, David proposed. Happy though Ruth was, she brought up the subject of his family. The engagement would have to be unofficial, he said, because "until you've been properly introduced to the family they might object if I suddenly said I was marrying someone from a nightclub." There was one other snag: Ruth still was legally married to George Ellis and it would be eight months before the divorce became final.

David's proposal, as Cliff Davis would say later, "put her in the promised land." But it was obvious to Davis that Ruth wouldn't stay there long, if only because of the hold Humphrey Cook's money had on his stepson. Davis remarked of Cook, "He wouldn't have sanctioned the marriage between them. He certainly would have cut off the bread."

That was the last thing David Blakely wanted to happen. Frugality wasn't his style. He'd spent most of his inheritance, and the money he earned at Silicon Pistons was nowhere near enough to cover his playboy lifestyle or to complete the Emperor project. The sports car was a money sink; not only did David owe Ant Findlater 10 pounds each week—which he often paid late—but there was constant outlay for parts as the design evolved. To make matters worse, Humphrey Cook was once again being dif-

At a table crowded with bottles and glasses, Ruth Ellis sits between Desmond Cussen and Court Club hostess Vicki Martin *(far right)*, while an unidentified admirer leers between the two women. Seated at the left is Jackie Dyer, a barmaid at the Little Club.

While young Andy cowered in the bedroom, Blakely accused Ruth of sleeping with Desmond Cussen only to get the money for the boy's boarding school. Ruth snarled that David had no right to reproach her since he was "poking Carole Findlater, though what you can get out of screwing that scarecrow, Christ only knows. Does she pay you for it?"

Blakely pushed Ruth out the door, telling her that Carole Findlater would settle the matter. As they climbed into David's gray Vanguard wagon, Cussen drove up unseen and trailed them to the Findlaters' apartment at 29 Tanza Road. Blakely had forgotten that the Findlaters were in Brighton for the holiday, but he had a key and let Ruth and himself in. Cussen waited for an hour outside the apartment and then returned to Goodwood Court to attend to Andy and to Ruth's guests. Ellis spent another exhausting night with David and told Cussen the next day that Blakely had threatened suicide if she left him.

The day after Christmas, Blakely raced at Brands Hatch, a track southeast of London. The Emperor was ready at last, and he placed second in the 1,500-cc. class. It was the highest he had ever finished. And when *The Motor* magazine rated the car "an impressive challenger," David and Ant Findlater were in seventh heaven. But before long, problems with Ruth cast a pall on David's high spirits.

On New Year's Eve he took her to the Crown pub in Penn, having made sure beforehand that the married woman he was sleeping with wouldn't be there. He had failed to check on his mother, however. David spotted Annie Cook entering the Crown as they drove up, so he went on to another pub, the Red Lion, where he and Ruth had a drink with some coworkers at Silicon Pistons. When they returned to the Crown, David went in alone to see whether the coast was clear. His mother was still there, which put him in a bit of a bind. Not daring— or caring—to introduce Ruth, Blakely stayed long enough to buy a drink for Ruth and take it out to the car, where she was waiting and fuming. They went back to the Red Lion and got drunk. Then they fought, and Blakely punched her in the eye.

Ruth knew it was futile to expect things ever to get better between them. But even in bed with Cussen all she could talk about was Blakely. "I think I've been a fool," she told him one night. "He's just a little drip. There are

cheap skates and cheap skates and I think I've met the cheapest of skates." She added wearily that she thought he'd sleep with every woman possible.

"I shouldn't worry about it, darling," replied Cussen.

"He really is the lowest of the low. Just a little skunk. He's rotten to the core. He has the nerve to call himself the social life of Buckinghamshire," said Ellis.

"Just go to sleep, darling," said Cussen.

"I don't want to go to sleep," insisted Ruth.

"You want more, do you?" asked Cussen.

"Yes, darling," Ruth laughed, her voice husky from alcohol. "More. Much more. More. More. More. Much more."

On January 8, 1955, Ellis and Blakely battled so violently in their room at the Rodney that other guests complained about the noise. When they parted, Blakely went to Penn. When Ellis didn't hear from him after two days, she called him to say that she intended to confront the married woman he had been seeing in Penn and to tell his mother about them. Next, she sent a telegram to him at Silicon Pistons: "PERSONAL MR D AND D BLAKELEY SYLICUM PISTONS LTD PENN-BUCKS—HAVENT YOU GOT THE GUTS TO SAY GOODBYE TO MY FACE—RUTH."

Terrified that his allowance would be cut off if she carried out her threat to see his mother, Blakely caved in. He begged her to forgive him and promised, "Things will be better once we're married."

The episodes of rancor and reconciliation continued. At Goodwood Court on February 6, while Cussen was at work, Blakely and Ellis had sex, then flew into jealous rages. She scratched his face. He punched and kicked her, blackening an eye and bruising her arms, legs, and left hip. In the melee, she sprained her ankle. But she could hobble around fast enough to snatch up his car keys when he tried to leave.

Blakely phoned Ant Findlater, who was working on the Emperor with a friend, Clive Gunnell, to come get him. The rescuers found Ruth hysterical and David whimpering, "She's an absolute bitch. She tried to knife me." At the Findlaters, Carole treated Blakely's scratches and gashes and asked him, "Could you, with your background, really be happy with that common tart?"

When Cussen got home, Ellis made him drive her to Tanza Road. They followed Blakely, Gunnell, and the Findlaters when they came out of the apartment and drove to the Magdala Tavern, a pub about five minutes away. Ellis and Cussen waited outside. At closing time, they followed the foursome back to Tanza Road, where Blakely dropped off the others and sped away. Desmond and Ruth trailed David to the Old Park in Penn. Still seething with fury, Ruth banged on the door of his apartment. The nanny answered, as a pajama-clad David hovered behind her. He panicked, bolted out the door, leaped into his car, and raced away, Ruth screaming obscenities in his wake.

Back in London, at Goodwood Court, Ruth lay awake in a fury all night. By now, her eye had swollen shut and Cussen pleaded with her to have it attended to. "Not until I get an apology from that bastard," she grated, and at 11 a.m. she had Cussen drive her back to Penn. On the way, they saw Blakely's car parked outside the Bull, a pub in the village of Gerrards Cross. Cussen went in alone, collared Blakely, and yanked him outside. While Ellis cursed him, Cussen called Blakely a coward and demanded, "What about hitting a man instead of a woman for a change?" Blakely fled in his car.

A few hours later, the standard bouquet of carnations arrived at Goodwood Court, along with the usual penitent note: "Sorry, Darling, I Love You. David." Two days later, Ruth and David, signing as Mr. and Mrs. Ellis, moved into a furnished room at 44 Egerton Gardens, a sort of bed-and-breakfast in central London. Ruth paid the weekly rent of seven pounds with money she'd borrowed from Desmond Cussen.

Within a week, the two were quarreling bitterly again. Ruth showed everybody the red marks on her neck; David claimed self-defense and sniveled that she had come at him with a gin bottle in a fit of jealousy.

When he left for work in the mornings, Ruth sat there drinking, consumed by the idea of catching Blakely with another woman. One night toward the end of February, David failed to return to Egerton Gardens. Early the next morning, Ruth had Cussen drive her to Penn. They parked outside the married woman's house and waited. Blakely strolled out at nine o'clock, saw Cussen's car, and scurried back inside. A few minutes later, he emerged with his lover, who he probably hoped would serve as protection. After a few heated words, Ruth let

A frequent spectator at David's races, Ruth Ellis appears at a meet in conventional sporty attire. Initially ignorant of the dress code for such events, she embarrassed herself by wearing a cocktail dress to her first race.

David proudly shows off the Emperor, the prototype for what he and his partner, Ant Findlater, hoped would be a commercially successful sports car. Blakely cadged money from his stepfather for the project.

One of Ruth's birthday
presents to David was
a charm in the shape of
an antique car.

After Ruth's ankle was broken in a quarrel, David sent red carnations and this note.

him go off to work and quietly apologized to the woman for "so much trouble." The woman told Ruth, in apparent sincerity, "I'm very sorry. It's all my fault, I did not know David had anything so important in London." But the woman didn't end their affair, and Ruth's jealousy became increasingly poisonous.

At the end of March, Ruth discovered she was pregnant once again and told David. At best, he was indifferent to her condition. One night, after a bitter row over the woman in Penn, Ruth told him, "It is no good David, in my condition, I cannot stand all this. I am feeling ill. You will have to go out of my life." Blakely's response, recalled Ruth, was to punch her in the cheek with his clenched fist, then grab her by the throat and drive his fist into her stomach. "He was like a mad man," she related. "The expression on his face was frightening. He said, 'One of these days, I will kill you.' I said, 'You have done that already.' "

A few days later she miscarried. Blakely didn't even ask how she felt, and his callousness hurt and angered Ruth. "I'll stand so much from you, David, but you can't go on walking over me forever," she told him.

"You'll stand it because you love me," he answered.

Bleeding and feeling feverish from the miscarriage, on Thursday, March 31, Ruth made a 200-mile trip with Blakely for a race in which the Emperor was entered. The car broke down during a practice run, and Blakely furiously turned on Ellis. "It's your fault. You jinxed me!" he yelled.

Upon her return home to Egerton Gardens on Sunday, April 3, Ruth went straight to bed with a high fever: Her temperature was 104°F. It was Easter recess, and Andy was with her; the faithful Desmond Cussen had gone up to the boy's boarding school to pick him up while Ruth was off traveling with Blakely. For two days Ruth stayed in bed brooding, without a call or a visit from David.

She had once been good company and fun, but she'd turned into a surly, miserable woman—David's fault, she felt. "I was growing to loathe him, he was so conceited and said that all women loved him," she recalled later. "He was so much in love with himself."

By Wednesday Ruth was feeling better, and Blakely, in one of his mood swings, was exultant. He'd just begun working as an assistant on the Bristol Works team that was slated to race at Le Mans in June, and he had his photograph taken while he was on the job.

On Thursday, April 7, he brought Ruth an enlargement of the photograph inscribed, "To Ruth, with all my love. David." She was delighted with the photo and urged David not to sell the damaged Emperor as he thought he had to, since he didn't have the money to repair it. "Surely we can raise the money somehow," she said earnestly. Seizing on the opening she'd given him, David brazenly suggested that perhaps she could borrow the necessary 400 pounds from his rival, Desmond Cussen; it is not known if Ruth acted on David's outrageous proposition.

Ruth recalled that they spent a companionable evening at the movies, and David said he wanted to take Andy out with them on Saturday night. They were, she remembered later "on the very best of terms."

But only for the moment. At lunch at the Magdala Tavern with the Findlaters on Friday, Blakely told them that he was desperately unhappy and increasingly frightened of her violent tantrums. "I'm supposed to be calling for Ruth at eight tonight," he said. "I can't stand it any longer, I want to get away from her."

Carole Findlater told Blakely to go ahead and do it. "For God's sake," she said, "don't be so bloody spineless and silly. Any man can leave any woman. What can she do about it?"

In February 1955 Ruth Ellis and David Blakely rented a furnished room at 44 Egerton Gardens
in London, passing themselves off as a married couple.

"You don't know her. You don't know what she's capable of," said David.

Ant Findlater, having witnessed Ruth's fury, invited Blakely to stay the weekend with them at Tanza Road. "If Ruth comes round and kicks up a scene, Carole and I will deal with her," he said.

That evening, Ruth waited for David until 9:30 p.m. and then telephoned the Findlaters. Their 19-year-old live-in nanny answered. When Ruth asked whether Blakely was there, the young woman replied that she was alone with the Findlaters' infant daughter, Francesca. Ruth called again in an hour. This time, Ant answered. He told her that Blakely wasn't there. Ruth said she was worried about David. Ant snickered, "Oh, he's all right."

"I knew at once David was there and that they were laughing at me behind my back," said Ellis later.

Over the next few hours, Ruth Ellis alternated between telephoning the Findlaters and Desmond Cussen. Now, when Ant heard her voice, he simply hung up. Desmond didn't get home until after midnight, but he agreed to drive Ruth to Tanza Road. Parked on the street near the Findlaters' apartment was Blakely's gray Vanguard wagon.

Ruth rang the bell and hammered on the front door. No answer. She ran to a public phone and called. Ant picked up—and hung up. Ruth ran back to the Findlaters' and held her finger on the buzzer. Still no answer. She thought she heard a woman giggling in the apartment upstairs.

A wave of rage washed over her. She hurried back to Cussen's car, where he sat observing the scene. She grabbed a large flashlight from the glove compartment, ran over to Blakely's car, and began smashing its windows with the flashlight.

Ant Findlater, in pajamas and robe, came down the steps. Ruth demanded to see David. Findlater insisted that he wasn't there. As they argued, a police car pulled up; Findlater had called the cops. Unwilling to intervene in what looked like a domestic squabble, the officers politely advised Ruth to calm down and left.

No sooner had the police car turned the corner than Ellis furiously banged in two more of the Vanguard's windows. Findlater again called the police. But by the time they arrived, Ruth had left with Cussen. "I did not

sleep that night," she said. "I just sat and howled. I no longer thought of David as the man I loved, but as someone who was trying to make a fool of me. I felt humiliated and frustrated."

At 8 a.m. Ruth again phoned the Findlaters. Someone picked up the phone and promptly hung up on her. She took a taxi to Tanza Road and hid in a doorway. At 10 a.m. she saw Blakely and Findlater drive off in the Vanguard. Ruth hailed a taxi and told the driver to take her to Cussen's place at Goodwood Court. Guessing correctly, she twice rang the garage where Blakely and Findlater were repairing the windows. Ant answered both times and hung up. Ruth asked Cussen to call. Findlater hung up on him. Finally, Cussen reminded Ruth that her son was alone at Egerton Gardens. Desmond took her home to fix lunch.

At two o'clock, they dropped Andy off at the zoo in Regents Park and continued on to Hampstead. They spotted Blakely's Vanguard outside the Magdala Tavern. Cussen then drove to Tanza Road. The house across the street from the Findlaters' apartment was for sale and Ruth, pretending to be a prospective buyer, got herself invited in for tea. From the second floor bay window, she saw Blakely and the Findlaters return home from the tavern and minutes later leave again with little Francesca and her nanny.

Ruth said thank you for the tea and hurried downstairs. Cussen had been driving around while she was inside, and when he returned they headed back to Egerton Gardens. Ruth told Cussen that she was certain David was getting it on with the Findlaters' young nanny. "He's up to his old tricks again," she said bitterly.

At 10 o'clock that night Cussen once again drove Ruth to Tanza Road. She heard David's voice and then a woman's giggle float through an open window. It enraged her. She watched the apartment until after midnight, when she saw a figure pull down the shades in one of the front rooms and switch off the lights. There was no doubt in Ruth's mind that David was in the darkened room with the nanny.

At Egerton Gardens, Ruth sat up all night, smoking cigarettes and shaking with wrath. Later on she recalled the bitter review of what her passion for Blakely had brought her to: "When I first fell in love with David," Ruth said, "I was a successful manageress of a prosper-

Wearing his racing costume, a proud David Blakely sat for this portrait after being invited to take part in the 1955 race at Le Mans. On April 6 he presented Ruth with an enlargement of the photograph and inscribed it affectionately *(inset)*.

To Ruth with all
my love
David

Trying to distance himself from Ruth, David spent the last week-end of his life at the Findlaters' apartment at 29 Tanza Road.

ous club. I had admirers, money in the bank and a lovely flat. Now all I had was a bed-sitting room, no money, no job. A man who beat me in private and abused me in public. A man who was relieved when I lost the child he had fathered. I had a peculiar desire to kill David."

On the evening of Easter Day, Cussen drove Ruth Ellis to Penn in search of Blakely. Failing to find him, they went back to London, where Ruth resumed her vigil outside the Findlaters' apartment. She could hear music from a record player in the apartment. Blakely's Vanguard was nowhere in sight, so Ruth went on to the Magdala Tavern to look for him. The Vanguard was parked nearby. Ruth reached into her handbag for her thick-lensed spectacles, put her face close to the window, and peered into the pub. She shivered when she saw Blakely, accompanied by Clive Gunnell, downing the last of a gin and tonic.

Ruth put her eyeglasses back in her purse and took out a long-barreled .38-caliber Smith & Wesson revolver loaded with six nickel-plated bullets. She pressed against the wall of the tavern. Blakely came out carrying a quart of beer and fumbling for his car keys. Gunnell followed a few steps behind with two bottles of beer.

"David!" called Ruth.

Blakely ignored her. She moved toward him calling his name. "David! David!" He turned to face her, eyes suddenly widening in terror when he saw the outstretched .38. He spun around and started to run.

Ruth Ellis squinted carefully along the barrel and fired one shot. She squeezed the trigger and fired again. Blakely staggered against the Vanguard, smudging the side panels with blood. The beer fell from his hands and foamed at his feet. He screamed, "Clive!" and lurched toward Gunnell.

"Get out of the way, Clive," Ruth commanded as she chased Blakely around the car. He staggered down the street and collapsed facedown in the gutter. Moaning and cradling his head with his right arm, he raised himself up on his left elbow. Blood flowed from his mouth. Ruth Ellis stood over him and fired three more times.

Then she raised the .38 to her right temple and squeezed the trigger until the hammer cocked with a click. She wavered. Her hand dropped and the pistol fired, the bullet ricocheting off the pavement and nicking a bystander in the right thumb.

Off-duty police constable Alan Thompson was sitting at the bar when someone rushed into the Magdala Tavern shouting, "A bloke's been shot outside!" Thompson walked out and saw Ruth holding the gun. She swung around and said, "Call the police."

"I am the police," replied Thompson as he took the gun from her hand.

David Blakely was dead before the ambulance arrived at the hospital. Of the four bullets that hit him, two had caused only superficial wounds. But one nickel-clad slug had entered his lower right back, penetrating his abdomen and liver before exiting below the left shoulder blade; a second bullet had perforated the left lung, aorta, and windpipe before lodging in the muscles of the tongue. A pathologist put the cause of death as "shock and hemmorrhage due to gunshot wounds."

At the police station, Ruth told officers, "I am guilty. I am rather confused." But she was not too confused to claim that she'd been given the pistol three years before by a Little Club patron as security for a bar debt. The police were skeptical about that and made some preliminary inquiries. But the investigation was cursory. To authorities, the case was clearly the vengeful act of a lower-class woman rejected by an upper-class lover. The report concluded, "On meeting Blakely and realizing that his class was much above her own, and finding he was sufficiently interested to propose marriage, it seems she was prepared to go to any lengths to keep him. Finding this impossible, she appears to have decided to wreak her vengeance upon him." The following afternoon Ruth Ellis was charged with the murder of David Blakely and remanded to Holloway Prison.

"When I was told she shot him I always thought it would have been him killing her," said barmaid Jackie Dyer, who was one of Ruth's first visitors at Holloway. "Are they going to hang me?" Ruth asked her friend, and added, "I don't mind, but go and see him and tell me what he looks like."

Dyer tracked Blakely's body to a funeral home and reported back that the body was laid out in a white satin-lined coffin. Ruth was pleased "that he was being properly cared for." She requested a photograph of Blakely and a Bible; she taped the photo to the wall of her cell and kept the Bible opened to a passage from Deuterono-

As Blakely walked out of the Magdala Tavern he was felled by two bullets. Ellis then fired three more times.

Ruth Ellis used this long-barreled .38-caliber Smith & Wesson revolver to kill her lover.

my describing how crime is to be punished—life for life, eye for eye, tooth for tooth. She wrote a misspelled letter to Blakely's mother, revealing her bitter, tortured state of mind: "The two people I blame for David's death, and my own, are the Finlayters. No dought you will not understand this but *perhaps* before I hang you will know what I mean. I shall die loving your son. And you should feel content that his death has been repaid."

Ruth's apparent indifference to her fate frustrated John Bickford, an experienced criminal lawyer hired by the Mirror Group of newspapers in exchange for exclusive rights to her life story. At their first meeting, Ellis asked Bickford to convey the message to Desmond Cussen that she'd told the police she got the gun from a Little Club patron. Bickford went to see Cussen, who confessed that it was he who had supplied Ruth with the Smith & Wesson and had shown her how to shoot it. The lawyer apparently didn't quiz Cussen as to why he'd given Ruth the pistol, and Cussen seems not to have volunteered an explanation. Considering his relationship with Ruth, the likelihood is that she asked and he simply gave, as he had over and over again.

Whatever the case, Bickford hurried back to Ruth with Cussen's story. She corroborated it but said, "I don't want it brought out in court." As to why Ruth wanted to shield Cussen, it may well have been because she wanted him to continue caring for Andy. If Cussen were to lose his freedom, Ruth's son would lose his guardian and protector. Against his better judgment, Bickford suppressed the information about the gun.

Ruth Ellis offered Bickford no more assistance with her defense. "I took David's life and I don't ask you to save mine," she said. "I don't want to live." Her mother, Bertha, begged her to plead insanity. But Ruth refused. "It's no use, mother," she said, "I was sane when I did it and I meant to do it, and I won't go to prison for ten years or more, and come out old and finished."

As the June 20, 1955, trial date approached, Ruth attended to a problem that was important to her—the brown roots of her hair were beginning to show. Holloway warden Charity Taylor allowed her to send out for the necessary materials, and two prison matrons, along with Jackie Dyer, helped her set matters right.

Bickford and the other members of the defense team had hoped to portray Ruth as the physically ravaged victim of a violent lover. But that idea fell apart on opening day when Ruth entered the jam-packed Old Bailey Number One courtroom, her platinum crown agleam. She wore a modish black suit with a lamb collar, a white silk blouse, and black high heels. She looked like a movie star—or a high-priced West End call girl.

The trial itself took little more than a day. John Bickford and his colleagues did no more than a cursory cross-examination of the Findlaters and other prosecution witnesses. The lawyers were afraid, they said, that too many tough, probing questions "would be interpreted as mud-slinging." The prosecution rested its case before the lunch recess.

When Ruth took the stand later that afternoon, she thwarted all attempts by her lawyers to depict her as a jealous woman provoked beyond reason into murdering her lover. She was asked about the beatings by Blakely. "I bruise very easily, and I was full of bruises on many occasions," she shrugged. When her attorneys asked why she had killed Blakely, she replied dispassionately, "I do not really know, quite seriously. I was just very upset." Under cross-examination, the prosecution narrowed the question: "When you fired that revolver at close range into the body of David Blakely, what did you intend to do?" Her answer didn't disappoint the opposing counsel: "It was obvious that when I shot him I intended to kill him."

At 10:30 the following morning, the presiding judge instructed the jury of 10 men and two women that under British law, unlike that of France and some other countries, "transport of passion and loss of self-control" was not a defense to the charge of murder. It took the jurors barely 23 minutes to find Ruth Ellis guilty. They didn't recommend mercy. In accord with tradition, the judge wore a black cap when he condemned Ruth to death by hanging. The execution was set for July 13, three weeks away.

That same afternoon Ruth was moved into the constantly lighted brown-and-pink cell reserved for the condemned, adjacent to the gallows shed at Holloway Prison. She ordered Bickford not to appeal and asked her family to smuggle poison or sleeping pills to her. But they disobeyed on both scores and petitioned Britain's Home Secretary, Major Gwilyn Lloyd George, for a stay of execution.

On July 11, two days before her scheduled execution, Lloyd George scribbled across Ruth Ellis's file: "The Law Must Take Its Course."

For once, Ruth's icy composure deserted her. She pounded on her prison bed shrieking, "I don't want to die, I don't want to die." Her earlier insistence on protecting Desmond Cussen also vanished. Later that day, when Bickford came to visit, she spat at him: "I've been wondering what your game was. I know now. You've been taking money from Cussen to see that I go down and he goes free." She demanded another lawyer, Victor Mishcon, who had represented her in the divorce from George Ellis.

Mishcon saw Ruth briefly that night and returned with a clerk the following morning. Her hysteria had given way to calm. She received her guests while smoking a cigarette affixed to a long holder. "She was quite remarkable," Mishcon remembered. "I shall never forget it. She was in a dressing gown, quite a resplendent one, over her prison clothes. When we walked in she stood up and like a gracious hostess said how kind it was of us to be there."

Ruth had told Mishcon that she wished him to know certain facts. And while the clerk took it down, she offered her version of how she had come into possession of the pistol: "I had been drinking Pernod (I think that is how it is spelt) in Desmond Cussen's flat and Desmond had been drinking too. I had been telling Desmond about Blakely's treatment of me. I was in a terribly depressed state. All I remember is that Desmond gave me a loaded gun. Desmond was jealous of Blakely as in fact Blakely was of Desmond. I would say that they hated each other. I rushed out as soon as he gave me the gun. I rushed back after a second or so and said, 'Will you drive me to Hampstead?' He did so, and left me at the top of Tanza Road."

At teatime, while Mishcon presented Ellis's signed statement to the Home Office hoping for a last-minute reprieve, a small, amiable man named Albert Pierrepoint checked in with warden Taylor. The owner of a pub called Help the Poor Struggler, Pierrepoint doubled as a public executioner, carrying on a family tradition initiated by his father and an uncle. He peered into the condemned cell through the "Judas hole," an incon-

David Blakely's friends Clive Gunnell *(far left)* and Ant Findlater arrive at London's Old Bailey courthouse for Ruth Ellis's murder trial. Gunnell saw her shoot Blakely.

spicuous crack in the wall, to study Ruth Ellis and compare her stature with the height and weight figures listed in her prison file.

As Ruth was led out of her cell and into the prison yard for her daily exercise, Pierrepoint entered the adjacent gallows shed. He scanned the calibrated table of drops and rigged a sandbag to test the spring-loaded trapdoor. There was an audible whir and a plop, and he was satisfied.

When Pierrepoint had departed, Ruth was led back to her cell. In the evening, her family visited her for the last time, and she asked her mother to place carnations—six red and six white—on David Blakely's grave.

By midnight, it was clear that Mishcon's mission would fail. Desmond Cussen couldn't be located, and in any case, Lloyd George refused to stay the execution. As he later remarked, Ruth's final statement "made no difference. If anything, it made her offense all the greater. Instead of a woman merely acting suddenly on impulse here you had an actual plot to commit murder." And there the matter rested. The police would never investigate Ellis's allegations against Desmond Cussen. If he did supply her with the gun, he never suffered any penalty for it. For him, life went on as usual.

At 6:30 a.m. on July 13, 1955, Ruth Ellis received communion from the prison chaplain. She refused breakfast, but she did accept a glass of brandy. Outside the walls of Holloway, more than 1,000 people had gathered, some weeping and chanting "Give her a reprieve," others simply waiting for the death notice to be posted on the massive oaken gates. At one minute before nine, hangman Pierrepoint and warden Taylor came to collect Ruth. In Blackpool, to the north, an effigy of her in a black evening gown was being installed in the waxworks museum's Chamber of Horrors.

Dressed a plain cotton shift, her platinum blond hair tied in a ponytail, her hands strapped behind her back, Ruth walked unassisted the few paces to the scaffold.

Standing on the *T* mark of the trapdoor, she fixed her eyes on the crucifix on the wall while her feet were being bound together. She puckered her lips as if trying to smile. A white hood was pulled down over her head and the loop of rope placed around her neck. Pierrepoint adjusted the knot. Then, he stepped quickly around Ruth Ellis and pulled the trapdoor lever.◆

Daily Mirror

WED JULY 13 1955

1½d

No. 16,045

FORWARD WITH THE PEOPLE

CASSANDRA talks to YOU about—

THE WOMAN WHO HANGS THIS MORNING

By CASSANDRA

IT'S a fine day for hay-making. A fine day for fishing. A fine day for lolling in the sun-shine. And if you feel that way—and I mourn to say that millions of you do—it's a fine day for a hanging.

If you read this before nine o'clock this morn-ing, the last dreadful and obscene preparations for hanging Ruth Ellis will be moving up to their fierce and sickening climax. The public hang-man and his assistant will have been slipped into the prison at about four o'clock yesterday afternoon.

There, from what is gro-tesquely called "some van-tage point" and unobserved by Ruth Ellis, they will have spied upon her when she was at exercise "to form an impression of the physique of the prisoner."

A bag of sand will have been filled to the same weight as the condemned woman and it will have been left hang-ing overnight to stretch the rope.

Our Guilt . . .

If you read this at nine o'clock then—short of a miracle—you and I and every man and woman in the land with head to think and heart to feel will, in full responsibility, blot this woman out.

The hands that place the white hood over her head will not be our hands. But the guilt—

and guilt there is in all this abominable business —will belong to us as much as to the wretched executioner paid and trained to do the job in accordance with the savage public will.

If you read this after nine o'clock, the murderess, Ruth Ellis, will have gone.

The one thing that brings stature and dignity to man-kind and raises us above the beasts of the field will have been denied her—pity and the hope of ultimate redemp-tion.

The medical officer will go to the pit under the trap door to see that life is extinct. Then, in the barbarous wickedness of this ceremony, rejected by nearly all civilised peoples, the body will be left to hang for one hour.

Dregs of Shame

If you read these words at mine at mid-day the grave will have been dug while there are no prisoners around and the Chaplain will have read the burial service after he and all of us have come so freshly from disobeying the Sixth Commandment which says thou shalt not kill.

The secrecy of it all shows that if compassion is not in us, then at least we still retain the dregs of shame. The medieval notice of execution will have been posted on the prison gates and the usual squalid handful of louts and rubbernecks who attend these legalised killings will have had their own private obscene delights.

Two Royal Commissions have protested against these horrible events. Every Home Secretary in recent years has testified to the agonies of his task, and the revulsion he has

felt towards his duty. None has ever claimed that executions prevent murder.

Yet they go on and still Parliament has neither the resolve nor the conviction, nor the wit, nor the de-cency to put an end to these atrocious affairs.

When I write about capi-tal punishment, as I have often done, I get some praise and usually more abuse. In this case I have been reviled as being "a sucker for a pretty face."

Well, I am a sucker for a pretty face. And I am a sucker for all human faces

because I hope I am a sucker for all humanity, good or bad. But I prefer the face not to be lolling because of a judicially broken neck.

Yes, it is a fine day.

Oscar Wilde, when he was in Reading Gaol, spoke with melancholy of "that little tent of blue which prisoners call the sky."

THE TENT OF BLUE SHOULD BE DARK AND SAD AT THE THING WE HAVE DONE THIS DAY.

RUTH ELLIS: *CASSANDRA SAYS: "In this case I have been reviled as being 'a sucker for a pretty face.' Well, I am a sucker for all human faces—good or bad. But I prefer them not to be lolling because of a judicially broken neck."*

EXECUTION EVE
Crowd break police cordon round gaol

DAILY MIRROR REPORTER

MORE than 400 people staged amazing scenes outside Holloway Gaol last night—the eve of Ruth Ellis's execution. There were even attempts to storm the prison gates.

Police were drawn up outside, but time after time sections of the crowd —mostly women—broke through the cordon and hammered on the massive oak doors.

They demanded to see Mrs. Ellis, crying: "We want her to kneel in prayer with us."

Once anti-capital pun-ishment leaflets were thrown in the air. They

fluttered down through the shafts of light from the prison windows.

Women wept as people began shouting: "Give her a reprieve."

And one woman clutch-ing a bunch of flowers kept repeating: "There, but for the grace of God, go I."

Despite official state-ments that "there would be nothing to see" the crowd refused to disperse.

One section chanted "Evans—Bentley—Ellis" and the chorus was taken up by the rest of the crowd.

Police on foot and in patrol cars tried to move people back, but the crowd

Continued on Back Page

Two articles that fill the front page of London's July 13, 1955, *Daily Mirror* reflect the storm of protest that Ruth Ellis's pending execution pro-voked among opponents of capital punishment.

CERTIFICATE OF SURGEON

(31 Vict. Cap. 24)

I, *George Ralph Percy Williams*, the Surgeon of Her Majesty's Prison of *Holloway* hereby certify that I this day examined the Body of *Ruth Ellis*, on whom Judgment of Death was this day executed in the said Prison; and that on that Examination I found that the said *Ruth Ellis* was dead.

Dated this *13th* day of *July* *1955*

(Signature) *RW Cunniffe*

No. 279

On the morning of Ruth Ellis's hanging a crowd waits outside Holloway Prison for her death certificate *(inset)* to be posted on the prison gate. She was the last woman executed in England.

I*t's not going to end until one of us is gone.*

DAN BRODERICK

4

Forever

"Fight back, be confident, be romantic," Betty Broderick repeated to herself as she steered her car around the curves of La Jolla's Soledad Mountain Road on her way to her husband's law office in downtown San Diego. That's what a wife must do when she suspects her husband is having an affair, her girlfriends told her: Let him know you exist. Don't just stand by and let it happen. Don't take it lying down.

It was November 22, 1983, Dan Broderick's 39th birthday, and Betty had with her the makings of a surprise party for two. There was a chilled bottle of Dom Perignon in a silver ice bucket, a dozen red roses, and a joke gift—a 24-karat-gold tire-pressure gauge to go with Dan's brand new $37,000 red Corvette. His midlife crisis car, she called it. Betty had dressed carefully for the occasion; she wanted to look perfect, to be perfect for him. She was wearing a California-chic outfit, a ruffly, flowered Diane Fries party dress—size eight, not bad for a 36-year-old mother of four—and matching Bruno Magli pumps.

Betty angled the rearview mirror so she could see herself. Her recent face peel had healed, leaving her skin pink and, if not dewy, at least taut and unblemished. The procedure hadn't done anything for the faint wrinkles at the corners of her blue eyes, but with her artful makeup, she thought, they were scarcely noticeable. She'd grown her hair long again, the way it was when she and Dan had met 18 years before. Only now its ash-blond color came from a bottle.

At Dan's office, Betty introduced herself to his newly hired receptionist, who smiled and said, "They went out to lunch at eleven. They're not back yet."

"Who?" asked Betty.

"Just them," the receptionist answered. "Dan and Linda."

Betty said she'd wait for Dan and headed toward his office. As she passed the closed door of the office next to his, her eye was caught by the inscription on the brass nameplate—LINDA KOLKENA. The new office assistant—22 years old, blond, beautiful. The one she'd told Dan to fire. Without hesitating Betty opened the door and walked in. The office was handsomely appointed with a mahogany desk, damask-upholstered furniture, and a high-tech stereo system. The late-afternoon sun streamed through floor-to-ceiling windows with a panoramic view of San Diego Bay. Elegant quarters for a well-heeled lawyer, but not what one would expect for a glorified receptionist who couldn't even type. Betty's eyes lingered on a photograph adorning one wall, a photograph she knew well. Taken when Dan was a 22-year-old bachelor—before there was a Mrs. Broderick—it showed him in the saddle of a rearing white horse. Dan must have given it to Linda, and Betty had no doubt what that meant. The photograph confirmed what she'd suspected for months.

Seeing Dan's office made her feel even worse. Streamers and balloons decorated the ornate oak roll-top desk Betty had special-ordered for her husband. On it sat the remnants of a chocolate mousse cake, an empty bottle of wine, and two wine glasses. Betty picked up one of the glasses and ran her finger over its pattern. It was her wedding crystal. As if in a trance, she sat down in one of Dan's plaid armchairs to wait for him.

By sunset neither Dan nor Linda had returned to the office, and Betty gave up and started for home, hurt and with rage welling up inside her. Back at the house, she stalked into her and Dan's second-floor bedroom and flung open the doors of his mirrored wall of closets. "I'll help him pack," Betty muttered angrily to herself. "I'll get him out." One by one she ripped Dan's custom-made suits from their wooden hangers. Then a new thought struck her. Instead of fetching suitcases, Betty carried armloads of suits out onto the balcony of their bedroom and threw them over the railing onto the back lawn. It took several trips. Finished with the suits, she collected Dan's monogrammed, handstitched shirts and his ski clothes from the closet and tossed them down onto the pile below.

"Mom, Mom, what are you doing? Stop it, stop, Dad's gonna kill you," pleaded her 13-year-old daughter, Kim. Standing in the bedroom doorway, watching the scene and weeping, was Betty's younger daughter, 12-year-old Lee.

"Get out of here," shouted Betty. "Just get out."

The contents of Dan's dresser drawers came next—polo shirts, pajamas, boxer shorts. Her work finished in the bedroom, Betty rushed downstairs to the garage and grabbed a can of gasoline. She soaked the heap of clothes with the fuel, lighted a match, and stood transfixed by the blaze as tears streamed down her face.

When the flames died down, Betty got a can of brown paint from the garage, carried it out to the smoldering pile, and poured the contents over what remained of Dan's wardrobe.

Betty could hardly have done anything more dramatic, more emphatic, more serious to express her overwhelming anger at Dan. Short of killing him.

Betty Broderick's symbolic assault was a stroke of wifely genius; after 14 years of marriage, she knew instinctively how to get to Dan. His lavish wardrobe mattered a great deal to him, as did the other big-ticket items that his seven-figure income provided: the candy-apple-red Corvette, the powerboat, the five-bedroom house with a swimming pool, the vacation condos, the private schools for their children, country-club memberships, trips to Europe, Caribbean cruises. Of such stuff are images made and, Dan Broderick often reminded his wife, image is everything.

To people who moved in the moneyed professional circles of San Diego and La Jolla, Betty and Dan Broderick appeared to have everything going for them. His track record in personal injury and medical malpractice lawsuits made him the envy of other lawyers, and he was becoming a powerful figure in the San Diego County Bar Association. Betty—Bets to her husband—seemed content to bask in her husband's reflected glory. Witty and energetic, the quintessential suburbanite, she chauffeured the four kids in her Chevy Suburban Blazer with the "LODEMUP" vanity plate to soccer games, music lessons, and catechism classes. She took cooking lessons,

entertained Dan's colleagues, juggled engagements on their social calendar, planned family trips, and managed household affairs while her husband made their ambitious dreams of wealth and social standing come true. "They were everything we all wanted to be," said the wife of one of Dan Broderick's colleagues. "They looked about as good as it gets."

It seemed impossible that a union that looked so right would turn out to be so murderously wrong.

Elisabeth Anne, the third of Frank and Marita Bisceglia's six children, was born on November 7, 1947, and grew up in Eastchester, a pleasant suburb north of New York City. Her father, the jovial, ruddy-faced owner of a successful construction company, was a thoroughgoing family man. Frank helped get the children dressed, fed, and off to school in the morning; he took his turn shuttling them to dancing lessons and scout meetings whenever he could, and he did much of the family's grocery shopping.

But it was mother Marita who ruled the roost, according to Betty. A Phi Beta Kappa college graduate and a former third-grade teacher, Marita Bisceglia was a traditionalist who raised her three daughters to be gracious wives. "She taught us how to do things right," remembered Betty. "She was socially aware. She knew the right stationery, the right china, the right everything." That included the right clothes—Villager dresses, Hermès scarves, Pappagallo shoes—and understated jewelry, such as gold circle pins. By the age of 13, Betty was a poised, willowy knockout with silky ash-blond hair, long legs, and a glowing complexion. She had even landed a part-time job modeling at Bonwit Teller, an exclusive department store.

The Bisceglias were devout Roman Catholics and sent all of their children to parochial schools. At her all-girls high school, Betty excelled in athletics, taking part in golf, tennis, horseback riding, and riflery. After her graduation in 1965 she went on to another Catholic all-female institution, Mount Saint Vincent College in nearby Riverdale. During her college years Betty continued to live at home, and her social life was conducted under her mother's watchful eye. Marita was unbending on the subject of boyfriends, since in her view they were all potential suitors: They had to be Catholic, and they had to

have a family history unblemished by divorce. Betty had no quarrel with such restrictions, remarking in later years that she wouldn't have dreamed of marrying any other kind of man.

In the fall of her freshman year, a girlfriend's brother invited Betty to Notre Dame University in South Bend, Indiana, for the biggest football game of the season, against the University of Southern California. After she had assured herself that Betty would be well-chaperoned, Marita gave her daughter permis-

Confronted with evidence of Dan's infidelity, Betty dumped his clothes onto the lawn from the rear balcony of their La Jolla house, then set them on fire.

sion to go. Notre Dame was, after all, a Catholic school.

Betty was at a post-game party on Saturday night when a fellow hanging around the table where she was sitting asked her for a pen. "I, of course, being the proper little Catholic schoolgirl, always had in my purse a handkerchief, a dime to get home, and my little gold Parker pen," she recalled more than two decades later. By way of introduction the young man wrote "Daniel T. Broderick III MD (A)" on the tablecloth. The

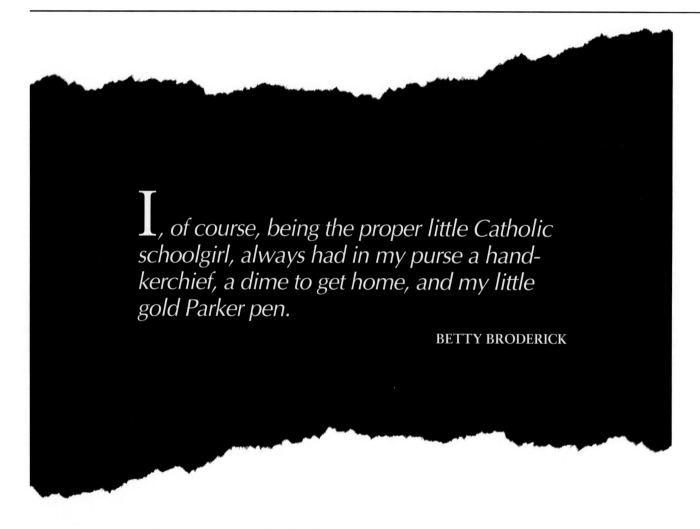

I, *of course, being the proper little Catholic schoolgirl, always had in my purse a handkerchief, a dime to get home, and my little gold Parker pen.*

BETTY BRODERICK

letters after his name, he explained, stood for "Medical Doctor Almost." He was a senior at Notre Dame and would enter Cornell University Medical College in Manhattan the following autumn.

Betty Bisceglia was only mildly interested. She thought Dan Broderick looked like a nerd, with his long, skinny sideburns and round tortoiseshell glasses. He was also shorter than she was—the five-foot-ten-and-one-half-inch Betty was accustomed to dating athletes, big guys. Still, he had a solid square jaw and bright blue eyes, and she liked his dimples and boyish smile. Betty didn't turn him down when he asked for her name and address, though she really didn't expect to hear from him.

She had misjudged Dan Broderick. In the following months Betty got phone calls, telegrams, and letters signed "Love, D" with a scribbled *X*, for a kiss. She wrote back, but she didn't take him seriously. When she saw Dan again, however, soon after he arrived in New York in the fall of 1966 to start medical school, it was a different story. Betty would say later that she fell in love with him on their first date.

Betty and Dan seemed to have a great deal in common. Both were bright, funny, and full of drive, and both had grown up in large, old-fashioned Catholic families. Daniel T. Broderick III was born in Pittsburgh on November 22, 1944, the oldest of nine children—five boys and four girls. He grew up knowing how much his parents expected from him as the firstborn male. Gender and hierarchy counted for a great deal in the Broderick household, and there wasn't any doubt who the head of the family was. The elder Dan managed a lumber brokerage. The grandson of an Irish immigrant and the first member of his family to attend college, he was an autocrat who demanded strict obedience from his wife, Yolanda, and his children. The daughters were expected to help their mother run the household. While they cooked and cleaned, the boys took care of what were considered properly masculine chores such as lawn mowing. That was one of young Dan's favorite assignments, and he continued to enjoy tending the lawn when he was grown.

Although Dan may have felt the pressure to excel more than his brothers did, the importance of making one's mark in the world was drummed into every Broderick boy. Dan's brother Larry once remarked, "Our will to succeed is inherited. It's genetic." So, it seems, was a sense of masculine superiority. The boys jokingly referred to their sisters as "yucks—too wet to step on, too low to kick." Such distinctions between the sexes were maintained in the education of the Broderick offspring. All nine of the children attended single-sex Catholic schools—Notre Dame for the boys and its affiliate, St. Mary's, for the girls.

When Dan first introduced Betty to his family, they were completely charmed. "She was so worldly, so sophisticated—a glamorous New York model," recalled Dan's sister Kathleen. "She was so witty and gracious." To the Broderick clan she seemed to be a very good match for Dan, and Frank and Marita Bisceglia were just as pleased with their prospective son-in-law. He was Catholic, he wasn't from a divorced family, and he was going to be a doctor—a good provider for Betty and the children that were bound to come along. Everything seemed to fit.

The young couple's large formal wedding took place on April 12, 1969, at the Immaculate Conception Church near the Bisceglia home. Still a virgin after numerous boyfriends and a long engagement, Betty was looking forward to an exquisitely romantic wedding night. According to her account, however, Dan was a hasty, thoughtless lover who virtually raped her on their first night together. Moreover, she claimed that immediately after they arrived at the Caribbean island of St. Thomas to honeymoon in the villa a friend had lent them, he dismissed the servants. Although Dan told her it was so they could be alone, it was Betty's opinion that Dan was sending her a message: She was now a wife, and wives were supposed to be housekeepers—even on their honeymoons.

Back in New York, the newlyweds moved into Dan's tiny dormitory room at the medical college, where they had to share a bathroom with the student next door. A month later, Betty found out she was pregnant. Her sheltered Catholic upbringing had left her completely ignorant on the matter of contraception, as well as other aspects of sex. Eight more pregnancies would follow in the next 10 years.

Betty had started teaching school after graduating from college four months before her marriage, and she stayed on the job until January 24, 1970, the day she gave birth to a baby girl. A dresser drawer was emptied out to serve as newborn Kimberly's crib, and Marita Bisceglia bought a layette for her at Saks Fifth Avenue. The young family was strapped for money, so soon after Kim was born Betty found work taking care of another couple's infant. As for Dan, he drove a taxi and worked in a medical laboratory at night. He wanted to handle the family finances himself, and Betty was happy enough to simply hand over whatever she earned to him.

By the time Dan got his degree, in 1970, he'd decided he didn't want to practice medicine. He would become a lawyer and take advantage of his medical background by specializing in malpractice and personal injury cases. At first unhappy at the thought of three more years of student poverty (the senior Brodericks and the Biscaglias agreed that the young couple would have to foot all the bills themselves) Betty came around to Dan's point of view that a hardscrabble present would pay off handsomely in the future.

Dan won admission to Harvard Law School, and he and Betty took a shabby basement apartment in Somerville, an industrial town outside Boston; they couldn't afford anything closer to the campus. Dan immersed himself in his studies and Betty, pregnant a second time, worked at a restaurant at night while Dan was

Dan, shown here in a photograph from the Cornell Medical College yearbook, earned his degree in 1970. Three years later he appeared in the Harvard Law School yearbook *(inset)* as a member of the graduating class.

Betty was both a mother and the family's principal breadwinner by the time this snapshot was taken, during Dan's stint at Harvard Law School.

at home studying. They had so little money that they qualified for food stamps.

Their second daughter, Lee, was born July 27, 1971. Trying to take care of two children and struggling to make ends meet stressed Betty beyond measure. Moreover, she felt that Dan was neglecting her. He often stayed out late at night, drinking with fellow law students and professors and forging professional contacts. But she apparently kept her anger under wraps, for Dan was taken aback when she sprang the news on him one day that she'd consulted a divorce attorney. Even then, she refused to spell out her complaints. According to Dan, she would only say, "If you don't know what I'm upset about, then you've got a real problem. I don't want to talk about it. I want to be divorced." Not that Dan thought everything was rosy. Years later, he would tell his close friend Brian Monaghan that he'd regretted his marriage to Betty while they were still honeymooning on St. Thomas. "He knew he had done the wrong thing," Monaghan remembered. "But he was Catholic and he was stuck."

For better or worse, Dan and Betty soldiered on. One

bright interlude in their law school years was the summer they spent in California while Dan was working for a Los Angeles law firm. One Saturday they settled their babies into their Volkswagen Beetle and drove around Mission Bay in San Diego. After two years of Boston winters, the bright sun, the ocean breezes, the miles of Pacific coastline, and the tanned surfers, joggers, and bicyclists enjoying the outdoor life enchanted Betty and Dan. They were determined to come back.

Soon after the Brodericks left California and went back east for Dan's final year at Harvard Law School, Betty found out that she was pregnant again. Although she'd been taught to regard abortion as a sin, she didn't think she could face having a third baby in three years with no money. When she told Dan she wanted an abortion, he was so upset that he broke down in tears. He promised he would make more time for her and the children and help out more at home, and Betty went through with the pregnancy.

The baby, a little boy, was born six weeks prematurely and died within a few days. About three months later Betty discovered that she was pregnant yet again. This time she had an abortion, and without consulting her husband beforehand. Dan cried when Betty told him what she'd done.

Dan graduated from Harvard in 1973 and he, Betty, and their two daughters were off to California, this time for good. He was exactly the kind of recruit the partners of the old, high-profile San Diego firm of Gray, Cary, Ames & Frye were looking for. He had earned his medical and law degrees at two of the country's most prestigious institutions. He was brilliant, brash, and ambitious. He was married to a beautiful, outgoing woman, and they'd already started a family. The partners of Gray, Cary liked family men. "They wooed us like royalty," Betty recalled. Nevertheless, Dan's starting salary was a modest $17,000 a year, so he and Betty had to settle for a commoner's existence for the time being. To boost their income Betty went to work, first as a part-time teacher and later as a hostess on the night shift at a steak house. During her teaching stint she got pregnant again and had her second abortion.

Gray, Cary got the lion's share of Dan's energy. He often worked late, logging 14-hour days and billing more hours than the other newly minted lawyers. That was the way to get ahead. It was assumed that family matters wouldn't intrude on work time. "Anybody who calls home is a wimp," a senior attorney advised Dan. Nor were wives' calls welcome, so Betty held the fort at home alone. After hours, the Brodericks' social life revolved around the firm. Dan's friends were almost all attorneys, and Betty's friends were their wives.

The Brodericks had been in California for two years when a defective television set sparked a fire that destroyed the modest house they'd been renting in Clairemont. The family escaped unharmed, and what at first seemed a disaster for them turned out to be a boon. With the large settlement they received from their insurance company, they had enough money for a down payment on a place of their own—a five-bedroom, three-bath house on Coral Reef Avenue on Mount Soledad in La Jolla. It had a three-car garage, a rooftop sundeck, and a Jacuzzi. The house wasn't in the choicest neighborhood in that glossy town, but it was several significant rungs up the ladder from Clairemont.

On February 23, 1976, some two months after their old house burned, Betty gave birth to Daniel T. Broderick IV. Dan's salary had increased enough that she could finally do what she'd always wanted—be a stay-at-home suburban housewife and mother. But she wasn't ready to quit working altogether, so she opened a backyard daycare center for neighborhood children. It was as much for her own pleasure as it was for making money, since she charged only a dollar an hour. The women who took advantage of her service were impressed at Betty's devotion to children. "Kids were her whole life. She was a complete Mother Earth type," one of the women observed. "Betty would do anything to make a little kid laugh." The earth mother was also a born teacher, and Ann Dick, a neighbor and friend whose child Betty cared for, noted approvingly that she "always had the latest in any toy that was educational." Kim and Lee were both in school by then, and Betty became a perennial and indefatigable volunteer.

As happy as she was to be able to devote herself full time to her family, Betty was dissatisfied with Dan. She craved more attention from him, and she wanted him to spend more time with the children. It wasn't strictly his responsibilities at Gray, Cary that were keeping Dan away from home. He often went to meetings of the county bar association, and he liked to relax after work at Dobson's, a downtown San Diego watering hole favored by lawyers, judges, politicians, and stockbrokers. He also joined the Friendly Sons of St. Patrick, an Irish-American society that carried a banner in the annual St. Patrick's Day parade and gathered to drink and sing sentimental Irish songs.

Betty, who enjoyed a glass of wine at meals but otherwise drank very little, began writing off Friday nights as a lost cause. Sometimes Dan didn't get home until four in the morning, and on at least one occasion Betty had to collect him from the San Diego jail's drunk tank. Saturday mornings often found a tired, grumpy, hungover Dan sitting outside in a lawn chair flipping through a lapful of legal briefs with a highlighter pen. But at least, Betty was forced to admit, he spent most Saturdays and Sundays at home. He would play with the kids a little, water the yard, and cut neat parallel swaths up and down the lawn with his power mower. Dan took a lot of pride in his lawn.

Nevertheless, there wasn't much communication be-

Chubby-faced Rhett, the baby in the Broderick family, snuggles between sisters Lee (*left*) and Kim. At right is Danny, the third of the four children.

tween husband and wife, except when they quarreled, and that was happening more and more. When Betty learned that one of the local Catholic churches was sponsoring a weekend-long retreat called Marriage Encounter, she persuaded Dan to take part. The program's purpose was to encourage honest dialogue, which the Brodericks sorely needed. Assigned to write letters to each other, Betty and Dan voiced their complaints and hopes and also defended themselves. Admitting that he had shortcomings as a husband and father, Dan nevertheless contended that he had "to earn a decent living, establish myself as a lawyer, acquire certain necessary possessions before I can indulge in the luxury of being an attentive, thoughtful person." Having more money, he argued, would erase many of their difficulties. "It will enable us to do a lot of things like travel to Europe that will be shared experiences we will, I hope, enjoy and never forget." He expressed the conviction that being able to provide lavishly for the family "will make me happy and secure and will make me a more loving and more lovable person."

Betty didn't dwell on money as a cure for their problems, instead lamenting their growing estrangement.

Dan was, she wrote, "the most important person I have in the whole universe, bar absolutely none, and I'd be lost without you." She felt frightened and insecure, as if she was "speeding along, wasting time, not seeing what is ahead—anticipating a terrible thing to happen to us at any second. Losing touch with the world. Unable to cling to anything secure." Betty suggested that things might improve between them if they would spend 10 minutes every day writing each other love letters. But she doubted that Dan would think much of her idea. "I honestly can't believe you'll do it," she wrote. "You're too tough, too cool, too hard to write a love letter every day and let me know you care." Whatever good effects the weekend retreat had on them soon dissipated, and the anxiety Betty had expressed about the future would in time seem prophetic.

Dan continued his professional ascent, and by 1978 he'd become Gray, Cary's star attorney in the areas of medical malpractice and personal injury—and the bane of the medical community. "If I ever get sick and need a doctor," he once joked to Betty, "be sure and get me out of town." As good as he was as a litigator, he had his detractors. One San Diego attorney said of Dan, "He's the

coldest man you'll ever meet, unless he wants something from you." Such remarks probably didn't give the ambitious Dan Broderick pause; to his way of thinking, being tough was part of the game.

Tired of making money for other people and earning a salary of only $32,500, Dan left Gray, Cary and opened his own law practice in 1978. In short order the Broderick income skyrocketed. Some of the cases Dan won involved multimillion-dollar verdicts, and a victory could mean a fee of $300,000—all for him, since he was the boss and sole practitioner. After a few such fat rewards, he took to calling himself the "Count du Money," and Betty gleefully told her friends about the "major money" Dan was bringing home.

It was an exhilarating change, and within a year the Brodericks could afford to construct a swimming pool in their backyard—an early sign of their new prosperity. There was something else to celebrate in 1979—the birth of their second son on February 15. He was named Rhett, after the flamboyant character played by Clark Gable in *Gone with the Wind,* Dan's favorite movie. Dan also named one of the family's cats Scarlett in honor of the film's heroine, and he hung a poster of Gable on the wall in his den.

Rhett would be the Brodericks' last child. Between Danny's birth and Rhett's, Betty had had two miscarriages, and she'd suffered from phlebitis while pregnant with Rhett. Deciding it was time to call it quits, she underwent a tubal ligation, with no protests from Dan.

If the money that was rolling in in such large sums didn't buy the happiness Dan had predicted during the 1976 Marriage Encounter retreat, it at least distracted the Brodericks from their marital problems. Always interested in clothes and the figure he cut, Dan began to indulge in expensive hand-tailored suits. His taste ran not to somber pinstripes but to lively pinks and greens and plaids that he carried off with aplomb. For black-tie affairs such as the annual Blackstone Ball, a fundraiser obligatory for up-and-coming San Diego lawyers, Dan fitted himself out with a top hat and a black cape lined with red silk.

To enhance his image further Dan took speech lessons, traded his glasses for contacts, and had plastic surgery on his nose. Rail-thin in earlier years, he had filled out by his middle thirties, and the added weight was be-

coming. Altogether, he looked as successful as he was.

According to Betty, her husband was very vain about his appearance and "couldn't pass a mirror" without checking himself. In the mornings, she said, "Dan got up and tweezed his eyebrows and puffed his hair. I was never allowed in the master bedroom while he was doing his toilette." However critical she was about Dan's habits, Betty reveled in their wealth. She initiated expensive renovations of the kitchen and the children's playroom and became a welcome customer at La Jolla's most fashionable boutiques; after a while she thought nothing of paying $2,000 for an outfit. "By 1982, my budget was unlimited," Betty reminisced wistfully six years later. Dan still took care of family money matters, as he had from the early days of their marriage. "I didn't do bills," she noted. "I didn't have any interest in money beyond spending it."

And the spending went on. The Brodericks joined the La Jolla Beach and Tennis Club and the Fairbanks Ranch Country Club, and several times a year Dan and Betty threw a dinner dance for as many as 200 guests. At fashionable charity events, they could be counted on to host a large table of friends and business associates. Photographs of the sleek couple often appeared on the society pages of the local newspapers, the *La Jolla Light* and the *San Diego Union.*

At home the Brodericks' masks fell away. Wilma Engel, a friend and neighbor, said Betty seemed like a different person around Dan. She was quiet and serious and proper, repressing her usual, sometimes manic, sense of humor. "She almost seemed afraid of him," Engel remarked. She also reported that when Dan was due home Betty would "run around the house, picking up all the children's stuff because she said Dan hated to have it underfoot." The conflict between the couple was obvious to an English teenager who spent the summer of 1980 with the Broderick family as a mother's helper. In a letter to her parents the girl observed that Dan habitually got home so late that the family almost never had dinner together. She called him "cold and unfriendly" and said that Betty sometimes cried about the evenings Dan spent "tippling with the lads."

The children couldn't ignore their parents' unhappiness, and the older they grew the more sensitive they became to it. Kim would say later, "I never heard either of

The Brodericks were regulars on the San Diego legal community's glittery social circuit. A top hat was Dan's trademark on formal occasions.

them say, 'I love you,' to each other. I never saw an affectionate kiss." Even with his children, Dan had a hard time expressing his love—except, Kim said, when he was drunk. The children knew to stay out of their father's way when he came home from the office in a bad mood. Danny and Rhett seemed especially vulnerable to his moods, perhaps because they were younger than the girls. Maria Montes, the family's full-time housekeeper, noticed how frightened and silent the boys often were when Dan was around. "He would just scream and say 'sit down' and they would," she remembered.

Betty and Dan made some attempts to keep their differences private, often fighting behind their locked bedroom door. Nevertheless, the children repeatedly witnessed their parents' violent, sometimes physical, eruptions of anger. Kim was present when Betty picked up a stereo and threw it at Dan, and on another occasion the girl saw her mother launch a ketchup bottle at him when he was late for dinner. Dan had his own furious outbursts, several of which writer Bella Stumbo describes in her saga of the Brodericks, *Until the Twelfth of Never.* At one time or another Dan battered a malfunctioning lawn mower with a hammer, hurled an empty aquarium off the balcony, and ripped a sliding glass door off its track.

The specter of divorce began to haunt the house. Dan would say later that Betty threatened to end the marriage hundreds of times. Perhaps he exaggerated, but more than once Betty declared to Kim that she was going to get a divorce. "Who are you going to live with?" she would ask her daughter.

But that was just talk. Unhappy though she was, Betty Broderick was a woman who'd married forever. And Dan Broderick seemed just as averse to divorce—Catholic and stuck, as his friend Brian Monaghan said.

But that was before Linda Kolkena.

In the summer of 1983 Betty took the four children on a month-long camping trip around the West. Dan chose to stay in San Diego and work, though he joined them for two weekends, at the family's ski condo in Keystone, Colorado, and in Flathead, Montana. On both occasions Dan was moody, short with the kids, and gruff with Betty. She brushed it off, telling herself he was preoccupied with some professional problem.

But Dan wasn't any mellower when Betty and the children returned. The day after she got home, as she and Dan were driving to a wedding in their Jaguar, he dropped a bombshell, telling her that he was unhappy with their life together. "He said our house was tacky,

During a vacation she and Dan took to Europe in the summer of 1984, Betty tried to put a good face on their crumbling relationship.

our friends were boring, and I was old, fat, boring, ugly, and stupid," Betty recalled. It was a direct, personal affront, and one that Betty thought she in no way deserved. At 35, she was still slim and pretty, and few people would have called her boring or stupid: On the contrary, she was bright, well-read, lively, a good conversationalist. Something was very wrong, but Betty didn't know exactly what.

Soon afterward, in September, Dan announced to Betty that he'd hired Linda Kolkena as his office assistant. Betty was instantly on the alert: Kolkena, she knew, was a receptionist who worked for Dan and several other lawyers on his floor. Betty had first seen Kolkena at a cocktail party earlier that year, and she'd heard what Dan had said about the tall, willowy blonde to another man that evening: "Isn't she beautiful?" Dan wasn't a womanizer, and it was out of character for him to make such a comment. The remark had made Betty faintly uneasy. She'd seen Linda Kolkena a second time, when Dan's parents were in town and Betty had taken them to watch their son in action at court. Linda was there, following Dan's performance with an admiring gaze. She was wearing, Betty later recalled snidely, a "little navy chino suit from J. C. Penney's." She went on, "She had on these little, spaghetti-strap heels. Clickety-clack, clickety-clack, whenever she walked." A tacky bimbo, in Betty's estimation.

But a dangerous one. Several friends reported seeing Dan at lunch or having drinks with a tall, attractive blonde who looked young enough to be his daughter. Betty felt sure the unfamiliar swimsuit her housekeeper, Maria Montes, had found beside the family's pool while she and the children were away camping belonged to Linda; Dan had brought her to the house. And now he was paying her $30,000 a year.

Betty gave Dan an ultimatum: "Get rid of the little bitch by October 1 or get out." He refused to fire Kolkena and told Betty she was imagining things. "This is my house," he said. "If you don't like things my way, you can get out." It was a stalemate.

When Dan came home with a new red Corvette, Betty was convinced that her husband, who would be turning 39 on November 22, was having a midlife crisis. "A lot of these attorneys in town, they all have affairs with their secretaries or these young girls," she told her friend Candy Westbrook. "But they don't divorce their wife for them." Betty tried hard to convince herself that Linda was out of her league. "I am prettier, smarter, classier," Betty wrote in her diary. "She is a dumb, uneducated tramp with no background or education or talent."

Dan continued to deny there was anything between him and Linda Kolkena and, according to Betty, he accused his wife of being "crazy" and "delusional." Nevertheless, his harsh words haunted her like a terrible refrain—old, fat, boring, ugly, and stupid. Thirty-five wasn't really old, but at 22 Kolkena was undeniably young and had all the voluptuous advantages of youth. Determined to make Dan eat at least some of his words, Betty began to lose weight, and she had a face peel to rejuvenate her complexion. And she started letting her hair grow out; Kolkena's hair was long, just as Betty's had been when she was 22.

On Dan's 39th birthday, Betty made her valiant effort to reclaim Dan's affection by romancing him at his office and ended up setting fire to thousands of dollars worth of his clothes and scorching the lawn he took such pride in. When he got home that night at eight o'clock, Kim recalled, he went to the backyard and "picked up the few pieces that weren't burned or ruined." He didn't even raise his voice. The family sat down together for a birthday dinner featuring two of Dan's favorite foods— roast beef and homemade chocolate cake. Then, according to Kim, "they went to bed, like everything was normal." But Betty feared that nothing was normal, even though Dan tried to convince her he'd been at a deposition all afternoon; she said later that she'd "caught him with his pants down. If he was innocent and he came home and his nutsy wife had burned his clothes, wild horses couldn't have kept him there. He was as guilty as anything." And he'd pay for it.

On a trip to New York City in late 1983, Betty found Dan calling Linda from a pay phone in the lobby of their hotel. The following day she went shopping on Fifth Avenue and bought a pink Bob Mackie evening gown on sale for $7,000. She also came away from a high-fashion shoe salon with several pairs of $250 sandals. Betty had been an avid shopper before, but this was different—this was getting even.

As the months wore on and her suspicions of Dan's infidelity mounted, she snapped up merchandise in posh

At Thanksgiving in 1984 the fashion-conscious Brodericks turned the girls out in Yves St. Laurent dresses and clothed the boys in outfits by Ralph Lauren.

shops as if she were picking up bargains in flea markets. She bought more clothes than she could ever possibly wear, by designers such as Oscar de la Renta and Adolpho, First Lady Nancy Reagan's favorite. Many of her purchases she simply stuffed into the closet with their price tags still attached. An early riser, Betty got some of her buying done before breakfast via phone calls to the East Coast, where stores were usually open by 7 a.m. California time. Dan confiscated Betty's credit cards, but that didn't stop her—she knew the account numbers and expiration dates by heart. Just to spite him, she ordered a $10,000 diamond-studded watch from a La Jolla jewelry store and had the bill sent to Dan at his office. In time one of Betty's friends would refer to her punitive, out-of-control extravagance as "alcoholic spending."

Dan was spending a lot, too, but he did his best to keep certain expenditures secret. While they were vacationing in England in the summer of 1984 on what Betty had hoped would be a second honeymoon, he had roses, a color television, and emerald jewelry delivered to Linda Kolkena for her birthday. He'd lent his Corvette to her while he was out of town, and later that year he gave her a Toyota convertible. When Kolkena bought a condominium, he cosigned the loan. They shared a MasterCard, with Linda's name listed below Dan's.

But it would be months before Betty had to face such indisputable evidence of Dan's unfaithfulness. For the time being, she was buffeted by her suspicions and his insistence that she was wrong to accuse him of violating their marriage vows. More than anything, she wanted to believe him, but that was becoming more and more difficult. Sometimes she thought Dan was trying to maneuver her into suing him for divorce. In retrospect Betty would say sourly that breaking up the family "didn't fit into his self-image as Mr. Wonderful, Mr. Ethical, Mr. Catholic family man."

Still, Betty tried to convince herself that Dan might be nearing the end of his midlife crisis. Without a squawk he'd agreed to buy a condominium she wanted as a family weekend retreat at Warner Springs Ranch, a nearby mountain resort. She'd also persuaded him to visit a physician to discuss the possibility of having her tubal

ligation reversed; perhaps a baby would do the trick, restore their relationship, banish Linda Kolkena. But the prognosis wasn't encouraging; there wouldn't be another pregnancy.

So Betty set her sights on something else that smacked of family togetherness. She and Dan had been talking for a long time about buying a new, much grander house in a better neighborhood. Before they could sell the Coral Reef Avenue house, however, Dan said they'd have to get its cracked foundation repaired. It was a major job best done without the family living there, so the Brodericks moved into a rental house.

On Christmas Day, 1984, the Brodericks were still in the rental house, and before the day was out, Dan and Betty were more at odds than ever. She had expected him to give her something very special, very expensive, to make up for what he'd put her through over the last year and more. But his gift to her was what she termed a "rinky-dinky little ring." She was furious. As the children watched, Betty threw the ring at him and said it wasn't even worth the gas it would take to return it.

Betty would have been even more upset had she

Betty later crossed out Dan's face on the family's 1984 Christmas portrait. It would be the last in which both parents appeared with the children.

known of a decision Linda Kolkena made that day, one that involved both Dan Broderick and Steve Kelley, a young, handsome editorial cartoonist for the *San Diego Union*. Linda had been dating Kelley at the same time she was seeing Dan Broderick. According to Steve, Linda "talked all the time about her boss, what an incredible guy he was." Like Betty, Kelley realized that Linda must be romantically involved with Dan when he saw her luxurious office and the photograph of her employer on horseback, looking, Kelley said later, "like a knight in shining armor." When he challenged Linda, she admitted that she and Dan often had sex at her condominium at lunchtime. Despite her confession, however, Steve didn't want to lose Linda. He was in love, and he had asked her to marry him. But he had also demanded that she decide between him and Dan Broderick by Christmas. To Kelley's sorrow, Linda declined his proposal and chose Dan.

Two months later, on February 28, 1985, Dan told Betty he was moving back to their house on Coral Reef Avenue—alone. According to Betty, he merely said he needed "more space" and denied that his decision had anything to do with Linda Kolkena. That wasn't the way Dan remembered what went on between him and Betty that night. He insisted he was honest about his reasons for leaving: "It's been bad too long between us. This is not going to work." By his own admission, however, he said nothing about wanting a divorce. Perhaps he was still too much of a Catholic to face where he'd been heading for years.

But Dan wasn't quite gone. On St. Patrick's Day, not three weeks after he'd left Betty, he spent the night with her at the rental house. She thought her husband would return to her for good.

Nothing of the sort happened. As the days crept by and Dan stayed away, Betty tried to put a good face on things and hide her humiliation and sense of betrayal from friends. But the stress generated by Dan's absence was becoming intolerable and, on the Saturday before Easter, Betty cracked. Kim would say later that her mother "lost it" when she asked her to drive a friend home. Ordering 15-year-old Kim to pack her bags and not bothering to call Dan, Betty drove her daughter over to the Coral Reef Avenue house and left her there. Dan said later, "I came home and found Kim in this empty house, crying. I couldn't believe Bets had done that to her own child." Nine-year-old Danny's turn came the next day, and Lee and Rhett followed six weeks later. "They were hysterical—holding onto her, crying and screaming, 'Don't leave us here,'" Kim remembered. Unmoved, Betty told her children, "Your dad's not going to get away with this. Let him try to deal with four kids."

When Dan tried to talk to her, Betty declared, "They're yours. You want to be apart from me. Well, see what it's like raising a family by yourself."

Betty's friends were aghast that a woman who'd been so committed a mother would dump her children on the doorstep of a father who'd walked out on the family and who spent a workaholic 14 hours or more at the office each day. Betty, however, felt what she'd done was perfectly justified. "No way I'm going to be a single mother with four children," she declared.

If Betty had hoped her tactic of saddling Dan with the children would make him recognize that they needed a mother and a father in a reunited family, she was mistaken. Whatever regard he'd had for her as a competent, loving mother vanished. In his eyes, Betty had proved

herself unfit to raise the children. He would manage it himself, with the help of a housekeeper. If Dan realized that he'd done something just as upsetting to the children when he left the family, he didn't let on.

Betty went to the house on Coral Reef Avenue frequently to see her children. One day in June she arrived to discover that Dan had undertaken some redecorating. She was infuriated that he would change anything in the house they'd owned and lived in together for almost 10 years without consulting her first, and she went on a rampage. She shattered a full-length mirror, smashed a hole in a bedroom wall, and sprayed black Rustoleum paint around the master bedroom, a bathroom, and the family room.

Dan feared that Betty's emotional attachment to the family home would mean more such episodes. The solution seemed obvious: They would move ahead with their plans to sell the house and buy places of their own. Betty went house hunting and, with a $140,000 down payment from Dan, bought a $650,000 house with a spectacular ocean view in La Jolla Shores, one of the town's most desirable neighborhoods. She moved in in July, telling people that she and Dan had big plans: They were going to tear the house down and build a multimillion dollar residence on the site. In the meantime, she initiated some outdoor improvements, including a new pool house, a putting green, and a volleyball court, for the enjoyment of the reunited family she envisioned.

The house wasn't Betty's only major expense in the first months after Dan's departure. She'd been spending with abandon for such extravagances as a $40,000 lynx coat, and by late summer her credit-card balances had swelled to gigantic proportions. Determined to put a stop to her binges, Dan made an appointment with Betty. It apparently didn't occur to her that they might be meeting as adversaries. She had reconciliation on her mind, and she dressed up for the occasion and resolved to be pleasant and agreeable. Dan, however, was all business. He said he'd pay off her current credit-card debts and would continue to take care of her taxes, insurance, and country-club dues. To cover all of her other expenses—mortgage, food, clothes, trips—he said he would send her a check for $9,036 each month. For the life Betty had become accustomed to, the sum was a pittance—her mortgage payment alone would eat up half

The campaign of vandalism Betty waged against Dan included shattering a glass door at the family home with a wine bottle *(above)*. Despite her anger, she could still flash a cheerful smile for the camera *(right)*.

of it—but that evening she was determined to avoid a quarrel. Besides, Dan had always handled money matters. She agreed to the amount, but it would soon become one more bone of bitter contention.

On September 23, 1985, just weeks after he'd put Betty on a budget, Dan filed for divorce. He was soon subjected to another of Betty's rampages. In the kitchen during a visit to the children, she saw a Boston cream pie on the counter—Dan's favorite. In answer to Betty's query, the housekeeper told her that Linda Kolkena had made it. Betty appropriated the pie and carried it upstairs to Dan's bedroom, where she smeared it on the bedspread, the carpet, a mirror, and some of his sweaters and shirts.

Her action violated a standard order the divorce court judge had issued barring estranged spouses from harassing each other. Dan saw opportunity in the pie assault, and he went to court to request a temporary restraining order forbidding Betty to come within 100 yards of his person or property without his permission. If she violated it, she risked criminal contempt charges and jail. Before a judge had a chance to issue the restraining order, however, Betty made another assault on the Coral Reef Avenue house, shattering a glass door with a bottle.

After two years of telling Betty she was imagining things, Dan went to see her one evening in October and admitted his affair with Linda Kolkena. He was, he de-

clared, in love with her. Betty collapsed in hysterics so extreme that Dan feared she might attempt suicide. But she collected herself and, several days later, went to Los Angeles to see Daniel Jaffe, a well-seasoned divorce lawyer. She'd already scoured San Diego for someone to represent her and claimed that the ones with the best qualifications had all declined to take her case because they knew Dan. On her first trip to Los Angeles to consult with Jaffe, she assured him that Dan would send him $10,000 as a retainer. After their meeting she celebrated by buying a used maroon Jaguar for $15,000. Back in La Jolla, she took a neighbor, Brian Forbes, for a spin. As they were driving around, he recalled, Betty remarked that she'd "like to shoot Dan's balls off." She laughed when Forbes protested. "Oh, well," she said, "they're too small to hit anyway."

Daniel Jaffe found Betty Broderick a frustrating client, for she repeatedly violated the restraining order against her. In a series of violent forays to the Coral Reef Avenue house, she broke a window with an umbrella, smashed lamps, ripped a sliding closet door off its track, upended a television set, and threw a rock at Dan's car. As the year drew to a close, Jaffe wrote to Betty, "This wanton-damage nonsense has to cease. I cannot spend what talents I have and what little time I have trying to justify to a court the unjustifiable." He urged her to seek psychiatric help. She disregarded his advice.

Christmas of 1984 had been miserable, but at least Betty had been with her family. This year she was alone for the holidays. Dan had taken the kids to a ski resort in Park City, Utah, where they'd all gone together in better times. Worse, Linda Kolkena was with them. It seemed to Betty that Dan was now flaunting his affair as brazenly as he'd once denied it. She interpreted the switch as his latest tactic in a long campaign to drive her crazy: If she were to lose her mind, every-

body would agree that Dan had a good reason for divorcing her, and he wouldn't have to worry that his image would be tarnished.

Before Dan and the children came home from Utah, Betty went to their house alone. She found a Christmas present with Linda's name on the tag and ripped it up. When Dan saw the mess, he lodged another complaint against her.

Linda and Dan's relationship was now in the open, and in January 1986 she became part of the household, moving with Dan and the children into an imposing Georgian-style house he'd bought in Marston Hills, an area near downtown San Diego. He and Betty had agreed on an asking price for the Coral Reef Avenue house, and they'd gotten several good offers. She turned all of them down, even though Daniel Jaffe had negotiated for her to receive more than half of the proceeds. He warned Betty that Dan could legally sell the house himself if she wouldn't cooperate.

That was exactly what happened. On February 4 Betty got a phone call from Jaffe, who told her the house had been sold. Her parents and a friend from Canada were visiting, and she was preparing pork roast and mashed potatoes for dinner. Saying she'd be right back, Betty jumped into her Chevy Suburban and drove to Marston Hills boiling over with rage. When Dan arrived home an hour later, Betty was there waiting for him, but he wouldn't discuss the transaction. "Talk to my lawyer," he said. "Get out of my house." Betty drove back to La Jolla, but instead of going home to get dinner on the table she went to the empty Coral Reef Avenue house, doused the hall carpet with gasoline, and lit a match. Before the fire was well started, however, she realized how stupid it was to burn down her own house and stamped out the flames.

Betty's fury hadn't abated, however, and she headed back to Dan's. She sped up the driveway, hurtled across the porch, and slammed the Chevy into the front door, knocking it off its hinges. Dan, Kim, Lee, and Danny were all in the kitchen when they heard the crash. "It sounded like a chain saw and everything started shaking," remembered Kim. Dan and Lee ran toward the sound of the crash, while Danny and Kim rushed out the back door and hid in a ravine behind the house.

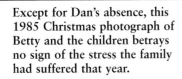

Except for Dan's absence, this 1985 Christmas photograph of Betty and the children betrays no sign of the stress the family had suffered that year.

151

As Dan reached the car and flung open the driver's door, Lee saw her mother lunge for a butcher's knife under the front seat. Dan grabbed Betty and pulled her out of the car, and she hit him on the head with her brass key ring. Lee rushed over and tried to separate her parents, but Dan shoved his daughter out of the way and hit Betty in the chest with his fist. She fell back gasping for breath, then became hysterical. Dan summoned the police, who wrestled Betty into a straitjacket. Kim rounded the house just in time to see her mother being taken away in the backseat of the cruiser. "Mom stuck her tongue out at me," Kim recalled.

Betty spent the next three days in a mental hospital, hurt and angered that her parents didn't visit her and left for New York before she was released. To the doctors who examined her Betty denied being suicidal and said of Dan, "I'm not crazy, he is. I am madder than hell and I want to kill him for being lied to and cheated." Labeled "histrionic," "narcissistic," and "immature" in her hospital record, she was classified as a borderline personality, meaning that her sense of identity was extremely shaky. Betty Broderick didn't care for such terms.

Shortly after Betty was released, Daniel Jaffe resigned as her attorney. He'd grown weary of her refusal to follow his advice, and he was also unhappy that he'd never received his $10,000 retainer. Although Dan hadn't agreed to pay it, Jaffe had assumed he would, since it is customary in divorce cases for the income-earning partner to pay the spouse's attorney fees up front and to seek reimbursement later under the property settlement. Betty subsequently contended that Dan had withheld the money because he didn't want a first-rate lawyer like Jaffe representing her.

Whatever Dan's reason may have been, in the four months between Jaffe's resignation and the Brodericks' divorce hearing on the 16th of July, Betty didn't get a new lawyer. In fact, she didn't even show up for the hearing. The judge granted Dan a divorce by default and awarded him sole temporary custody of the children. Betty was allowed to see the children only with his approval, and she was reminded that she was not to come within 100 yards of Dan's house. At Dan's request, the property settlement, alimony, and a final decision on custody were bifurcated, a legalism meaning that they would be settled at a later hearing. Until there was a rul-

ing on alimony, Betty would be at Dan's mercy financially; he could reduce or even cut off her monthly allowance if he wanted to, leaving her nothing to live on except what she was earning from the part-time job she'd taken at a La Jolla art gallery. She denounced the bifurcation order as "bifornication."

Betty herself had handed Dan an extremely effective weapon to use at the divorce hearing, and it was one he would wield over and over—her obscene language. Her friends couldn't remember her using lewd terms and curse words until her marriage was nearing collapse; then foul language started popping out of her mouth, an audible symptom of her growing rage and loss of self-esteem—and, Dan argued, a measure of her mental instability. In the months after he left, Betty began leaving obscene messages on Dan's answering machine, and in the fall of 1985 he'd gotten a restraining order in an attempt to make her stop. She wasn't deterred. At the hearing, Dan presented transcripts of messages and conversations larded with vulgarities that he'd taped with the answering machine at his house. Linda had recorded the greeting on the machine, so whenever Betty called she was automatically reminded that Linda was living with Dan and the children. "Don't you have a toilet to live in of your own?" Betty snarled in a message to her successor. "Idiot, answer the phone," Betty commanded Dan in another message; "The whore won't mind if you answer the phone."

"Whore" was Betty's mildest label for Linda, and she didn't hesitate to use four-letter words in her conversations with Rhett, then seven years old, and Danny, 10. Besides weakening her case for getting custody of the children, her vulgarities provided Dan with an opening to attack her financially. Shortly after the divorce he wrote Betty: "I am tired of finding messages full of obscenities. You are violating a court order. From now on, when you leave a message or call and use any vulgar or obscene language, you will be fined $100 per offensive word. These fines will be withheld from your support checks." A man of his word, he docked her September allowance because she referred to Linda with what he called "a disgusting and unseemly word" during a telephone conversation.

Steeper fines followed as Dan expanded them to punish violations of the restraining order against coming onto his property. It cost Betty $250 to step into his yard, $500 to cross the threshold of the house. Dan also announced that she'd be fined $1,000 whenever she picked the kids up for an unscheduled visit.

In October, Dan didn't send Betty a cent. He wrote her a note explaining that her various offenses had wiped out her entire $9,036 allowance for the month and left her $1,300 in the red.

Betty read the letter and drove straight to Marston Hills, where Dan and Linda were dressing for the Blackstone Ball, the legal community's annual black-tie affair. It was a special night for him, since he'd just become president of the San Diego County Bar Association. "What am I supposed to do? How am I supposed to live?" she demanded. Dan gave her 10 seconds to get off his property. When she didn't budge, he called the police and had her arrested.

While Dan was at the ball basking in the presidential limelight, Betty spent the evening in the Las Colinas Women's Detention Facility. It was Bradley T. Wright who came to sign for her release from jail. Six-foot-three, blue-eyed, tan, and seven years younger than Betty, Brad was an avid sailor with a ready smile. He owned a fence-construction business. He and Betty had met earlier in 1986 at the home of a neighbor of hers in La Jolla Shores and had hit it off immediately, finding in each other an easy companionship. "He was incredibly supportive," remembered Betty's friend Vicki Currie. "He was always there waiting to take her places and help with the kids."

Inevitably, Betty compared this attractive, caring man to Dan. He didn't measure up. According to another of Betty's friends, Helen Pickard, "She would never accept him as he was, because he wasn't the lawyer, doctor, Notre Dame, Cornell, Harvard background. That was important to Betty," Pickard said.

But there were other factors that muted Betty's attachment to Brad. For one thing, the difference in their ages

Exterior and interior photos document the damage done when Betty rammed her car into the front door of Dan's newly purchased house in San Diego.

embarrassed Betty. "I didn't want to be the other half of the midlife joke," she once explained in an interview, recalling her view of Dan's infidelity. And then there was the matter of sex. Even though Dan had been gone for a year by the time Betty and Brad met, she wasn't ready to forget her marriage vows. Not until after the divorce would she sleep with Brad. He jokingly nicknamed her the Dinosaur because of her old-fashioned notions about sexual behavior. Even though she enjoyed sex with Brad, Betty later said she'd never felt as comfortable with him as she had with Dan "because Brad wasn't my husband. At least with Dan, even if it wasn't much fun, I felt like it was *right*."

As fond as she was of her new boyfriend, the focus of Betty's emotional life was Dan; she couldn't shake her obsession with him, even after he'd demonstrated his enmity by slashing her allowance and having her jailed. Those events did, however, underscore how desperately Betty needed a lawyer, and she renewed the search. After a couple of false starts—including a consultation with a big-time Los Angeles lawyer who demanded, as an on-the-spot retainer, the gold and diamond necklace she wore to his office—she hired divorce attorney Tricia Smith. In February of 1987 Smith secured official, court-ordered support for Betty amounting to $16,100 a month—a total of $193,200 a year. It was better than $9,036, but far short of the minimum $25,000 a month that Betty had wanted. Dan's personal monthly income at the time was more than $100,000 and she thought she deserved much more than she was getting.

Smith's major ongoing task was to help Betty fight the numerous contempt charges Dan brought against her for violating the various restraining orders. In the first six months of 1987 alone, Betty would receive 37 different notices and legal filings.

In March, Betty and Dan met separately with psychologist Ruth Roth, who'd been appointed by the court to mediate the custody dispute. Betty didn't make a good impression on Roth, who later described her as "the angriest person I ever saw." She referred to Dan and Linda by her customary obscenities and stated flatly that Dan had been and would remain hers. "I'm not going to be a single parent of four kids. He'll die first," she told Roth. The psychologist took Betty seriously and telephoned Dan to warn him of her threat.

The counseling sessions had no effect on Betty's behavior. That same month, Dan taped 34 minutes of a damning conversation between Betty and 11-year-old Danny. When she asked him where Linda was, he replied, "Nowhere, Mom. I don't know." Her response: "It's not time to come over and screw him yet, huh?" Danny repeatedly begged his mother not to use "bad words" and pointed out, in a pitifully mature way, that his father wouldn't let the children go to her house if she didn't stop. Both of them began to cry:

DANNY: You're going to get the kids that want to go to your house, forever, if you just stop saying stupid bad words! Mom, will you just stop? Mom?

BETTY: I hate Daddy.

DANNY: It's not going to do any good to keep saying bad words.

BETTY: We had such a nice family.

DANNY: I know, but you're just going to make it worse by saying bad words, Mom.

BETTY: We had the best family in the whole world and we were all so happy. All the kids and me were all so happy.

DANNY: I know, and we'll all be a lot happier if you just stop saying bad words.

BETTY: You tell that slimeball—

DANNY: See what I mean, Mom? You're saying it right now, and you'd better stop or else you're just going to make everything worse.

BETTY: You tell that slimeball to act like a man.

As Danny had predicted, Betty did make everything worse. Two months later, she was sentenced to 25 days in the Las Colinas Women's Detention Facility for five different counts of contempt of court. Released after serving six days of her sentence—Tricia Smith had successfully argued for a suspension of the rest—Betty sent the judge a lengthy diatribe on the failures of the judicial system along with photocopied dictionary definitions of "prostitute" and one of the four-letter words that had helped put her in jail in the first place.

Dan defended himself for having had Betty arrested and jailed. "What else can you do?" he said to two reporters from *The Reader*, a weekly San Diego news magazine. "Repeated warnings and she would come back and do it again. And pretty soon the judge had to say, 'This is a law-abiding society. You cannot act like this.

Dan Broderick's recent election as president of the county bar association put him in the spotlight with Linda Kolkena at the San Diego legal community's 1986 Blackstone Ball.

Making no secret of their relationship, Dan and Linda often appeared together at San Diego nightspots and in the society pages of the local newspapers.

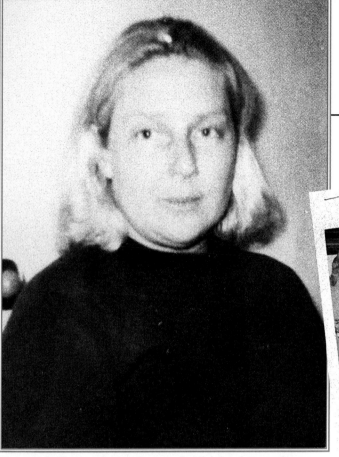

Overweight and ill-groomed by 1988 *(left)*, Betty claimed she got hate mail from Linda—including a picture of Linda and Dan from a newsletter, with a nasty note attached *(below)*.

Stop it.' " His tough stand seemed to bother him, at least enough to make him ask the judge at a contempt hearing that took place in May 1988 to fine Betty instead of giving her a jail term. In a later interview with the same reporters Dan said, "All I want is peace and quiet. She's filled with hatred. I left her and she's mad about it. It's not going to end until one of us is gone."

The year 1988 was all downhill for Betty Broderick. She was completely obsessed with Dan, with Dan and Linda, with what they did, where they went, whom they saw. She gained 60 pounds and ballooned from a size eight to a size 18. Her skin broke out in blotches. Stress made her unconsciously clench her jaws so tight that it gave her headaches, and she was worn out from insomnia. She cried in public and talked endlessly about Dan's heartless treatment of her. She showed her friends ads for wrinkle creams and brochures for weight-loss clinics that she claimed Linda Kolkena had sent to her anonymously. And she made them look once again at a page from a San Diego legal publication showing a photograph of Dan and Linda at an August 1986 party honoring him as president-elect of the county bar association. The photograph bore a typewritten barb: "It must KILL you to see these two happy together . . .

EAT YOUR HEART OUT, BITCH!!!" Linda had sent that, too, Betty asserted.

A few of her friends loyally stuck by Betty, but many more avoided her. Later on she would insist that she hadn't cared what people thought of her or how her reputation had suffered. "There's nothing more liberating than to realize that you don't have to live up to anything anymore," she said. In her opinion the six days she'd served in jail for contempt in 1987 had destroyed her image "so I didn't have to pretend anymore. I had nothing left to lose."

When she wasn't rehashing the wrongs done to her

with sympathetic listeners, Betty filled page after page in her diary. "There is no better reason in the world for someone to kill than to protect their home, possessions, and my family from attack and destruction," one entry reads. Addressing Dan, she went on: "You have attacked and destroyed me, my home, my possessions, my family. You're the sickest person alive. A law degree does not give you the license to kill and destroy, nor does it give you immunity from punishment. No one will mourn you." Her rage, unlike her image, was intact.

At times Betty was so overwhelmed by depression that she remained in her darkened bedroom for days, brooding, weeping, and turning the pages of photo albums. Pictures of her childhood, her wedding, her children at Disneyland or at the Colorado ski condo, the family home on Coral Reef Avenue—each snapshot brought back memories she hoped would cheer her. They didn't. She rummaged through boxes of Mother's Day cards, anniversary cards, and the children's school papers. They saddened her.

It didn't shock Betty when she learned that Dan, surrounded by a cheering crowd, had proposed to Linda on bended knee at happy hour at Dobson's and had given her an emerald-and-diamond engagement ring. Betty filed it away as another public insult, another assault on her wounded vanity. In an attempt to improve her spirits in the wake of the engagement, she had her forehead and her eyes lifted and the loose skin on her abdomen removed. "It made me feel better for an hour," she told her friend Candy Westbrook. Westbrook felt bad for Betty: "She was so completely nuts by then. Just nuts."

While she recuperated from the plastic surgery, Betty made notes on her legal strategy for the final divorce hearing, which was scheduled to begin December 27, 1988. Betty's most recent lawyer, Tricia Smith, had quit in desperation over her client's unpredictable behavior. Betty had decided she'd represent herself.

Not having a lawyer to defend her at the time of the initial divorce hearing in 1986 had had disastrous consequences, and this time Betty fared no better. Between Dan and his lawyer, she was totally outmaneuvered. There weren't any reporters or other outsiders to witness the proceedings; Betty had acquiesced to Dan's request to have the court records sealed in order to protect the children's privacy. The request also served Dan's in-

terests, since he didn't want his personal affairs to be aired in public. According to his arithmetic, by the time he subtracted taxes, overhead, Betty's allowance, and so on from his $1,332,444 income in 1985, the year they separated and the year he had picked as a basis for arriving at a property settlement and alimony, Dan claimed he had only $22,600 a month left over. Betty accepted his self-serving calculations without protest, even though she was seeking monthly alimony of $25,000 and Dan's monthly income by late 1988 was well in excess of $100,000.

The questions Betty directed at her ex-husband in court were painfully inept and amateurish, but she was far more concerned with exposing his moral shortcomings than with finances. Thus she asked him: "You're totally unaware of Danny and Rhett looking in the door at Linda and you in bed with her legs up in the air many times?" Dan denied such occurrences, just as he denied her claim that Linda paraded around the house in see-through nightgowns or that he drank too much and had smoked marijuana in medical school.

The judge at the hearing questioned all four children before making his decision about custody. Twelve-year-old Danny said he wanted to live with his mother and thought about it every day. Rhett, aged 9, felt the same way, and when the judge asked him why, the boy replied, "Because Mom is there when I need her." Despite the temporary custody arrangement, Lee was then living with Betty and wanted to stay there. The 17-year-old said of her father, "He does not like to be around me." Only Kim said she preferred living with her father, but at 18 she was beyond the court's jurisdiction.

In early March the judge announced his decision. He awarded custody of Danny and Rhett to Dan, with Betty getting visitation rights on alternating weekends and holidays and for one month in the summer. Custody of Lee went to Betty, and Dan was ordered to pay monthly child support of $1,500. As to the property settlement, Betty got her $240,000 half of Dan's pension fund, which meant little because she wouldn't be able to draw on it until she was 65 years old; $127,000 from the sale of the family home on Coral Reef Avenue; and sole ownership of the Warner Springs Ranch condominium. Her alimony was set at $16,100 a month, subject to further order of the court. From painful past experience Betty well knew what that foretold—more legal attacks from Dan.

The separate cash award of $28,606.02 shocked and infuriated Betty; it was a tiny fraction of the tax-free $1 million she'd sought. Under California community property law, Dan had been allowed to deduct every penny he'd advanced Betty since their separation; her legal expenses alone amounted to more than $250,000. He also deducted half of the steep investment losses he claimed to have suffered since then. Much of the money he'd invested had been handled by his brother Larry, and Betty would later insist, perhaps rightly, that he and Dan had plotted to siphon off money in anticipation of the divorce and thus cheat her out of her fair share of their joint assets.

A comment Betty wrote on her copy of the hearing transcript encapsulated her anger: "Five years of *HELL* in court. Anyone would hate him or kill him."

Betty tried to get on with her life. But that was impossible. Still reeling from the judge's rulings, she was staring at another imminent trauma—Dan and Linda's marriage. The wedding ceremony was scheduled for April 22—just 10 days after Betty and Dan's anniversary, April 12. She thought Dan had chosen the date in order to hurt her.

On March 10, Betty dropped off Danny and Rhett at Dan's and found the guest list for the wedding on the hall table. She picked it up and took it home with her. Three days later, while Betty was at work, housekeeper Maria Montes arrived at Betty's to find a strange woman about to leave the house with some papers. It was Linda Kolkena, who had come to retrieve her guest list. She couldn't find the list, but in her search she had come across a 90-page autobiography Betty had written and a number of pages from her diary. She told Montes she was a friend of Kim's and went on her way. When Dan found out what Linda had done, he was enraged and ordered her to return the papers immediately. Montes, but not Betty, was at the house when Linda returned the pilfered documents.

When Montes told Betty what had happened, she decided to buy a gun. "It was self-defense," Betty claimed later. "She was breaking into my house. I felt so alone."

The day after Linda's foray, Betty went to a local gun shop and test fired several models. When the salesman complimented her on her aim, Betty explained that she'd been instructed in riflery in her high-school days and had attained the level of marksman. Settling on a five-shot, snub-nosed .38-caliber Smith & Wesson revolver, she filled out the required application to have her record checked for any felony convictions and paid the salesman $357.33.

Her record was clear. She picked up the gun at the end of March, along with three boxes of hollow-point bullets, a particularly lethal kind of ammunition that expands on impact. Back home, Betty showed the gun to her children and her housekeeper before hiding it in her lingerie drawer. Danny discovered the hiding place, however, so from then on Betty kept what she called her "teeny-weeny ladies' gun" in the large brown handbag that she carried everywhere she went. Danny was afraid that his mother might use the gun on his father and remembered Betty's cleaning it in his presence and her telling him, "This is what I'm going to use to kill your father and Linda."

As the wedding drew nearer, Linda Kolkena and Dan's brother Larry urged Dan to wear a bulletproof vest that day. He refused, but he did take the precaution of hiring security guards in case Betty appeared and tried to make a scene. On the day of the ceremony, Betty's friend Helen Pickard came over to keep her company, and later another neighbor, Gail Forbes, dropped by. Brad showed up and offered to take everybody out to dinner, but Betty didn't want to leave until she'd gotten a report from the kids. When they finally telephoned, Rhett suggested that his mother hadn't missed anything. "It was just a bunch of people standing around on Daddy's front lawn with his friend marrying him," he said. Kim commented, "It was really honky. You should see all her low-class friends." Her words probably gave Betty momentary solace. She'd often said that Linda was a "sleaze girl."

Linda was also an imposter, as far as Betty was concerned. There was only one Mrs. Daniel T. Broderick III, and it was she. Friends urged Betty to take back her maiden name, but she wouldn't do it, or possibly couldn't. A psychologist who interviewed Betty would say later that she lacked any core identity except what she took from being Dan Broderick's wife. If this diagnosis was correct, there was no Elisabeth Anne Bisceglia anymore—only Mrs. Daniel T. Broderick III.

There was hardly a breather from legal wrangles with Dan, since Betty decided to hire another lawyer to try again to get custody of Rhett and Danny. She was now all alone in the house, since Lee had moved out and was living with her boyfriend, Jason Prantil, in Pacific Beach.

Walter Maund, Betty's new lawyer, got a custody hearing scheduled, only to have Dan win a postponement to October. As that date approached, he wangled yet another delay. At the end of October, Dan, Linda, Kim, Danny, and Rhett flew to South Bend to see Notre Dame play the University of Southern California—the same teams that had squared off the day Betty and Dan had met, 24 years earlier. They'd often talked about going back to South Bend for a Notre Dame-USC game as a sort of anniversary celebration, but they'd never made the trip. Betty mourned to a friend, "It's like Dan's life has just gone on. I feel like Linda is living *my* life."

Depressed and lonely, Betty spent the weekend at her Warner Springs Ranch condo, then she returned home to start packing for her move into the $200,000 two-bedroom condo she'd just bought in a development on the outskirts of La Jolla, within sight of a traffic-choked freeway. It was a melancholy business. Betty had decided she could no longer afford to live in her big house with the ocean view on Calle del Cielo and had put it up for sale for $1.5 million.

The following Friday, November 3, Betty received two letters from Dan's lawyer—more trouble, she felt sure. Instead of reading them right away, she would testify later, she flung them onto the stack of legal documents she'd accumulated. Whatever bad news they contained would keep. To relax, she went shopping with Lee.

The boys arrived for the weekend, and on Saturday Betty took them for haircuts and laid in $400 worth of groceries; the boys complained about meals at their father's house, but they could count on their mother to serve their favorite foods. Helen Pickard stopped by in the afternoon and listened to Betty rant for an hour. Betty repeated her habitual refrain: "Linda is leading my life." As Pickard was about to leave, Betty asked her, "Is Linda pregnant?" Pickard wasn't friends with Linda and

didn't know the answer, but she felt very sorry for Betty. "I think her thought was, 'He is going to start another family,'" she said. "She just couldn't stand that."

Brad came over for dinner. For months Betty had been sleeping badly, and by early that evening she was dead tired. Right after supper she lay down on her bed and fell asleep in her clothes. The boys watched TV for a while with Brad, who slept that night in another room, perhaps because Rhett and Danny were there.

According to Betty's account of the events that took place the following morning—Sunday, November 5—she woke even earlier than usual, shortly after 4 a.m. Rhett had climbed into bed with her, and she slipped out of the room quietly and went to the kitchen. The letters she'd gotten on Friday caught her attention, and she decided to read them. One was a response to her proposal for custody of the boys. Through his attorney, Dan stated that the boys could live with her on a trial basis. But there was a string attached: She would have to agree that he could take them back anytime he wished. The second letter threatened her with more contempt of court citations for the latest batch of lewd messages on Dan and Linda's answering machine. More threats, more manipulation, more diversions and delays. She remembered Dan saying it would never be over; his charges that she was a crazy, unfit mother; the insulting way he'd described her just before Linda Kolkena exploded into Betty's awareness—old, fat, boring, ugly, stupid. She felt as though she'd become all of those things. Her birthday was two days away and, she said later, "I was just standing in that kitchen saying, you know, 'Jesus Christ! I'm turning forty-two years old! I have been put through this bullshit since I was thirty-five, seven years of my life wasted!'" It would be better to be dead than to go through more of the same nightmare.

On the bottom of one of the letters Betty started what sounded like a suicide note—"I can't take this anymore, them constantly insinuating I'm crazy"—then broke off. She left the house and got into her car. Her first impulse, she later recounted, was to go to the beach—taking an early-morning walk there had become a ritual for her. On the way, though, Betty

I *can't take this anymore, them constantly insinuating I'm crazy.*

BETTY BRODERICK

changed her mind. She decided she had to talk to Dan, tell him to stop tormenting her. If he wouldn't, she said to herself, "I'll splash my brains all over his goddamned house." The big brown handbag in which Betty kept her Smith & Wesson revolver was in the car because, she explained later, she always locked it up there whenever Danny and Rhett stayed with her. She sped along the freeway to downtown San Diego, and in less than 20 minutes she pulled up in front of Dan's house.

Betty had Kim's key to the back door; she testified later that it was in a box of miscellaneous items she had put in her car to move to the new condo. She let herself in and, with the gun in her hand, climbed the stairs to the master bedroom. Heavy draperies were drawn across the windows, and in the near darkness Betty could barely make out Dan and Linda lying side by side in bed. One of the

sleeping figures stirred—Linda, Betty thought—and then it seemed that someone screamed, and she panicked and began firing into the darkness. She pulled the trigger five times, until the gun was empty. She then ripped the telephone out of the wall and fled from the house, gun in hand.

At 7:20 a.m., Lee Broderick and Jason Prantil were wakened by the telephone. Betty was on the line, sobbing hysterically, but Lee was able to make out what her mother was saying: "I shot your father. I shot the sonofabitch."

Betty was at a pay telephone at a gas station in Clairemont, the town where she and Dan had lived so long ago, in another time. Rambling and incoherent, she called her friend Dian Black and told her she'd been at Dan's house and might have shot him. She would have shot herself, Betty said, but she'd emptied the gun. Telling Betty to stay put, Black hung up and got hold of Brad Wright at Betty's house. He ran down the street to the home of Gail and Brian Forbes. Although the couple knew how to get to Dan's Marston Hills house, they didn't know the street number. Brad and Brian left for Dan's and Gail called 911. But she was calling from La Jolla and asking them to investigate a possible shooting in San Diego, at an address she didn't even know. The police thought it might be a hoax and were slow to re-

Betty bought this Smith & Wesson revolver, shown actual size, eight months before she killed Dan and Linda.

160

The circle on this police photo of the back of Dan and Linda's house marks the location of their bedroom.

spond. Thus it was Brad and Brian who got to Dan's house first. After ringing the bell, trying the doors, and shouting, Brian climbed in through a window. Calling out to let Dan and Linda know they weren't burglars, the two men went upstairs and into the bedroom.

Dan and Linda were dead. She had been hit twice, first in the chest and then, as she turned reflexively, in the back of the head. Her brainstem had exploded, spewing blood over her black-and-white polka dot shortie pajamas and the bed's blue-and-white quilted coverlet. The single bullet that struck Dan had ripped through his bare back, broken a rib, and pierced his right lung. The autopsy would reveal that Dan had survived at least a few minutes and perhaps as long as a half-hour before suffocating on his own blood. The other two bullets had smashed harmlessly into a nightstand and the wall behind the bed.

From Clairemont, Betty drove to Lee's apartment. Talking very fast in a trembling voice, she anxiously paced back and forth and gave a disjointed account of what had just occurred. It was too dark to know whether she'd shot Dan, she said, but she'd heard him say, "Okay, you shot me. I'm dead." Lee didn't know whether to believe her mother or not. Jason Prantil later testified, "She wasn't making a lot of sense. She looked like she had been up for a couple days. She looked like she was sick, like she was panic-stricken."

From Lee's place Betty called her parents' house and talked to her father. "Dan is driving me crazy," she sobbed. "He's driving me up the wall. I feel like committing suicide." She said nothing about the shooting; perhaps she couldn't bring herself to confess to Frank Bisceglia what she'd done.

Soon afterward, Dian Black telephoned Lee's apartment with the name of a lawyer who'd agreed to walk Betty through the booking at the police station. Betty unclasped her $10,000 diamond necklace and handed it to Lee, along with a personal check for $10,000. Lee and Jason drove Betty to meet Dian, who then escorted her to lawyer Ron Frant's office. Later that same day, accompanied by Frant, Betty turned herself in at the police station in downtown San Diego, where she was charged with two counts of first-degree murder. From San Diego, Betty was taken to the Las Colinas Women's Detention Facility, the county jail where she'd served six days

Linda Broderick's body sprawls facedown at
an angle across the bed, obscuring the bullet
wound in her chest *(above)*. Dan, perhaps

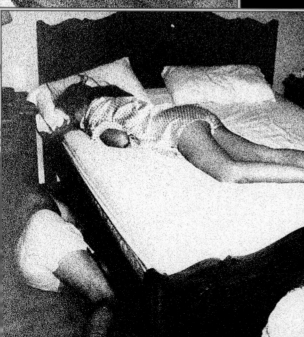

in 1987 because of her vulgar telephone messages.

Five days after the shootings, more than 600 mourners attended the joint funeral of Dan and Linda Broderick at St. Joseph's Cathedral in San Diego. Their twin caskets, his covered with red roses and hers with white, were placed before a large floral arrangement in the shape of a shamrock. Dan was eulogized as a "man of unquestioned integrity" and Linda as the woman who offered him "a new life, a second chance." The service would rankle in Betty's memory for years. Calling it "a fraud," she railed, "The sonofabitch hadn't stepped foot in a church all the years he'd been in San Diego and they bury him like he's the pope. Why is he being buried like a good Catholic father when he deserted his family?" After Dan died, Betty continued to refer to him in the present tense, as if he were still alive.

Betty Broderick's request to be freed on bail was denied after Deputy District Attorney Kerry Wells convinced the judge that she was "an absolutely uncontrolled and angry woman" who would use her freedom to terrorize Dan Broderick's relatives and friends. For the next two years Betty would remain an inmate at Las Colinas. With neither father nor mother to care for them, 13-year-old Danny and 10-year-old Rhett went to live with Dan's brother Larry and his wife in Denver.

Betty Broderick never denied that she had shot her husband and his new wife, and she vigorously justified what she'd done in the interviews she gave while awaiting trial. It wasn't murder, she said, but "the most sincere, honest act of self-defense that there can be in the world. It was justifiable homicide against a weapon you can't see—and nobody can tell me Dan Broderick and his cheap little bitch sidekick didn't have a weapon. His weapon was the legal system. I was under constant attack." It angered her that people thought of Dan and Linda as victims. "Me and the kids were the victims," she told a *Los Angeles Times* reporter. "There are two dead people, but there were five victims."

The trial began on October 22, 1990, almost a year after the killings, and Betty's lawyer for the proceedings, Jack Earley, defended her as the victim

of psychological, legal, and financial assault. Of her motive in going to Marston Hills early on Sunday, November 5, 1989, the lawyer asserted that Betty hadn't intended to "execute two people asleep in their beds." She had come to talk to Dan, Earley went on, to "try one more time before killing herself."

Prosecuting attorney Kerry Wells, however, called Betty's act a premeditated cold-blooded execution committed when her victims were asleep and at their most vulnerable. "Killing Dan and Linda Broderick was something she had thought about for a long, long time," Wells said. The prosecutor wanted to see Betty Broderick found guilty of first-degree murder and sentenced to life without parole. Although the death penalty is legal in California, the district attorney's office had announced earlier the decision not to seek such punishment because the Broderick children might be called to testify for the prosecution.

Wells hammered at the repeated threats Betty had made against Dan and Linda. Kim Broderick, who sat at the trial with her Broderick relatives, testified that her mother had told her, "I'm going to kill them. I'm going to shoot them." Ruth Roth, the psychologist brought in to mediate the Brodericks' custody dispute in 1987, repeated what Betty had told her then: "I'm not going to be a single parent of four kids. He'll die first." The tapes of Betty's foul, sometimes violent messages and conversations were used by the prosecutor so often that reporters covering the trial began referring to the recordings as "The Best of Betty."

Taking the stand in her own defense, Betty Broderick poured out a detailed recounting of her childhood, courtship, married life, and divorce. She wept as she said, "Dan's opinion of me was really all I cared about." As for what she termed the accident that took place in his and Linda's bedroom, her impressions were vague. She thought Dan might have said something like "You've shot me" or "Don't shoot" just before she discovered that the gun was empty and she couldn't shoot herself as she'd set out to do.

After some three weeks of testimony, the case went to the jury of six men and six women. Three days of deliberation convinced the jurors that reaching a unanimous verdict was going to be impossible—10 of them had voted to convict Betty Broderick of murder, but the other two were holding out staunchly for manslaughter. On November 20 the judge declared a mistrial. One of the holdouts, a 60-year-old retired Air Force engineer, thought Betty Broderick had been terribly victimized by her husband. Of the shooting, he asked, "What took her so long?"

Once again denied bail, Betty was returned to Las Colinas and confined in a wing for women who were violent, retarded, or in protective custody. "I'm a no-bailer," she remarked in an interview. "In the hierarchy of inmates, that's as bad as you get." During the 11 months between her first and second trials, she recounted her disastrous marital history on a television news program and was interviewed by reporters from three well-known magazines. The case received still more notoriety from a TV movie aired during the same period.

Betty Broderick's second trial began October 14, 1991, and prosecutor Wells was successful that time around. On the 10th of December the jury found Betty guilty of two counts of second-degree murder—meaning that her actions were not premeditated but that she intended to kill Dan and Linda when she shot them. She was sentenced to two consecutive terms of 15 years to life plus two years for illegal use of a firearm; she would have to serve a total of 21 years, counting from the date she was arrested, before becoming eligible for parole in the year 2011.

"I'm outraged," stormed Larry Broderick after the judge pronounced Betty's sentence. He spoke for all the friends and relatives of Dan and Linda Broderick who thought his former sister-in-law was guilty of premeditated murder and should have been imprisoned for life, with no possibility of parole.

In 1992, after three years of incarceration for shooting her former husband and his second wife, Betty Broderick was still strenuously defending her actions. When an interviewer raised the question of remorse, Betty resented the implication that she had done something wrong. "I never made a decision to hurt those people, much less kill them. I never made that choice. So how can I feel the remorse for a choice I never made?" She said she was sorry they were dead, but for a very different reason. "You know, I want them to see that I survived. I want them to see no matter what they did to me, a little pilot light in me wouldn't give up."◆

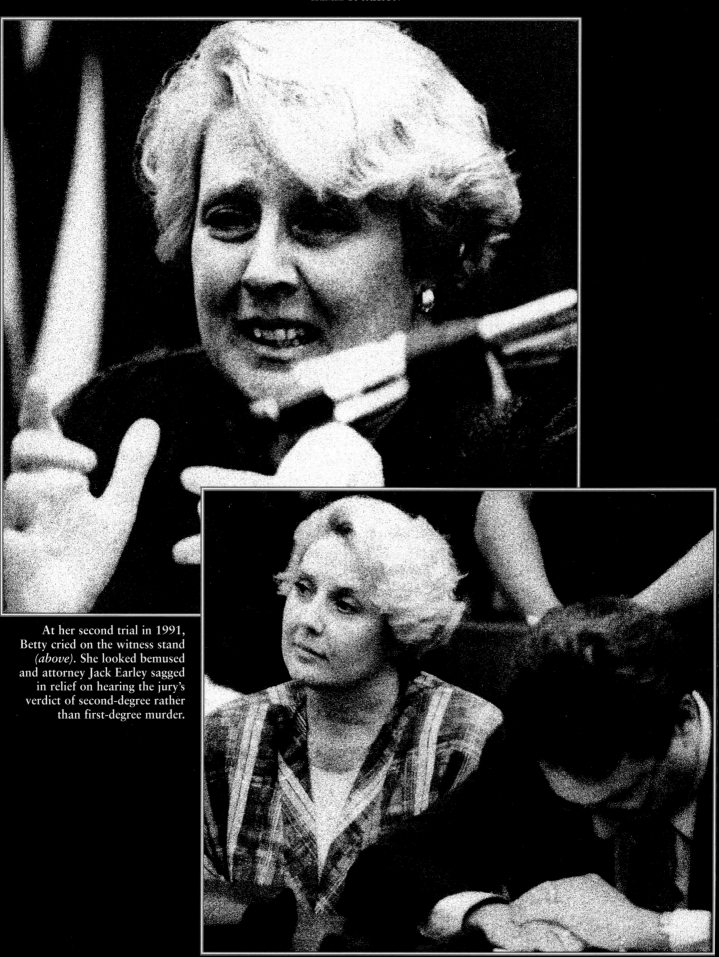

At her second trial in 1991, Betty cried on the witness stand *(above)*. She looked bemused and attorney Jack Earley sagged in relief on hearing the jury's verdict of second-degree rather than first-degree murder.

Betty maintained a brave, smiling front for press photographers as she was escorted from the courtroom after the verdict was announced.

Picture Credits

Time-Life Books is a division of TIME LIFE INC.

PRESIDENT and CEO: John M. Fahey Jr.
EDITOR-IN-CHIEF: John L. Papanek

TIME-LIFE BOOKS

MANAGING EDITOR: Roberta Conlan

Executive Art Director: Ellen Robling
Director of Photography and Research:
  John Conrad Weiser
Senior Editors: Russell B. Adams Jr., Dale M.
  Brown, Janet Cave, Lee Hassig, Jim Hicks,
  Robert Somerville, Henry Woodhead
Director of Technology: Eileen Bradley

PRESIDENT: John D. Hall

Vice President, Director of Marketing:
  Nancy K. Jones
Vice President, New Product Development:
  Neil Kagan
Director of Production Services: Robert N. Carr
Production Manager: Marlene Zack
Supervisor of Quality Control: James King

Editorial Operations
Production: Celia Beattie
Library: Louise D. Forstall
Computer Composition: Deborah G. Tait
  (Manager), Monika D. Thayer, Janet Barnes
  Syring, Lillian Daniels

Library of Congress Cataloging in Publication Data
Crimes of passion/by the editors of Time-Life Books.
    p.   cm. — (True crime)
    Includes bibliographical references and index.
    ISBN 0-7835-0029-7
    1. Crimes of passion—United States—Case
studies. 2. Murder—United States—Case studies.
I. Time-Life Books. II. Series.
HV6053.C66 1994
364.1'523'0973—dc20   93-35976
                                          CIP
ISBN 0-7835-0030-0 (lib. bdg.)

TRUE CRIME

SERIES EDITOR: Janet Cave
Administrative Editor: Jane A. Martin
Art Director: Christopher Register
Picture Editor: Jane Jordan

Editorial Staff for *Crimes of Passion*
Text Editor: Sarah Brash
Associate Editors/Research: Mark Lazen, Terrell
  Smith
Assistant Art Director: Sue Pratt
Senior Copyeditors: Elizabeth Graham, Barbara
  Quarmby, Colette Stockum
Picture Coordinator: Jennifer Iker
Editorial Assistant: Donna Fountain

Special Contributors: Cyndi Bemel, Chris Hoelzl,
Catherine Harper Parrott, Susan Gregory Thomas,
Kathy Wismar (research); George G. Daniels,
Margery A. duMond, Laura Foreman, Jack Mc-
Clintock, Daisy More, Bob Speziale (text); John
Drummond (design); Mel Ingber (index).

Correspondents: Elisabeth Kraemer-Singh (Bonn);
Christine Hinze (London); Christina Lieberman
(New York); Maria Vincenza Aloisi (Paris); Ann
Natanson (Rome). Valuable assistance was also
provided by Judy Aspinall (London); Elizabeth
Brown, Katheryn White (New York); Ann Wise
(Rome).

Other Publications:
WEIGHT WATCHERS® SMART CHOICE
  RECIPE COLLECTION
THE AMERICAN INDIANS
THE ART OF WOODWORKING
LOST CIVILIZATIONS
ECHOES OF GLORY
THE NEW FACE OF WAR
HOW THINGS WORK
WINGS OF WAR
CREATIVE EVERYDAY COOKING
COLLECTOR'S LIBRARY OF THE UNKNOWN
CLASSICS OF WORLD WAR II
TIME-LIFE LIBRARY OF CURIOUS AND
  UNUSUAL FACTS
AMERICAN COUNTRY
VOYAGE THROUGH THE UNIVERSE
THE THIRD REICH
THE TIME-LIFE GARDENER'S GUIDE
MYSTERIES OF THE UNKNOWN
TIME FRAME
FIX IT YOURSELF
FITNESS, HEALTH & NUTRITION
SUCCESSFUL PARENTING
HEALTHY HOME COOKING
UNDERSTANDING COMPUTERS
LIBRARY OF NATIONS
THE ENCHANTED WORLD
THE KODAK LIBRARY OF CREATIVE
  PHOTOGRAPHY
GREAT MEALS IN MINUTES
THE CIVIL WAR
PLANET EARTH
COLLECTOR'S LIBRARY OF THE CIVIL WAR
THE EPIC OF FLIGHT
THE GOOD COOK
WORLD WAR II
HOME REPAIR AND IMPROVEMENT
THE OLD WEST

*For information on and a full description of any of
the Time-Life Books series listed above, please call
1-800-621-7026 or write:*
Reader Information
Time-Life Customer Service
P.O. Box C-32068
Richmond, Virginia 23261-2068

This volume is one of a series that examines
the phenomenon of crime. Other books in the
series include:
Serial Killers
Mass Murderers
Mafia
Unsolved Crimes
Compulsion To Kill
Most Wanted
Death and Celebrity

TIME®
LIFE
BOOKS